LORDS OF THE NIGHT: Vampires

BOOK ONE OF THE DARKNESS RISING SERIES

CREDITS
Author: Karis

Editor: Mark Roddison
Cover Art: Ralph Horsley
Interior Art by: Ralph Horsley, Brannon Hall and Andy Mason
Graphic Design: Jason Barr Sawyer
Katharein Concept: Gavin Birch

Thanks to: The Guild of Wizards, Aldo Ghiozzi, Impressions, Patterson Printing

Extra Special Thanks to:
James Wallis (for helping me to believe it could be done)
Andrew Girdwood (for his continual support)
Betty Brandon and Pamela "Blonde" Thames (for putting up with my constant phone calls)
Matthew Skipper (for all those rules edits)
Brannon Hall (for being available just about all of the time)

The Guild of Wizards: Chris Dolan, Emily Douglas, Jessica Jones, Orion Kroulek, Derek Lloyd, Chris Pearson, Joy Pearson, Adam Skipper, Matthew Skipper, Brett Williams, Tom Williams, Mark Worthy, Charles Young

First Printing: **March 2003**

BOTTLED IMP GAMES

"Putting the Game into Gamers - everywhere!"

Visit our website at http://www.bottledimpgames.com

DARK WATCHER

My name is Phillian Artus Alucidan. I have lived in the City for as long as I can remember, choosing to hide here when it was nothing more than a tiny hamlet. I call it the City, although it goes by many names, each of them as empty and meaningless as the last. For although the surroundings change, only I am eternal.

I do not use the word eternal lightly, for I am in so far as I am aware immortal, living until I am slain or choose to die. I have seen wars and famine, flood and disaster, life and death. I am as endless as the blackness of night and as unreachable as the stars. The people of this City do not know me; I am more permanent than the towering cathedral or the foundations of this townhouse in which I reside.

I am fifty three years of age. One thousand, five hundred and fifty three, or thereabouts. It may seem like an eternity when your heart beats out the ticks of endless time and every moment is precious, but to me the years have passed in a blur, a heady whirl of intoxicating sensation and desperate loneliness. I no longer count time in the passing of hours or days, or even years.

But in centuries...

I am scholar and sorcerer, seer and prophet.

I am also a vampire.

How I came into my second unlife is another story, but suffice it to say that I have lived here in the City for countless years, hiding from those who would find me, and watching others of my kind as they pursue their endless games with the *Powers of Light*.

I say *Powers of Light*, for they are opposite to us in every way. They cherish life; we dwell in darkness. They devote their lives to destroying evil, while we ally ourselves with the shadow, true creatures of the night. They revere love and compassion; we embody pain and suffering.

But I am above them. I have no master. While I am no longer mortal, neither am I a monster. I lie in a middle state, requiring blood to feed, yet retaining my mortal mind. Yes, the cold Void of necromancy pulls at me - whispering of darkness, of great powers and terrible lusts - but I do not listen. I rise above such things. I rarely use my powers, drink sparingly from the blood of mortals, and it always helps to know the spells that keep the Void at bay. I know that to succumb even once to the darkness will be to fall into shadow, and I must retain my mortal mind, my conscience and my sanity if I am to withstand the task given to me.

I must continue to watch for as long as I am able.

I am watcher, historian and teller of truth, as much of it as I can see. I sit here in darkness, writing with not even a single candle to cast back the gloom. My eyes need no light to see - I am a vampire and darkness is my friend, the shadow my ally.

And it is my only ally, for I have no affinity with others of my kind. Those who know of my presence leave me alone, choosing not to see any merit in my existence or value in my destruction. So I am left to remain here, watching and writing what I see.

Yet I do not study the vampire races. I have my eyes firmly fixed on the mortal realms. A shift in the balance of power between good and evil looms ever closer and the time for mortals hangs on a knife-edge.

But this story begins with a man called Devin. And he is a cleric of the *Powers of Light*. His first life is almost over, but the choices he makes before he falls into shadow will shape the mortal realms forever.

A great darkness is rising. And I intend to be right in the middle of it.

Watching...

Note from the Author: What this book is about

Foreword

It's not real. It's only a game. Vampires don't exist. They really don't! Sure – there are some people who really, really want to believe… But remember – vampires don't exist! People don't drink blood or sleep in coffins. Remember exactly who you are when you put this book down - a living, breathing person.

Definition of a Vampire

He who drinks blood to survive. It's as simple as that. Well ok, there's a bit more too it than that perhaps, but essentially, vampires were once living creatures that have been raised from death by necromancy. Not all vampires have fangs or claws, some look far from human. While a great majority may be evil, not all want to drink the blood of virgins or to live in a nightmarish castles, despotic masters of all they survey. You will find many vampires in this book, not all of them conform to the traditional view of the walking dead.

Playing The Lords of the Night: Vampires

The Lords of the Night: Vampires can be played on many levels. It can be about power; a player could be openly saying 'cool, I'm a vampire now!' - content to play in a world with new powers and strange creatures of evil. Other players might be eager to stew in their own personal darkness - doomed by the knowledge that they have been corrupted by necromancy and separated from the lives they once knew.

Being a vampire can be a journey of self-discovery or it can be about donning the mantle of dark avenger. It might even be fun to play an evil character for awhile, although that *isn't* what this book is about.

So what *IS* this book about?

This book is also about becoming a vampire. It's about fear, about discovering a darker world that is teeming with evil. The PCs will discover that the creatures of the night are preparing themselves, gathering their numbers in readiness for something terrible. Exactly what is unknown - but they have been hiding for a very long time and their plans are about to come to fruition.

In addition, this book is about creating something that's deliciously sinister. The abilities and powers listed here are designed to stir those creative juices to help you create something wonderful, dark and definitely vampiric. But remember, they are only guidelines. It's your world; no one can tell you how to run your game. So take what you will, change everything if you like. Nothing is set in stone, least of all names, places and *especially* numbers.

It's your world, have fun with it.

Just remember - vampires can be anywhere! Before you turn off the light tonight, make sure you check under the bed and inside your closet!

The Beginning

As the Darkness Rising series progresses, the PCs may find options to shed off the curse of vampirism and become something greater: hero vampires who have retained their mortality and become creatures of tremendous power. But until those options reveal themselves the PCs will be forced to face despair and the cold darkness of undeath.

Not all of the answers are contained here. The PCs do not have the option to become hero vampires in this book. That mystery remains unanswered, at least for now. Let your vampires discover a new world, a world of shadow and evil and let them choose their side, or least let them choose what side they believe to be the right side. As the Darkness Rising series progresses a great many things may change…

When all around you is bathed in shadow, it is hard to make out the truth.

Darkness Rises…

CHAPTER ONE: A TREATISE ON VAMPIRES

I shall begin by speaking about the vampire races in general. There are two distinct types of vampire. Although similar in many ways, in reality they could not be more different. One group has existed since the beginning of time, a force of elemental nature that has always been. The other arrived with the appearance of Vangual, the self-proclaimed god of vampires.

I have encountered many, though certainly not all of the vampire races over the centuries. While I cannot be wholly certain of the truth of my observations, I shall try and comment on them in as much detail as I am able.

Feral Vampires

Ever since mortals have existed, feral vampires have wandered the mortal realms under cover of darkness. Created by the raw forces of nature, by curse or magic, feral vampires will certainly exist long after the mortal races have passed to dust. Without any form of leadership, they are solitary creatures, little more than animals, driven solely by their necromantic urges to find blood. They have precious little society and are creatures to be kept by a wizard, the subject of research or to be put to use as a powerful bodyguard.

Children of Vangual

The comparisons between the Children of Vangual and their feral brethren are many. They have the same dead flesh, share many of the same powers, but while they may hold the name vampire, they are very different.

Their history is both bloody and terrible, an example of shining devotion turned to darkness. The Avystyx Prophecies tells of an order of the purest good that discovered the rise of a recently awoken god known only as Vangual. Hunting down his followers, the order traced the evil back to a city filled with necromancers in a remote region of the world. Rather than rout the evil, the order razed the city to the ground in a conflagration of purifying flame. Thousands were slain: necromancer, slave, sinner and innocent alike. And it was all done in the name of justice...

Bereft of his followers, Vangual cried out for justice. He called out to the gods, but they turned away and would not hear his cries for revenge. Standing in the ruins of the burning city, Vangual gave out a scream that even now rings out at the edges of reality. He called upon the powers of the most terrible darkness, uttering words that had not been spoken since before the time of creation. He called out to any power that would aid him, no matter what the price.

His agony drifted out into the universe - and was answered by the deadly enemy.

The Void...

The Avystyx Prophecies say that Vangual was once a vampire himself; a creature that became so powerful he was elevated beyond the status of mere undead and granted godhood.

Armed with the greatest of the *Powers of Darkness*, Vangual transformed the living order into vampires, creatures that looked like mortals and had fearsome powers. Denied sanctuary in the mortal realms, these beings fled deep into the earth beneath the city of Veil where they became the First, the progenitors of the vampire races.

At Vangual's insistence, the First created Avystervan, the subterranean *City of Graves*; a place of screams and terrible suffering where the living exist in fear and where vampires reside far from the prying eyes of the *Powers of Light*. It is a realm of darkness and undead, of screaming mortals and endless caverns where the sun never shines.

But Vangual was far from done. He took one of his chosen and shaped them into a new form, the Vangaard, a creature filled with rage and cold fury. The Vangaard he commanded to be both bodyguard and defenders to the vampire races, and that was their task. Hulking monstrosities, the Vangaard take what they want and prey on both younger vampires and mortals alike. Battle has seen an end to many of their number, but they can still be found in Avystervan, bodyguard and protectors to the Black Council.

But they were not the end of Vangual's creations. The First found a wizard who had been burned beyond imagining in the razing of the great city. Vangual breathed unlife into his tortured flesh, returning him from death as a horribly charred and smouldering spirit. Joined with the powers of flame, this vampire became the embodiment of fire, and was vengeance and destruction incarnate.

Today, they are known as Fire Vampires and are demons bound with hellfire and malice. They can appear as a mote of flame or a pillar of fire. They are truly monstrous, taking great delight in destroying everything in their path. They rarely assume physical form, but when they choose to do so, appear as the hideously burned individuals that they were at the moment of their first deaths.

As the flames of the city died, the remaining dead fell around the ruined city. Some, touched by disease were corrupted by Vangual's malevolence. They arose as the Ravenous, desperately hungry vampires with a craving for mortal flesh. These creatures carried their disease over into undeath, and sought the safety of Avystervan and its darkness to heal their wounds. Today the Ravenous are disease-ridden creatures that feast on health and youth. They are mistrusted even by other vampires, for they are considered filthy and the bringers of plague. Ravenous travel the world, seeking out the strong and the powerful and feasting upon them, leaving behind a diseased and enfeebled victim. Ravenous are always hungry, their lurid eyes blaze with an appetite that cannot be sated.

Next, Vangual awoke the shadow. He ordered the First to bring to him the drow they found in the underworld. Willing or not, he transformed them into Shadow Vampires, insubstantial creatures that only half reside in the mortal realms. They exist in part on the shadow plane and consist of swirling darkness and frigid cold. Filled with wickedness, they travel at night, stealing the breath from children while they sleep. They are dark assassins and evil murderers, stealers of warmth and hope.

Mock Vampires or the *mocked* are ghoulish creatures whose bodies have not successfully survived the transition from mortal to vampire. They have remained dead for too long before their *Second Waking* and have suffered both physical and mental degeneration in the grave. Dripping gore, the *mocked* are often mistaken for zombies. Many are completely bestial, devoid of any intelligence whatsoever. They typically have no masters - or at least anyone who will claim them. Subject of much amusement, the mocked live in sewers or places of filth where their stench of decay is not so noticeable.

At the height of Vangual's power came the most terrible of his children. Ash Vampires: they who feast upon life itself. Draining the very essence from the living, plants wither and the ground turns to dust as they pass. These emotionless vampires are given mortal form in return for performing despicable acts in the name of the lord of blood. It is said those of the ash are the most powerful of Vangual's creations, and that he could only create them when he had sufficient followers amongst mortals and vampires alike.

Finally came the Lost, divine beings that have fallen from the grace of their celestial realm and cast to earth. Retaining a fragment of their memory and a shard of divinity, these creatures are perhaps the most tragic of all the vampire races. Forced to drink blood and to eat ash, they wake to darkness knowing they have done wrong, but not what. Perhaps they can find redemption, but most Lost spend their unlives brooding over their mysterious past and punishing themselves for a transgression they cannot remember. While they are not one of Vangual's creations, the god of blood eagerly accepts them as his own.

I shall speak now of lesser vampires, for these creatures certainly exist and in growing numbers.

Dhampyre or half-vampires are the result of a joining between a vampire and a mortal. They are able to walk in daylight and are almost totally impervious to the forces of necromancy. They have many of the vampiric strengths and few of their weaknesses. They can perceive the undead, and it is that power which singles them out for subjugation (or destruction) by the forces of darkness. Dhampyre live well beyond the life span of normal mortals, but are rare indeed. I would imagine there are but a handful of Dhampyre in existence and those that will not ally with the *Powers of Darkness* are quickly slain.

The Dhampyre are wild cards in the vampiric world. They may well turn the tide of the coming darkness for good or ill. As yet, none can say...

In time, Vangual showed his vampires how to create children of their own. Vampire Scion are created by a single draining of a mortal's blood without following the ritualistic process of the *Black Kiss*. These creatures are devoid of the uniqueness of a true vampire and are typically created as a result of a careless encounter with a mortal. A Vampire Scion can become a true vampire should their master be slain, although the outcome of this is uncertain.

The *vampire touched* are those mortals bitten on one or more separate occasions by the Children of Vangual. In this blood-drained state, death is close. A third visitation and the victim will rise up as a vampire a few nights later (provided the victim is slain in the process). Symptoms include weakness, pale and cold flesh, aversion to sunlight, disorientation and a desperate and unquenchable thirst. The *vampire touched* may even gain the semblance of a vampire's strengths and weaknesses - from their heightened senses to a fear of holy items and garlic.

On other Vampires

I have no doubt that the terrible Black Cabal - the guild of vampire wizards - has created its own form of vampiric life. But they are hardly the only undead monsters that have taken the name vampire. There are forces in the universe that are more complex and unfathomable than even the Children of Vangual arrogantly believe themselves to be.

I have heard the name Iliari whispered on many lips. There are so many rumours surrounding these mythical creatures, I wonder if I can give any accurate information about them at all. Supposedly created by the *Powers of Light* - the Iliari are 'bright' vampires - opposite to our kind in every way.

Those that have allegedly encountered them have spoken of a brilliance akin to that of the sun and powerful holy magic.

Rumours whisper that the Iliari carry the secret to vampiric restoration within their blood. I remain sceptical to such claims until I see one of these 'bright' vampires with my own eyes.

The Avystyx Prophecies also mention the coming of the Kethax, evil vampires of hellfire and brimstone from the Ash Plane. I have not seen one of these creatures, so I can only presume the Avystyx Prophecies are either incorrect, or the time for these creatures has not yet come to pass.

The Black Kiss

To create a vampire the Children of Vangual must slay their mortal victim by draining every last drop of blood from their body. This is a task in itself - for drinking to the point of death can be extremely difficult. However, this process is not done all at once. The Children of Vangual must come to a mortal three times if they are to turn them into a vampire. This process is called the Visitation and is steeped in ancient ritual and ceremony.

On the third Visitation, the vampire must drain not only all of the blood but the last vestiges of life energy from their victim. The dead and cold corpse will then rise up as a fledgling vampire a few days later. If the master does not (or can not) follow this process *exactly*, the slain mortal will become a Vampire Scion, cursed to eternal stagnation and endless subservience.

The Second Waking

On the fourth night of death, a fledgling vampire will rise from the grave. Occasionally this process can happen more quickly, other times, somewhat longer. The necromantic processes are mysterious and cannot be predicted, even by the most learned of sages.

Shock and Madness

Finding oneself buried alive is distressing enough to shatter any remaining sanity a newly risen vampire might have. It is enough of a shock for the unprepared to feel their transformed flesh, dead and lifeless, animated solely by force of will.

Many vampires do not survive this early period. Disoriented and lacking direction, they simply remain by their place of death, burning with the dawn when the sun rises. This is especially true of Vampire Scion that may rise from their graves long after their master has departed. Without direction, their chances of survival are slim indeed.

It is because of this that most vampires select their prospective progeny very carefully, ensuring that they are suitable for the *Black Kiss*. They will make preparations to steal them away; transforming them to vampires in their own lair to ensure the transition to undeath proceeds as smoothly as possible.

Newly risen vampires experience the Strength of the Grave, a burst of super-vampiric strength that allows them to crawl from the ground, tearing up the earth in their attempt to break free from their place of internment. I have known vampires able to tear through rock and stone to reach freedom.

While formidable, this strength wanes shortly after their first feeding and even if a vampire does not feed, fades before sunrise.

Vampire Physiology

These are the most general facts about vampires physiology:-

* **Waxy Flesh:** All vampires have pallid, waxy and unnatural seeming flesh. This can have the appearance of porcelain or be scarred and marked with wounds from their first death.
* **Foul Breath:** Although vampires do not breathe, they must draw breath to speak. A vampire's breath is foul, reeking of clotted blood and stinking gore. This diminishes as a vampire ages and their internal organs rot to naught but dust.
* **Luminous Eyes:** All vampires have eyes that gleam in twilight. Attuned to shadow, undead perceive the night in a monochrome where life-force shines more brightly than the brightest wake. Vampires can see with mortal sight when they choose, but such vision is hazy and even candlelight can be blinding.
* **Great Strength:** Vampires are superior to mortals in many ways. They have incredible strength, do not tire and can endure wounds that would slay even the greatest of warriors. They are resistant to many forms of magical and physical attack and only powerful enchanted weapons can harm them..
* **Stench of the Grave:** This foul smell surrounds the vampire, the stench of death, decay and rot. Only the eldest vampires no longer smell of anything but ancient time. Their bodies are nothing but dust held together by endless magic.
* **Chill of the Grave:** A freezing aura of necromancy surrounds every vampire. Like a cloak of ice, the Chill is the one thing they cannot easily hide. It strikes unease into the living and terror into animals. Fuelled by the Void, the Chill is a vampire's greatest strength, but it is also a terrible weakness. It gives them their incredible powers, but it also separates them from their mortality and drives them toward darkness.

Vampire Anatomy

Vampires have no working organs. Their flesh is icy to the touch. Sustained by blood and negative energy, they can toil all night, do not rest, sweat or need sleep. They do not breathe. They cannot easily drink any liquid other than blood.

They cannot eat: it is only with great force of will that foods are kept down for any continued period. They are immune to alcohol and poisons and cannot submerge their despair in ale or narcotics.

Vampires appear far from human. Even the most normal-seeming has a deathly pallor about them. Many have dirt-encrusted flesh or broken veins marking the skin, remnants of their first burial. Those vampires who were not buried fare better, but their eyes still gleam like the pits of the abyss, filled with malice and the cold darkness of the Void.

Blood

The one unalterable fact that binds all vampires is that they must consume the life essence of the living in order to survive. They do not need to do so every day, but grow steadily more famished the lower their reserves become. Vampire blood is magical; they can perform amazing feats with it, and it is linked to their age. The older they are, the more powerful they become.

Death of the Corpse

Killing a vampire is not a simple matter. Inflict enough physical damage and they turn to mist, dust, ash or blood. They must then retreat to their *place of rest* to recover and recuperate. Once in their coffins or places of darkness, they hide away, healing and plotting their revenge. Yet it is then that they are at their weakest; destroy a vampire while they lie in their sanctuaries and they are utterly vanquished, turning to dust in a moment.

Sunlight

Even with Vangual's blessings, the day still kills. A hint of sunlight can be fatal. It chars a vampire's flesh and clouds their powers. Of all the forms of damage they may suffer, it is the hardest to heal. With age, a vampire gains some modicum of resistance to the brilliance of the sun, but on the whole sunlight will be their greatest nemesis.

Sleeping

Nocturnal, vampires must sleep through the day. As dawn comes, they must return to their *places of rest* where they fall into a deathlike slumber until nightfall. When they wake, consciousness seeps back into their bodies and inert flesh is aroused once more. If a vampire does not sleep during the day, they suffer greatly. They do not heal and lose much of their immortal strength and mystical powers. The ties to the grave are formidable and only the eldest vampires can deny them.

The Eternal Quiescence

Vampires who expend all of their blood resources risk falling into the *black sleep*, a state from which many vampires never wake.

Sages speculate that thousands of vampires lie slumbering across the mortal realms even now, unable to find the life essence they need to rise from their deathlike state.

The Void

The Void is the embodiment of necromancy, darkness and utter corruption. Both life and unlife to a vampire, it is a power of malevolence and hatred. It twists their mortal minds into strange and wicked forms, dragging them ever down towards evil. One can struggle against the Void as it whispers of darkness, but eventually all things succumb to it. Only through magic or the Katharein can a vampire remain true to their mortality as the ages pass by.

Dark Gifts

The Children of Vangual have tremendous powers, magical abilities forged from the blackest wells of necromancy. They gain supernatural strength, can shift forms, melt into the night and even control the minds of lesser mortals. Vampires truly are the lords of the night.

Why are we here?

I cannot say. Vangual certainly has a purpose and an evil design upon the mortal realms. The Avystyx Prophecies make mention of a dark Eden, that the Black Bloods shall one day inhabit the earth. It also says that when the time comes, the dead shall rise up and reclaim the world of the living.

There are many who would say that in this telling I am betraying my own kind. To them I say this: I am as much mortal as I am a vampire. I am death wrapped in mortal flesh. I have gripped tightly to what remains of my first life and I shall not let it go.

Why do I write this?

I write this because I sense a darkness is coming. A darkness that the mortal races may not be able to fight alone. They will need every weapon, every ounce of faith if they are to survive the rising shadow.

I have sworn no allegiance to others of my kind, I do not choose to serve the *Powers of Darkness* or their minions. In the depths of my heart, in the one fragile shard of mortality that my death could not destroy lies a glimmer of truth. The Children of Vangual are an abomination, they, *we* should never have existed. I shall not allow the undead to destroy what sentimental fragments remain of my first life.

If I can do my part - however small - to grant the mortal races even a glimmer of hope, then so be it.

I shall do what I can.

CHAPTER TWO: THE CHILDREN OF VANGUAL

I remember the day I *met* him only too well. It seems like a lifetime ago now. But regret has faded into distant memory.

Regrets do not seem important now.

He was walking down the street, bold as brass, cane clicking on the cobbles. Big as a tree he was, and dark as pitch. It was like the light was afraid of him, or he was more real, because my lantern light seemed to shrink back from him and he was surrounded by shadow.

He walked right past me and I just stood frozen in place, staring open-mouthed like a babe. Sensing a palpable evil, I reached for my holy symbol, but at that moment, Auraran seemed far away, the gods of light insignificant against this terrible darkness.

As if reading my mind, the man stopped and turned, his dusky face pointed and not quite right, as though he was not entirely human.

His eyes… They were aflame, dancing as if all the fires of hell were behind them. Chilled me to the bone like nothing else I had ever seen. Or ever will…

He looked at me as though he had never seen my kind before, pursing his lips and studying me thoughtfully. It was as if he knew me somehow. Then he drew himself close, until his cheek was almost pressed against my own. I could feel a chill about him and he smelled like mothballs, only older and more faded. Ancient, somehow.

"Hello Devin." He said with a thick accent that I couldn't quite place. Gods, I could barely understand him, never mind tell you from where he came. He certainly wasn't from any place local. Then he drew himself upright and gave me a smile that could have been a sneer. It looked hungry. I felt like a rabbit about to be eaten by a wolf. It set my legs a quiver and my heart pounding. A trail of cold sweat ran down my neck. But the dark man didn't do anything to me, he merely reached forward and gave me a package. Something hard wrapped in black velvet.

"Take it." He said. "It contains the answers to all of your questions."

I wanted to flee, wanted to run screaming into the night. But his eyes… They burned. They were so big, so large and powerful. I could not resist him. I found myself reaching out and taking the package. I did it without question, willingly, eagerly. I tucked it into the folds of my robe and stood mutely before him.

Satisfied, he tipped his hat to me and vanished, right before my eyes into thin air.

Even though he was gone, I could still hear his voice in my ears.

"Darkness is rising." He said ominously. I blinked, and listened for a moment longer, yet the voice was silent.

Darkness is rising…

I wonder what he meant by that?

ASH VAMPIRES

Of all the vampire races, Ash Vampires (known as *Corrupters*) have the blackest hearts. Forged from the most concentrated source of negative energy, Ash Vampires are a corruption of nature. Their minds are shattered in the transition to undeath, leaving behind a great thirst for malevolence and a twisted delight in psychological torment. They have truly left their humanity behind, and are monstrous and inhuman creations.

Corrupters can destroy just about anything, living or inanimate. Their powers of entropy and decay grow as they age. Their touch is death; they can turn stone, rock and wood to dust in an instant. A brood of Ash Vampires can bring a walled city to its knees. An elder Ash Vampire can cause a hail of arrows to turn to cinders, and every sword blow rained upon him to crumble to dust.

The presence of an Ash Vampire is always evident to those who know the signs. Around a *Corrupter's* lair, the ground will be black and lifeless. Nothing will live in the sky or upon the ground.

APPEARANCE

Ash Vampires have dark or ashen flesh and pale, narrow black eyes. They are either bald or have very fine white or black hair. They exhale wisps of ash and dust when they speak. Their eyes burn like embers, twin points of piercing scarlet.

THE BLACK KISS

A *Corrupter* selects his victims carefully, never creating Scion, always true vampires. Rangers and druids are typically chosen. Those transformed are torn between their mortal love for the earth and being forever barred from it. Their very touch destroys flora and fauna - they have become the very antithesis of all they once valued. This realisation initially leads to a period of personal conflict while the fledgling vampire struggles to deal with who and what they have become. Most newly created vampires are taken to the Ash Plane where they remain until they come to terms with their dark powers. The Ash Plane quickly strips away mortal sentiment, transforming the *Corrupter* into a dark and emotionless creature in a short space of time.

SOCIETY

Ash Vampires have no society. They rarely gather in groups and when they do, do so for business rather than for any social reason. They do not have any particular base of operations in Avystervan, but many gather around the portal to the Ash Plane, where they occasionally stop to exchange secrets or information.

While they are not the most faithful to the Black Council, they are paid very well for any services rendered. Their powers of mass destruction make them an invaluable asset to any brood. Ash Vampires come to Avystervan seeking information, work, or for more nefarious reasons.

There are very few non-evil Ash Vampires. Their good souls are quickly devoured by the Void - and by the very nature of what they have become. Some with considerable effort learn to still the flows of negativity enough to be able to live in relative harmony with the world around them, although these are very few and far between and most are singled out for destruction by the Black Council.

The Black Council have been known to infiltrate Ash Vampires into hard to reach, holy or magically protected locations. They store the inert ashes of a willing *Corrupter* in a container and transport it through unsuspecting mortal merchants to its destination *(see Story and Adventure Hooks p.119)*. A few days later the Ash Vampire reforms ready to achieve its dark objective.

OUTLOOK

Ash Vampires are the least mortal of all the vampire races. They are considered monsters even by vampire standards. They have no allegiance except to their own, and seek to twist and manipulate those around them. Few are trusted, although they have worked successfully for the Black Council on many occasions without incident.

Corrupters have a very difficult time living in populated areas. At their passing, milk curdles and vegetation withers. Nothing grows in their immediate vicinity. The area of corruption can be as large as several hundred feet in all directions for the most ancient of vampires. Additionally, Ash Vampires drain energy from their surroundings at all times. This manifests as a withering of flesh and a temporary lowering of physical attributes. Mortals in their direct proximity will feel this effect as a weakness or a strange tightening of the skin. An Ash Vampire is wholly distanced from their mortal heritage and cannot even vaguely pass for human - there is just something too alien and disturbing about them.

ROLE-PLAYING AN ASH VAMPIRE

You are a shallow, despicable creature. Undeath has stripped away all mortal sentiment, leaving behind an empty void filled only with darkness. You are considered empty and devoid of emotion even by other vampires, but that simply isn't true. You take great pleasure in manipulation and the mental torture of others. You love to destroy everything around your victims: friends, family and lovers before feasting on their blood. You revel in causing fear and anguish, pain and suffering wherever you can. It's all so clear now. What else is there other than the emotional torture of others...?

CREATING AN ASH VAMPIRE

Ash Vampire is a template that can be added to any humanoid or monstrous humanoid creature. The creature's type changes to undead, and it uses all the base creature's abilities and special abilities except as noted here.

SPECIAL ATTACKS:

Ash Disintegration (Su): Instead of draining levels, Ash Vampires can focus their powers of entropy, using their slam (or touch) attack to deliver a powerful disintegration effect. Against living beings, *Ash Disintegration* does 1d8 +1d8 points of damage per *age* category. Against standard objects it works as per the *rusting grasp* spell only it effects any object living or inanimate. Ash Vampires can use this power once per round. A creature or object that makes a successful Fortitude save receives only half damage.

Note: Hit Points removed by this power can only be restored through powerful curative magic (*heal* or better) by a cleric of 15th level or greater, otherwise wounds heal naturally at half normal rate.

Blood Drain (Ex): As summarised on p. 30.

Domination (Su): As summarised on p. 59.

Energy Drain (Su): Living creatures hit by an Ash Vampire's slam attack suffer 3 negative levels.

SPECIAL QUALITIES:

Black Mantle (Su): Ash Vampires gain the Dark Gift, Black Mantle.

Damage Reduction (Su): Ash Vampires gain damage reduction dependent on their *age* category (see p. 127).

Destruction (Su): The only way to slay an Ash Vampire is to bury them in holy ground. Only when the *Corrupter* has lain in the earth for a year and a day will it finally be destroyed.

The final destruction of a *Corrupter* is a hideous affair. During its last days, the earth around the Ash Vampire blackens and those sleeping nearby suffer frightful dreams in which the endless wailing of the dead assault their ears. These blessed urns tend to be stored deep in the catacombs of holy places, where they are maintained by clerics until their destruction.

Fast Healing (Ex): An Ash Vampire's fast healing ability is dependent on their *age* category (see p. 127).

Favoured Class: Black Monk. When determining whether a multiclass Ash Vampire suffers an XP penalty, his highest-level black monk class does not count.

Invulnerability (Su): Ash Vampires are *very* hard to kill. Even sunlight does not slay them. Reducing an Ash Vampire to 0 hit points (or a stake in the heart) does not destroy them. They transform into ash and reform in 1d10 days (unless specific measures are taken to the contrary). A single point of blood will restore an Ash Vampire from death instantly (although they must feed immediately).

Resistance (Su): Ash Vampires have cold and electricity resistance 10/+5 per *age*.

Turn to Ash (Su): As a move equivalent action, an Ash Vampire can transform into a swirling cloud of dust and ash. They can reform as a move equivalent action, making them very difficult to kill. While in ash form they have a movement rate of 20 ft. (perfect) and are immune to physical attacks (although they can be turned - but not destroyed).

Note: The ash is almost impossible to destroy. If it is separated, scattered or blown apart, the *Corrupter* reforms from the greatest portion of ash; the rest becomes non-magical.

SKILLS

Ash Vampires receive a +4 racial bonus to Concentration, Intimidate, Listen, Move Silently, Search, Sense Motive and Spot checks. This bonus increases by +2 for every *age* they gain. Otherwise same as the base creature.

VAMPIRIC WEAKNESSES

Allergy: Iron, Allergy: Silver, Cannot Cross Holy Ground, Cannot Enter without Invitation, Chill of the Grave, Fear of Fire, Fear of Sunlight, No Reflection, Gravebound.

WEAKNESSES

Ash Destruction (Su): A cloak of entropy radiates out from an Ash Vampire in a 5 ft. radius per *age* category. Creatures with fewer than 1 HD are slain instantly. Birds will fall from the sky; insects will turn to dust. All vegetation will blacken, leaving a noticeable trail in rural areas. This destruction makes it hard for an Ash Vampire to conceal themselves in populated areas.

Note: This weakness can be temporarily negated with use of the Dark Gift, Stifle the Chill.

DEATH STATE

See invulnerability (above).

ADVANCED ENERGY DRAIN: STEAL ESSENCE

In addition to draining levels, a *Corrupter* can steal the very life essence from a victim. They must maintain contact for a full round to age their victim by 1d4 years. They can do this while feeding. This attack manifests as a withering of flesh and a reduction in physical abilities. Visible tendrils of energy can be seen passing between the Ash Vampire and his prey.

An Ash Vampire gains +1 to his Strength, Dexterity and AC and heals 1d4 hit points for every year drained. These benefits remain for a total number of minutes equal 1 + the amount of years drained. He can only benefit from 1 + twice his *age* years at any one time. If an Ash Vampire drains more than 4 years from a mortal within 24 hours, the target is immediately *exhausted*.

Example: An age 2 Ash Vampire successfully pins a fighter to the ground. At the end of the round, he drains 3 years from the fighter in a wash of life force. He gains +3 to his Strength, Dexterity and AC for 3 minutes as well as recovering 3d4 hit points. If in the next round he drains another year from the fighter, the fighter will be exhausted (see Exhausted, DMG).

Note: Only the most powerful restorative magic can recover the years lost to an Ash Vampire. A cleric of no lower than 15th level is needed with powerful restoratives, *dispel magic*, *heal* and *restoration*.

> *"In the midst of life we are in death.*
> *Earth to earth, ashes to ashes, dust to dust;*
> *in sure and certain hope of the Resurrection into eternal unlife.*
> *I don't know about the rest,*
> *but the ash part's just about right."*
> Kale Rayne, Ash Vampire

BLACK BLOODS

Black Bloods (or vampires) are the talk of every fireside story. Everyone knows at least one tale about the bloodsucking monsters that plague the living. Black Bloods are as much a part of mortal culture as elves or dragons and they have a long and bloody history spanning thousands of years. Few races have been in greater conflict with mortals, for they must drink the blood of the living if they are to survive. Standard vampires are known as Black Bloods - a term used by vampires to indicate their own kind. They are by far the most numerous of the vampire races and can be found in crypts and places of darkness all across the realm. They were the first of Vangual's creations and consider themselves the most favoured of his children.

Appearance

Black Bloods look similar to mortals, save for their pallid complexions and ashen features. They often have broken veins marking their flesh and deep glowering eyes. Many have clawed hands and protruding fangs. While they look the most like humans, they are also the most inhuman.

The Black Kiss

Black Bloods make up the majority of the Children of Vangual. The curse can be passed to any of the mortal races, from human, elf and dwarf, to the monster races: goblin, troll and ogre. There are Black Blood giants, drow and even vampire lizardmen lurking in darkness across the realms.

Society

Black Bloods live close to their prey, near villages where the hunting is good, or in cities in groups called broods. Broods consist of a number of lesser vampires controlled by one master. Solitary and prideful, vampires protect their broods fiercely and will not lightly tolerate the presence of others encroaching on their territory. Most Black Bloods live in Avystervan, under the protection of the Black Council where they gain safety and have access to all the food and resources they require.

Outlook

Black Bloods differ greatly in their outlook and beliefs. Where one individual might be shy and reclusive, another might be a power hungry tyrant with aspirations of world domination. They can be scholastic, or they can be extravagant and daring, willful in the face of the *Powers of Light*.

Role-playing a Black Blood

You are a Black Blood, first born of the children of Vangual. You are superior to your feral brethren and the Void is pure within you. Being taken from mortals, mortality is strongest within you. You appear human; and aside from the *Chill* and your deathly pallor, you can move amongst humans without too much trouble (although you are still unquestionably dead). You are the eyes and ears of the vampire community, the senses of the Black Council.

Creating a Black Blood

Black Blood is a template that can be added to any humanoid or monstrous humanoid creature. The creature's type changes to undead, and it uses all the base creature's abilities and special abilities except as noted here. Black Bloods gain 2 additional Dark Gifts at character creation and an additional 1 Dark Gift at each new *age* category.

Special Attacks:

Blood Drain (Ex): As summarised on p. 30.
Domination (Su): As summarised on p. 59.
Energy Drain (Su): Living creatures hit by a Black Blood's slam attack suffer 2 negative levels.

Special Qualities:

Damage Reduction (Su): A Black Blood gains damage reduction dependent on their *age* (see p. 127).
Fast Healing (Ex): So long as they have at least 1 hit point, Black Bloods heal hit points per round based on their *age* (see p. 127).
Favoured Class: Any. When determining whether a multiclass Black Blood suffers an XP penalty, his highest-level black class does not count.
Resistance (Su): Black Bloods have cold and electricity resistance 10/+5 per *age*.

Skills

Black Bloods receive a +4 racial bonus to Concentration, Hide, Listen, Move Silently, Search, Sense Motive and Spot checks. This bonus increases by +2 for every *age* they gain. Otherwise same as the base creature.

Vampiric Weaknesses

Allergy: Garlic, Allergy: Iron, Allergy: Silver, Cannot Cross Running Water, Cannot Enter Holy Ground, Cannot Enter without Invitation, Chill of the Grave, Fear of Fire, Fear of Sunlight, Gravebound, No Reflection, Stench of the Grave, Water Vulnerability

Weaknesses

Black Bloods do not have any specific race weaknesses.

Death State

Black Bloods turn to mist when reduced to 0 hit points or lower.

Advanced Energy Drain

Black Bloods do not have an advanced energy drain power.

---

*"We are the first, and the last; the alpha and the omega.
We have the wisdom of the ages and the power to become like gods.
With darkness behind us, there is nothing we cannot do."*
Andaine Gellor, Black Blood

FIRE VAMPIRES

Perhaps the rarest of all vampires, Fire Vampires (or *Infernos*) are those mortals horribly burned in life. They return to undeath as vengeful spirits intent on wreaking havoc on the world. Even cremation does not always prevent the *Second Waking*, a Fire Vampire's body reforms from ashes unless it was buried on holy ground. Pyromaniacs, they are imbued with hellfire, a crimson burning flame that accentuates their madness.

Fire Vampires have absolute command of fire. They can incinerate on touch, casting whole gouts of flame about them at a whim.

Appearance

Fire Vampires commonly appear as a mote of flickering fire or a column of raging flame. When they so choose, they can take mortal form, appearing as a horribly burned individual with still-smouldering flesh. When they grow angry or vengeful, they set afire, burning with crimson rage. Their eyes appear as points of scolding scarlet, and are visible in all of their forms. They do not stink of the grave, but of horribly rotting and charred flesh that remains with them until they are destroyed.

When not aflame, Fire Vampires tend to remain hooded or cloaked to hide their disfigurement. They are dark creatures with twisted, madness-torn minds. They are hateful of all life, and are slavishly obedient to the Black Council.

Fire Vampires are wholly bound with crimson flame the color of blood. This fire gives off a glowering darkness that sheds blood red light around them, but does not harm other vampires (although their spells and attacks can do so, should they desire it). Their presence sucks the very heat from the air and despite their flames, a room will grow cold upon their entrance.

The Black Kiss

Fire Vampires can create progeny, although they rarely choose to. To do so, they must drain all of the blood from a candidate while inflicting powerful flame attacks upon their bodies. They must incinerate their victim on the very threshold of death. Horribly disfigured, the mortal will then rise up as a Fire Vampire a few short nights later.

Society

Some *Infernos* are worshipped as gods of fire and flame. These 'deities' typically live in remote regions, elevated to godhood by the local shamanistic community who often do not realise the true nature of their 'deity'. Such Fire Vampires take full advantage of their status, demanding regular human and animal sacrifices and elaborate displays of devotion. In return, the Fire Vampire protects their domain from invaders, while controlling their people with an iron hand.

Outlook

Fire Vampires are thoroughly wicked creatures whose minds were shattered by the blazing conflagration that killed them. Insane, *Infernos* take great delight in setting whole areas of a city aflame, and picking off the stragglers or the wounded. They greatly enjoy the hunt and in causing as much damage and destruction as possible. Unlike other vampires, they do not have an energy drain attack but are instead capable of causing grievous damage with their Black Fire spells.

Fire Vampires have a great penchant for gems and jewellery. They adore rubies and precious stones, and demand these in payment for work done.

A Fire Vampire must assume mortal form to feed. They often appear as a will 'o' wisp, luring a single adventurer away from the rest of their group with the use of their charm powers and feasting upon their vulnerable flesh when they are alone.

Role-playing a Fire Vampire

Burned. Continually in pain, the memory of your first death never lessens. Vindictive, you want to make those who transformed you pay. It doesn't matter that your masters were the ones that mutilated you. They had their reasons. Mortals must pay. All of them. You cannot let them see you as you really are; you must conceal your true form, hide your ruined flesh. Until the time to strike, and to feed.

Creating a Fire Vampire

Fire Vampire is a template that can be added to any humanoid or monstrous humanoid creature. The creature's type changes to undead, and it uses all the base creature's abilities and special abilities except as noted here.

Special Attacks:

Blood Drain (Ex): As summarised on p. 30.

Domination (Su): As summarised on p. 59.

Special Qualities:

Damage Reduction (Su): Fire Vampires gain damage reduction dependent on their *age* category (see p. 127).

Fast Healing (Ex): A Fire Vampire's fast healing ability is dependent on their *age* category (see p. 127).

Favoured Class: Black Sorcerer. When determining whether a multiclass Fire Vampire suffers an XP penalty, his highest-level black sorcerer class does not count. The sorcerer must specialise in fire elementalism or else he does not gain this benefit. All Fire Vampire black sorcerers can cast one additional fire elemental spell of each level per day in addition to any other benefits they may receive.

Fire Command: An *Inferno* can empower any Black Fire spell at any time by expending 1 Blood point.

Fire Immunity (Su): Fire Vampires are wholly immune to all forms of fire, heat or flame. Additionally, any fire-based damage done to an *Inferno* heals it (on a hit point per hit point basis). An average size bonfire will restore a Fire Vampire's hit points at a rate of 5 per round. This healing is in addition to any benefits an *Inferno* enjoys from their fast healing ability.

Flight (Su): Fire Vampires gain the Dark Gift, Flight.

Immolate (Su): Fire Vampires are wreathed in Black Fire, a supernatural flame that burns but does not harm vampires. It has the appearance of a *Bloodlight* spell. Fire Vampires in mortal form can choose to extinguish this flame at any time. Anyone in melee with an immolated Fire Vampire suffers 1d4 (+1 per *age* category) points of Black Fire damage per round (see below) and must make a Reflex save (DC 16) or risk catching fire (see 'catching fire' in the DMG).

Resistance (Su): Fire Vampires have electricity resistance 10/+5 per *age* category.

Transmute to Fire: Fire Vampires can turn into a mote of fire, or a column of raging flame at will, as a move-equivalent action.

* *Mote of Fire:* A mote of fire cannot be affected by melee weapons, and has the trait *incorporeal*. It can fly at a rate of 40 ft. (good). It can attack, attempting to set a character aflame (Reflex save DC 16 to avoid). It causes 1d4 points of damage with a successful melee attack.

* *Column of Flame:* A column of flame is a roaring pillar of fire 10 ft. high and has the trait *incorporeal*. It can move at 20 ft. per round, and attacks for 2d8+6 points of fire damage (plus additional effects as per Immolate). All within 10 ft. of the column of flame suffer 1d4 (+1 per *age* category) points of damage per round from the intense heat.

Vampiric Charm: Fire Vampires can use their vampiric charm powers in any of their forms.

SKILLS

Fire Vampires receive a +4 racial bonus to Concentration, Hide, Listen, Move Silently, Search, Sense Motive and Spot checks. This bonus increases by +2 for every *age* they gain. Otherwise same as the base creature.

VAMPIRIC WEAKNESSES

Allergy: Garlic, Allergy: Iron, Cannot Cross Running Water, Cannot Enter Holy Ground, Cannot Enter without Invitation, Fear of Sunlight, Stench of the Grave, Water Vulnerability.

WEAKNESSES

Cold and Water Vulnerability: Cold based attacks do double damage to a Fire Vampire. Water based attacks do double damage to a Fire Vampire aflame. Holy water does triple damage to a Fire Vampire in mortal form and quadruple damage to a Fire Vampire aflame.

No Energy Drain Ability: Fire Vampires do not typically have the ability to drain levels.

DEATH STATE

An *Inferno* transforms into its mote of fire form when reduced to 0 or lower hit points.

ADVANCED POWER DESCRIPTIONS

Fire Vampires have tremendous control over fire. They can cast 2 plus their *age* category in Black Fire spells (see below) per night as a spell-like ability. These spell effects are free and do not cost the vampire any blood. Spells are cast with a DC of 10 + spell level + *Inferno's* Intelligence Modifier and require a standard action to activate.

Example: An age 3 vampire can cast up to 5 Blood points worth of spells from the Black Fire spell list below per night.

Additionally, Fire Vampires can choose to cast the following Black Fire spells at the cost of Blood:

* *Produce Flame:* 1 blood
* *Wall of Fire:* 2 blood
* *Fireball:* 3 blood
* *Flame Strike:* 4 blood
* *Fire Storm:* 5 blood

BLACK FIRE SPELLS

Black Fire spells are blood red in color and necromantic in nature. They are not true elemental fire. Spells and abilities that protect against heat or fire confer only half protection against Black Fire spells.

Fire Vampires cannot use Black Fire spells to heal themselves, but are wholly immune to their own magic (ie. they can center a Black Fire *fireball* on themselves with taking any damage).

THE LOST

These creatures are not and have never been mortal. Cursed by divine magic, they have fallen from whichever spiritual domain they once inhabited, given immortal bodies and doomed to live in exile amongst the undead. Once glorious spirits - now vampires - they must drink blood and devour ashes to survive.

Appearance

Lost Vampires take the form of beautiful winged humanoids, with large wide eyes that blaze a baleful crimson when angered. They have a look of divinity about them, although the perpetual scowl or shadow that seems to loom over them mars this. Their eyes are always questioning, and a mortal cannot gaze upon them for too long without experiencing the sadness of unfathomable loss. As the Lost age, they begin to take on an infernal appearance, with swarthy flesh and dark or crimson eyes, horns, claws or even hooves. Additionally, their wings grow with age, becoming more gnarled and twisted.

The Curse

The Lost are not true vampires. They were never 'turned' by another, but were instead cursed by powerful magic. Exiled, they appear in darkness with no clue as to who they are or from where they came. Occasionally, a divine being will visit them to inform them of their exile, but this will be brief and of little information to the grief-stricken Lost. Their minds and spirits are their own, but their memories are all but gone.

Society

The Lost do not work together. They loathe others of their kind as they remind them of what they have lost. They have no House in Avystervan and are tended solely by the Devoted Incarnate. The guild of evil clerics has expended considerable resources to look after any Lost that cross their path and to ensure their descent towards evil goes as smoothly (and quickly) as possible. Seeing all good Lost to be a potential threat, they ensure those they cannot turn to evil are quickly destroyed. When a new Lost is cast to earth, the vampiric forces of good and evil clash as they race to unmask the fallen celestial, and bring it into the fold.

Outlook

The Lost truly do not know who they are. They have little memory of their identity before they opened their eyes on their *Second Waking*. Cast adrift in a world that bears little resemblance to the heaven they once inhabited, they feel they have been torn from something wonderful into a world where even their own flesh betrays them.

Sunlight burns, divine magic strikes terror and they can never find the solace they so desperately crave.

Many Lost spend their unlives seeking redemption, torn between resentment for the *Powers of Light* and a desperate longing to be returned to the fold. This often makes them bitter and vengeful, especially toward good clerics. Those that do not fall to evil become shattered creatures, drifters and vagrants, impoverished and broken beings without place or purpose. Many spend their unlives in the gutter, drinking from the blood of vagrants and unable to resolve the missing portions of their lives.

Those who embrace evil desire revenge. They seek out the divine, destroying temples and defiling holy places with grim satisfaction. They take tormented pleasure in slaying priests and congregation alike whenever they find them. These sessions are always proceeded by a period of deep remorse and self-loathing when they cry tears of blood and sob wracking breaths of ash.

The non-evil Lost that exist are quickly sought out and destroyed by the Devoted Incarnate. Most Lost are too bitter and self-obsessed to spare any thought for others. When one must drink mortal blood to survive, a Lost quickly discovers that the divine rules of good and evil no longer apply.

The early stages of a Lost's development are very painful. Many Lost spend their first years in exile, refusing to accept what they have become and unable to piece together the fragments of their shattered past. Denied even their own destruction, the Lost wander the mortal realms, knowing they are cursed yet powerless to do anything about it. They scream to the gods for release, but the *Powers of Light* are oblivious to their cries.

Some Lost experience dreams, warnings and omen sent by the *Powers of Light* informing them of clerics who have fallen, or of specific quests that need completing. Feeling used, most Lost turn their backs on these dreams and rarely receive them after a century. These are the Lost that fall into shadow.

Others willingly take up the mantle of unholy avenger, becoming forces of shadow to drive back darkness. Having been given new purpose these vampires have their faith renewed, knowing the holy *Powers of Light* have not abandoned them - and that they can reclaim their lost glory - but such vampires are rare indeed.

It is said that those Lost who persevere, enduring all manner of torments are returned to the heavenly fold, vanishing in wash of golden holy light after a particularly difficult mission. The sad truth is that many Lost are unable to interpret their dreams, and spend their unlives divided between love and a burning hatred for the *Powers of Light*. Many Lost simply allow themselves to run out of blood and spend eternity in the *black sleep*, content to while away the centuries until they are destroyed or their deity takes pity on them.

Role-playing the Lost

You are cursed. Banished to darkness and stripped of all that was once glorious. Perhaps you were once a creature of incredible power and beauty, swathed in light and righteousness. The truth does not matter for all that remains now is a vague memory. This impotence tears at your soul, causing periods of terrible rage and agonizing pain. Perhaps you can seek a way back to your celestial domain, seek redemption for what you have done. If only you could remember what that was…

Creating a Lost Vampire

The Lost are a race. A mortal character cannot play one of the Lost unless he was previously a powerful celestial who was cast down from his planar home. The Lost gain the hit dice for their character classes and typically begin play at 1st level, having lost most of their former divine knowledge. The Lost can begin play at any alignment and undergo a Katharein like every other vampire.

The Lost are celestials that have been cursed by their god. While the player does not have to come up with a reason why they were so transformed, the crime must fit the punishment (and the sentence of vampirism is most grave indeed). Perhaps they will find redemption, but perhaps they will spend their unlives wallowing in self pity in a world that wants to use them as pawns in an army of terrible darkness...

Special Attacks:

Blood Drain (Ex): As summarised on p. 30.
Domination (Su): As summarised on p. 59.
Energy Drain (Su): Living creatures hit by a Lost Vampire's slam attack suffer 2 negative levels.

Special Qualities:

Damage Reduction (Su): The Lost gain damage reduction dependent on their *age* category (see p. 127).
Fast Healing (Ex): A Lost Vampire's fast healing ability is dependent on their *age* category (see p. 127).
Favoured Class: Black Cleric. When determining whether a multiclass Lost Vampire suffers an XP penalty, his highest-level black cleric class does not count.
Immortal Being (Su): Slain Lost awaken in another place within 1d4 days of their destruction. Range is not an issue but none can predict where the Lost will appear. They will have little or no recollection of their previous incarnations (although they may remember a painful glimmer of their past unlives). They may even have a completely different appearance (although they retain their previous *age* and abilities). No one knows how to fully destroy the Lost. Capturing what fragments of divinity remain in their shattered souls may forever prevent the Lost from awaking to unlife, but nothing is certain.

Resistance (Su): The Lost have cold and electricity resistance 10/+5 per *age* category.
Sense (Su): Lost Vampires gain the Dark Gift, Sense.
Wings (Ex): The Lost can use their wings to fly 40 ft. (good).

Skills

The Lost receive a +4 racial bonus to Concentration, Hide, Listen, Move Silently, Search, Sense Motive and Spot checks. This bonus increases by +2 for every *age* they gain.

Vampiric Weaknesses

Allergy: Silver, Cannot Enter Holy Ground, Cannot Enter without Invitation, Chill of the Grave, Fear of Fire, Fear of Sunlight.

Weaknesses

Create Scion: The Lost cannot pass on their curse to others. Theirs is a lonely existence.
Dreams: The sleep of the Lost is not filled with Void. They are plagued with fragments of their past, flashes of their home and lives before their fall. The Lost are truly tormented. They wake from sleeping, still hearing the echo of the celestial choir ringing in their ears.
Flashbacks*: The Lost must choose a patron deity (from their previous life). When faced with good clerics, the Lost may suffer unsettling flashbacks to their past. They must make a Will save DC 15. Against good clerics of their patron deity the DC rises to 20. They can only make one *Flashback* check when faced with clerics of the same religion per hour.
Fragmented Memory: The Lost have little recollection of who or what they were before they awoke. If they are new vampires, they have precious little understanding of the world of mortals. They can speak celestial but must learn other languages.
Turning Vulnerability*: Turning causes the Lost great agony, blistering their bodies and setting their flesh aflame. They suffer 1d4 points of damage for every level of the turning cleric (Will save at the cleric's turning level +4 for half damage).
Vulnerability to Divine Magic*: A powerful reminder of the divine, holy magic causes the Lost to recoil in pain and terror. The Lost suffer an additional point of damage per die from good divine spells as well as saving against such powers at -4.
Vulnerability to Holy Water*: Holy water does double damage against the Lost. Holy water from their (former) patron deity does *triple* damage.
Note: Weaknesses marked * can be bought off by good Lost as per other vampiric weaknesses (see p. 35). These weaknesses should be role played away, as the Lost gains inner strength and confidence with his new unlife and abilities.

Death State

A Lost vampire transforms into a glowering mist when reduced to 0 or lower hit points.

Advanced Energy Drain: Wisdom

In addition to draining levels, the Lost drain 1 point of Wisdom for every negative level they inflict. This gives them +1 to their Wisdom and Charisma for 1 turn per point of Wisdom drained to a maximum increase at any one time of 1 plus their *age* category.

Mock Vampires

Rotting skin, exposed ligaments and pustulating flesh, the *mocked* are the mongrels of vampire society. They have the appearance of a zombie, yet retain all the powers and abilities of a Black Blood. Dripping gore, they wear rags and often have misshapen limbs and greenish flesh.

The *mocked* have lain dead in the ground for too long. They are grotesque monsters with baleful eyes and foul stench. Some have dead greying flesh, others green, oozing skin. When they must travel beyond their caverns, they do so in thick robes with deep hoods to hide their terrible features.

The Black Kiss

No one knows exactly what creates the *mocked*, certainly there are many things that can influence the necromantic processes: holy ground, divine blessings, even nearby running water or a holy symbol casually tossed into a coffin. A poor first Katharein can result in the vampire rising as one of the *mocked*. Many Mock Vampires do not have the ability to speak in any more than guttural moans, their vocal chords all but rotted away. Some suffer delusions or insanity, although this is rare.

The *mocked* typically remain dead for at least a week longer than the typical 1d4 days, rotting while in the grave. They can restore any standard wounds they receive but the rot of the grave is permanent and cannot be healed without the use of powerful magic beyond even that of the Black Cabal.

Society

The *mocked* typically inhabit the lowest rank of vampire society and are treated like animals by other vampires. It is considered a great embarrassment to have one of the *mocked* in a brood. Despite their disadvantages, the *mocked* do have uses; they look like zombies, which means they are often mistaken for lesser undead in battle and are used as guards and watchers when the element of surprise is needed (or no one else will do the job). The *mocked* have their own caverns underneath Avystervan where they are thrown the scraps from the town.

Outlook

The *mocked* live in sewers out of sight of the other vampire races. Degenerated, they are permanently disfigured in unlife. They awake from the grave with reduced intellect and many are the subject of cruel jokes amongst vampire society.

While over the centuries, Mock Vampires gain some semblance of intelligence, some go to the other extreme and become wholly subsumed by darkness, becoming little more than beasts.

Role-playing a Mock Vampire

Rotten, oozing and foul, you are a monster. You have the appearance of a zombie, with pustulating flesh and dripping gore and this causes you great shame. You are responsible for mopping up the morsels left behind by the rest of vampire society and stick to the sewers under the *City of Graves*, out of sight of the other – true vampires. Vampire society has little use for you, yet you remain, having nowhere else to go. You have powers, though. Great powers. They will soon see.

Your time will come. Soon…

Creating a Mock Vampire

Mock Vampire is a template that can be added to any humanoid or monstrous humanoid creature. The creature's type changes to undead, and it uses all the base creature's abilities and special abilities except as noted here.

Special Attacks:

Blood Drain (Ex): As summarised on p. 30.

Domination (Su): As summarised on p. 59.

Energy Drain (Su): Living creatures hit by a Mock Vampire's slam attack suffer 2 negative levels.

Special Qualities:

Damage Reduction (Su): A Mock Vampire gains damage reduction dependent on their *age* (see p. 127).

Fast Healing (Ex): So long as they have at least 1 hit point, Mock Vampires heal hit points per round based on their *age* (see p. 127).

Regenerate (Su): Mock Vampires have powerful healing abilities but the *Powers of Darkness* are cruel. Although they cannot restore their disfigurements, they can expend Blood to rapidly restore any wounds they receive. As a standard action, the *mocked* can expend up to 1 plus their *age* category in Blood per round to restore 1d12 + their *age* category hit points per point of Blood expended.

Resistance (Su): Mock Vampires have cold, sonic and electricity resistance 10/+5 per *age*.

Sludge Form (Ex): Due to their fleshy bodies, the *mocked* only take half damage from slashing and piercing weapons.

Turn to Ooze (Su): The *mocked* can transform into a pool of greenish liquid as a move-equivalent action (at a cost of 1 Blood). While in this form they are immune to standard melee attacks. Area of effect attacks (such as burning oil, spells, holy water or the flame effect from a magic sword) will still damage them. They can extend two tentacles to attack their victims at their level, delivering their Slam attacks up to 10 ft. away. These tentacles have the Mock Vampire's Strength but can only drain 1 negative level per attack while in this form.

Skills

The *mocked* receive a +4 racial bonus to Hide, Listen, Move Silently, Search, Sense Motive and Spot checks. This bonus increases by +2 for every *age* they gain. Otherwise same as the base creature.

Vampiric Weaknesses

Allergy: Garlic, Allergy: Iron, Allergy: Silver, Cannot Cross Running Water, Cannot Enter Holy Ground, Cannot Enter without Invitation, Chill of the Grave, Fear of Fire, Fear of Sunlight, Gravebound, Stench of the Grave, Water Vulnerability

Death State

When the *mocked* are slain, they do not turn to mist, instead transforming into a greenish sludge that can move at 20 ft. If they cannot seek a hiding place, they are destroyed after 2 hours.

Advanced Energy Drain: Charisma

In addition to draining levels, Mock Vampires drain 1 point of Charisma for every negative level they inflict. This gives them +1 to their Charisma for 1 hour per point of Charisma drained to a maximum of 1 plus their *age* category. This Charisma gives them a more normal appearance, regenerating their wounds and smoothing over their flesh. While they cannot completely restore their disfigurements, they can temporarily negate the worst of the effects and have some semblance of mortality about them.

> *'Whoever said beauty's only skin deep was lying.*
> *It's plainly not true.*
> *I'm hideous inside as well..."*
> Ichabod Luthien, Mock Vampire

The Man Under the Stair

Beware, beware of the man under the stair
He's mean with just one goal.
And if you stay to chat today
He'll feast upon your soul.

So hurry, quick, ensure you're slick
And be so very brave.
Avoid the man under the stair
For he'll send you to your grave.

Don't stop to hear when old man sings
It will surely make you shiver.
For he'll take the chance to trip you up
And feast upon your liver.

(Song sung by villagefolk to warn children
of the dangers of talking to strangers.)

RAVENOUS VAMPIRES

Ravenous are disease-riddled monsters who feast on health and youth. Known as *Leeches*, they are mistrusted and reviled, even by other vampires who consider them a blight. The bringers of plague and decay. Some say they were created by the god of slimes and oozes, while others believe they are demons cast from the abyss and given mortal form.

APPEARANCE

The Ravenous are tall and thin with long angular faces, with a slight emerald caste. They have domed foreheads and little hair. Their eyes shimmer with a nacreous green and their lips are marked with an unhealthy sheen. Their faces gleam eerily in darkness. They are emaciated with thin limbs and protruding ribs - although this does not detract from their strength or agility. As Ravenous age they take on a more reptilian quality, which is particularly evident in their various shape-changed forms. They can grow filthy claws through which they can deliver their foul disease attacks.

THE BLACK KISS

When they so choose, the Ravenous can make their own. To do this the victim must be forced to drink a concentrated point of the *Leech's* blood. The victim will be fine - for a day or so. After 48 hours they will begin to get chills, feeling sick and losing a point of Constitution and Strength per day. This will continue throughout the next 2d4+1 days until their skin turns a greenish hue. Finally, facing uncontrollable convulsions, they lose a point of Constitution and Strength per hour until death comes. Only a *neutralise poison* spell cast by a cleric of no lower than 15th Level, followed swiftly by a *remove curse* will prevent death. Lost abilities are regained at a rate of 1 point per week.

SOCIETY

The Black Council created an order of Ravenous called the Blighted Heart. These despicable vampires live in cities, feasting on those in hospitals, poor houses and orphanages across the realm.

There they feed in secret, draining both youth and vitality until even the strongest fade away.

OUTLOOK

The Ravenous take great delight in travelling the world, seeking out the strongest and the fittest, devouring their life essence and leaving behind a diseased and crippled victim. Ravenous typically wear rags and take on the role of beggars, asking for alms and then quickly draining the vitality from any who come close enough to offer help. The Ravenous are few and far between, but they spread death and disease whenever they get the opportunity. They are the carriers of plague and have been known to pollute village water supplies, and to vomit great waves of toxins into rivers and streams.

They make their homes in city sewers, corrupting the environment and slaying any that cross their path. These places tend to quickly become disease ridden and many strange creatures are created from feeding on the waste left by the *Leeches*.

Unlike other vampires, the Ravenous cannot sustain themselves without blood. The hungrier they are, the more violent and deranged they become. A Ravenous will use their Noxious Breath attack to incapacitate their target before feeding. Disoriented, many victims are unaware that they have been subjected to any kind of attack. With any feeding, sickness and death inevitably follows.

ROLE-PLAYING THE RAVENOUS

You are forever hungry. The Void burns in your chest, a cold clamour that lingers in your mouth. You must feed and drink the blood of the living whenever you can. No matter how hard you try, you can never be sated. Even the purest blood does not still the craving, although it is the sweetest nectar that soothes your tortured psyche. When the Void claims you, you take great delight in torture and causing physical pain.

CREATING A RAVENOUS VAMPIRE

Ravenous Vampire is a template that can be added to any humanoid or monstrous humanoid creature. The creature's type changes to undead, and it uses all the base creature's abilities and special abilities except as noted here.

SPECIAL ATTACKS:

Contagion (Su): A Ravenous can deliver a touch attack to inflict a disease upon their target as per the *Contagion* spell. The Ravenous may choose the disease inflicted and the general severity.

Drain Blood (Ex): As summarised on p. 30.

Energy Drain (Su): Living creatures hit by a Ravenous Vampire's slam attack suffer 2 negative levels.

SPECIAL QUALITIES:

Damage Reduction (Su): Ravenous Vampires gain damage reduction dependent on their *age* category (see p. 127).

Fast Healing (Ex): A Ravenous Vampire's fast healing ability is dependent on their *age* category (see p. 127).

Gaseous Form (Su): Ravenous Vampires assuming their gaseous form transform into a noxious cloud of mist equivalent to the sorcerer spell *stinking cloud*.

Noxious Breath (Su): Ravenous Vampires gain the Dark Gift, Noxious Breath.

Resistance (Su): Ravenous Vampires have acid, cold and electricity resistance 10/+5 per *age*.

Scent (Ex): Ravenous have a heightened sense of smell. They gain the '*Scent*' special ability.

RCH 11-02

SKILLS

The Ravenous receive a +4 racial bonus to Bluff, Hide, Listen, Move Silently, Search, Sense Motive and Spot checks. This bonus increases by +2 for every *age* they gain. Otherwise same as the base creature.

VAMPIRIC WEAKNESSES

Allergy: Garlic, Allergy: Iron, Cannot Cross Running Water, Cannot Enter Holy Ground, Cannot Enter without Invitation, Chill of the Grave, Fear of Fire, Fear of Sunlight, Gravebound, Stench of the Grave.

WEAKNESSES

Blood Loss: When the Ravenous reach 0 blood, they collapse into a yellowish puddle of foul and highly toxic liquid that quickly dissipates in sunlight. At this point they are slain (however, someone could collect the liquid and reform the Ravenous at a later date, had he the proper knowledge to do so). The ichor dissipates in 2d4 rounds in bright sunlight, 2d4 minutes in shade, and 2d4 hours in complete darkness.

Blood Thirst: Each point of Constitution a Ravenous drinks satisfies only half a point of blood.

Cause Disease: There is a 20% chance +10% per *age* category that a Ravenous will transmit a disease to any mortal upon whom they feed as per the spell *contagion*. The target must make a Fortitude save (DC 10 + half the Ravenous' HD + Charisma modifier) to avoid the effects of disease.

Desperate Hunger: Ravenous burn two points of Blood per day.

Raving: When a Ravenous Vampire gets down to half his Blood total, he must make a Will save when he next sees mortals (DC 10+ the deficit in his blood). A *raving* vampire will attack the nearest possible victim regardless of the danger, seeking only to feed. He need only make this check once every day or every time he uses a point of Blood and encounters further sources of food.

Example: A Ravenous with a total Blood score of 12 is down to his last 4 points of Blood. The DC to avoid Raving will be 18. While he is amongst mortals, he will need to make a further raving check every time he expends Blood to power any of his abilities.

DEATH STATE

When reduced to 0 hit points, the Ravenous transforms into a cloud of noxious mist. This mist acts like the spell *cloudkill* (although the vampire can do nothing but return to his *place of rest* to heal). A Ravenous Vampire cannot consciously assume this form unless they have the Dark Gift, Cloudkill.

ADVANCED ENERGY DRAIN: CONSTITUTION

In addition to draining levels, the Ravenous can steal the vitality from a victim. The vampire need but maintain contact with their target for one full round to drain 1d4 points of permanent Constitution damage. The Ravenous gains additional temporary hit points equal to the HD of the drained victim x the amount of Constitution drained. These hit points last for 10 minutes +1 minute per hit point drained before dissipating at a rate of 1 per round. The Ravenous can only benefit from one set of bonus hit points at any one time.

Example: A Ravenous drains a level (and 3 Constitution) from an 8th Level fighter. The Ravenous gains 24 temporary hit points that last for 34 minutes.

The Monster

There's a monster in the sewers
My pa says it just ain't so
But I've seen its green eyes burning
All aflame with hungry glow

There's a monster in the sewers
My ma says it just ain't true
The Watch they keep on looking
And they don't know what to do.

I saw two Watchmen talking
One day and overheard
That some travellers were missing
And the townsfolk were real scared

There's a monster lurking somewhere
I know this to be right
For it ate my best friend Darryl
When he walked back home one night

My parents say he's missing
And I know and shake my head
I know the monster ate him
And I know for sure he's dead

The monster it is crafty
For it hides throughout the day
And it feeds upon the people
When the moon comes out to play

So if you go a looking
Down the dark and enclosed well
You might just find a monster
That has clawed its way from hell.

So if you see the monster
Its eyes all flame and black
Just turn and run right back home.
Don't stop and don't look back.

Written by Jonus Bellman
Age 12, Tiradale

SHADOW VAMPIRES

Shadow Vampires only half-reside on the mortal realms. Insubstantial, they exist in part on the Shadow Plane. Fearful of the sun, they travel at night, draining the heat from their victims and stealing the breath from children.

They are the assassins of the vampire races, bringers of fear and shadow. Their powers are of silence and darkness and they are given tasks that involve stealth and secrecy.

APPEARANCE

Shadow Vampires consist of swirling darkness and frigid cold. Their eyes are tiny pinpricks of piercing sapphire. They cast no shadow of their own and frequently have no physical form on the mortal realms. They appear as inky shades, silent and near-invisible. They can hide in cracks or appear as monstrous shadows, gnarled and twisted.

On the rare occasions when they choose to take physical form, Shadow Vampires appear as tall ebon or ashen-haired drow with angular features and long pointed ears. They love to clothe themselves in the most expensive fabrics and wear impressive ornamental swords and bejeweled crowns. Cold surrounds them and when they speak, they exhale plumes of glimmering frost. A frigid aura accompanies their passing. It is said they freeze their victims to death long before they have finished feasting upon their blood.

THE BLACK KISS

Shadow Vampires are drow that have been cursed by darkness. They were taken by Vangual and transformed into shadow. It is said that Shadow Vampires must give up their shadows to the god of vampires for purposes unknown. The eldest Shadow Vampires have not revealed any purpose to this or what Vangual does with the shadows he collects.

Shadow Vampires cannot make more of their own. Even if they follow the process exactly, they simply create a standard Black Blood. Believing in keeping their vampire line absolutely pure, they will never create a vampire of any race other than drow. Only the drow elder Avernuus has the authority to create new Shadow Vampires, and then only at Vangual's instruction.

SOCIETY

Shadow Vampires are rare. There are few in existence and most can be found in Avystervan or on the Shadow Plane. Shadow Vampires are the elite guards for House *Avanaar* or drow vampires on elite and dangerous missions for the Black Council. Many drow vampires desire elevation to Shadow Vampire. It is considered highly prestigious, but few are chosen.

Shadow Vampires ally themselves only with other Shadow Vampires or with those the Black Council bids them work. They are wicked, arrogant and power hungry. They have neither respect for their peers or for vampire authority. Although they work with the Black Council, they do not respect its ways.

Shadow Vampires have given the Black Council a great deal of information about their mortal drow brethren. It is because of this that the drow of the underworld are gravely concerned. The Black Council know the strengths and locations of the drow armies, as well as many of their magical secrets. Shadow Vampires have returned to the drow cities on occasion, putting out the offer to join the ranks of the undead. There has been a slow, but steady flow of defectors from the drow to Avystervan over the years.

The Black Council petitioned Vangual for a number of non-drow Shadow Vampires to be created, and he agreed. The creation of these *shadow elves* has greatly angered House *Avanaar*, and there is much animosity between the two groups of vampires. Elven Shadow Vampires still have the blackest flesh, but they aren't quite as tall nor are their features quite so angular.

Shadow Vampires have been known on occasion to team up with Fire Vampires. This has proved to be an excellent combination of powers and abilities.

OUTLOOK

Shadow Vampires consider themselves superior to all other vampires and are particularly cruel to the *mocked*. They hate all life and consider mortal drow especially weak, seeing them as unwilling to take the next evolutionary step toward greatness.

ROLE-PLAYING A SHADOW VAMPIRE

You are drow - the most powerful race in the world. You are the elite of your race, chosen by the *Powers of Darkness* for great things. There is nothing you cannot accomplish. Only sunlight is your enemy, and soon enough, even that shall be extinguished.

CREATING A SHADOW VAMPIRE

Shadow Vampire is a template that can be added to any humanoid or monstrous humanoid creature. The creature's type changes to undead, and it uses all the base creature's abilities and special abilities except as noted here.

SPECIAL ATTACKS:

Blood Drain (Ex): As summarised on p. 30.

Domination (Su): As summarised on p. 59.

Energy Drain (Su): Living creatures hit by a Shadow Vampire's slam attack suffer 2 negative levels.

SPECIAL QUALITIES:

Conjure Darkness (Su): Shadow Vampires gain the Dark Gift, Conjure Darkness.

Damage Reduction (Su): Shadow Vampires gain damage reduction dependent on their *age* category (see p. 127).

Eyes of the Night (Su): Shadow Vampires can see in *any* darkness, magical or otherwise.

Fast Healing (Ex): A Shadow Vampire's fast healing ability is dependent on their *age* category (see p. 127).

Favoured Class - Black Rogue/Assassin: When determining whether a multiclass Shadow Vampire suffers an XP penalty, his highest-level black rogue (or assassin) class does not count.

Frigid Aura (Su): A glacial cold surrounds a Shadow Vampire. While this causes no problems for the undead, it proves troublesome for living beings. Mortals suffer -1 to all actions while in melee with a Shadow Vampire. Spells and powers that protect against cold are not effective against a Shadow Vampire's frigid aura.

Resistance (Su): Shadow Vampires are immune to all forms of cold and have electricity resistance 10/+5 per *age*.

Return to the Shadow (Su): At the cost of 1 Blood, a Shadow Vampire can take a move-equivalent action to fully manifest on the Shadow Plane. They can return for free as a move-equivalent action but can only do so once each round.

Shadow Form (Su): Shadow Vampires gain the Dark Gift, Shadow Form and can use their dominate powers while in this form.

Stifle the Chill (Su): Shadow Vampires taking the Dark Gift, Stifle the Chill can temporarily reduce their freezing aura at a cost of 1 Blood per turn, thus allowing them to covertly move amongst mortals.

SKILLS

Shadow Vampires receive a +4 racial bonus to Balance, Concentration, Hide, Listen, Move Silently, Search, Sense Motive and Spot checks. This bonus increases by +2 for every *age* they gain. Otherwise same as the base creature.

VAMPIRIC WEAKNESSES

Allergy: Iron, Allergy: Silver, Cannot Cross Running Water, Cannot Enter Holy Ground, Cannot Enter without Invitation, Chill of the Grave, Fear of Fire, Fear of Sunlight, Gravebound.

WEAKNESSES

Chill: A Shadow Vampire deals 1d4 points of cold damage for every round it feeds on a mortal.

Light Vulnerability: Shadow Vampires take double damage from light based spells.

Shadowbound: A Shadow Vampire must return to the Shadow Plane when they sleep.

Shadowless: Shadow Vampires cast no shadow.

Sunlight: Sunlight slays a Shadow Vampire in half the normal time (minimum of 1 round).

Weakened in Light. Shadow Vampires suffer an additional penalty of −1 to their actions in dim light and −2 in bright light.

DEATH STATE

When reduced to 0 hit points or lower, Shadow Vampires transmute into an inky shadow that moves 40 ft. (good) and is immune to all forms of physical damage.

ADVANCED ENERGY DRAIN: DEXTERITY

Shadow Vampires wield a terrible cold that sucks the warmth from their opponents. This has the additional effect of stripping the victim of his bravery, striking terror into his soul. Every negative level conferred transfers 1 point of Dexterity from the victim to the Shadow Vampire. Stolen Dexterity lasts for 1 turn per point of drained Dexterity. A victim reduced to 0 Dexterity is slain and rises as a shadow 1d4 days later.

Characters whose levels have been drained by a Shadow Vampire suffer -2 to their Willpower saves (related to fear) for a number of hours equal to the vampire's *age* category (or until sunrise). Whenever the character must face any encounter that might cause him fear, he must make a fear save DC 10 plus half the HD of the creature he faces, or run screaming in fear as though he were *panicked*.

Kings and Crowns

"We are kings, nobles of the purest lineage.

We have ascended beyond the Veil,
granted the blessings of immortality by the Shadow.

We reside in the highest celestial realm,
above and apart from the lesser breeds.

We alone have seen the Void and gazed into its black heart.
We have mastered the Shadow and can see far into the blackest night. The sun cannot touch us, for we spread darkness wherever we go, a mantle blessed by the Shadow.

Should we desire it, we alone could take back the day.

We are the true lords of the night."

Illian Mort Drellian, Shadow Vampire

VANGAARD

The Vangaard are the largest of the vampire races. While they do not have powerful vampiric abilities, their sheer size and strength more than compensate for any weaknesses they may have. The Vangaard can trace their origins back to Toth, the First vampire barbarian and member of the Black Council. The Vangaard Toth is the only member of the Black Council who is not a pure Black Blood. No one knows why Vangual transformed Toth into a Vangaard; perhaps it was a capricious whim by the god of vampires.

APPEARANCE

Vangaard have thick, leathery skin and large dark eyes. Their slab-like bodies are much larger and heavier than even the largest mortals. It is not unknown for Vangaard to grow up to eleven feet tall. They typically wear clothes fashioned from human skin, adorned with the pelts of various animals.

Vangaard are both the least and greatest of the vampire races. The forces of necromancy sustain their great bodies, but flow weakly through them. They have fewer vampiric powers and cannot easily mimic even the lesser vampire abilities. Bodyguards to the First, they have no equal in battle. They have tremendous strength and speed and regenerate wounds quickly. Even the most powerful magical weapons cannot strike the eldest of the Vangaard.

THE BLACK KISS

Vangaard can create progeny. Bound in ritual, they will choose mainly barbarians, journeying back to their homelands in search of a suitable candidate.

They will challenge their chosen target to a duel; if they are somehow defeated, they will allow their victim to leave unharmed. If they are victorious, they will take their conquest back to Avystervan.

SOCIETY

Battle has seen an end to many of the Vangaard and their numbers continue to fall. Fewer Vangaard are being made, and the *Black Kiss* does not always work when performed on even the most suitable mortals. Some say the Void in their blood is dissipating although, why this might be, none can say.

Vangual recently ordered the creation of a new group of Vangaard, the Cruentus. This bloody order is made up of fighters, rogues and a few arcane spellcasters, although the Devoted Incarnate are reluctant to allow the creation of clerical Vangaard. There is a deep schism between Toth, the ancient Vangaard and these new creations.

OUTLOOK

Vangaard are rarely seen beyond the confines of Avystervan. They are simply too large to conceal themselves in populated areas. They have limited shapechanging ability and can use this in places where they wish to move undetected. Vangaard have something of a code of conduct. Unlike other vampires, the Void is not so strong within them. Although they are still monsters, they rarely feast upon mortals for pleasure. They take ritualistic satisfaction in the hunt, seeking out those they deem worthy and turning them into other Vangaard. These are typically great warriors, or more preferably high level barbarians.

It is said the Vangaard are more beast than vampire. With heightened senses, they live for battle, seeking out worthy opponents and destroying them in fair combat. They are masters of the hunt and without a doubt, the arm of the Black Council.

ROLE-PLAYING A VANGAARD

Ritualistic, ancient, you are of noble birth. All other races are lesser creations, spawned from mortal magic or happenstance. Because of this you are free to take what you want from those beneath you while fiercely proving your loyalty to your masters. The two worlds - the spirit and the mortal - are intertwined, and even though you have passed on to another cycle, you will still continue your work in darkness.

CREATING A VANGAARD

Vangaard is a template that can be added to any humanoid or monstrous humanoid creature. The creature's type changes to undead, and it uses all the base creature's abilities and special abilities except as noted here.

SPECIAL ATTACKS:

Blood Drain (Ex): As summarised on p. 30.

Domination (Su): As summarised on p. 59. Vangaard domination is weaker than the charm powers of other vampires. The DC falls to 5 plus half the Vangaard's hit dice + their Charisma Modifier.

Energy Drain (Su): Living creatures hit by a Vangaard's slam attack suffer 1 negative level.

SPECIAL QUALITIES:

Beastform (Su): Vangaard gain the Dark Gift, Beastform but they cannot assume a tiny form, and every form they choose is 10% larger per *age* category than a typical creature of that species.

Damage Reduction (Su): Vangaard gain damage reduction dependent on their *age* category (see p. 127).

Fast Healing (Ex): A Vangaard's fast healing ability is dependent on their *age* category (see p. 127).

Favoured Class: Black Barbarian. When determining whether a multiclass Vangaard suffers an XP penalty, his highest-level black barbarian class does not count.

Large (Ex): Vangaard are Large creatures (they must be at least 8 ft. in height). They suffer modifiers to their Strength (+8), Dexterity (-2), Natural Armor (+2) and AC (-1). These ability bonuses **are** included in the Master *Age* Chart on p. 127.

Resistance (Su): Vangaard have cold and lightning resistance 10/+5 per *age*.

Scent Skill (Ex): Vangaard gain the *'Scent'* special ability.

Skills

Vangaard receive a +4 racial bonus to Climb, Intimidate, Intuit Direction, Jump, Listen, Search, Sense Motive and Spot checks. This bonus increases by +2 for every *age* they gain. Otherwise same as the base creature.

Vampiric Weaknesses

Allergy: Garlic, Allergy: Iron, Allergy: Silver, Cannot Cross Running Water, Cannot Enter Holy Ground, Cannot Enter without Invitation, Chill of the Grave, Fear of Fire, Fear of Sunlight, Gravebound, Stench of the Grave, Water Vulnerability

Death State

When reduced to 0 hit points or lower, the Vangaard transforms into gaseous form.

Advanced Energy Drain: Strength

In addition to draining levels, Vangaard drain 1 point of Strength for every negative level they inflict. This gives them +1 to their Strength for 1 turn per point of Strength drained to a maximum of 1 plus their *age* category.

Cruentus Vangaard

Who knows what power Vangual used to create the new order of Vangaard. Certainly the two Vangaard types could not be more different, and the Blood Mages have catalogued them a wholly separate race. The Vangaard are calling them *mock* Vangaard.

The Cruentus are very different to their older counterparts. They are smaller and are only slightly taller and heavier than Black Bloods. Their vampiric powers are more closely aligned to standard vampires, and while their warrior powers are formidable, they have only a fraction of the Vangaard's great strength.

Certainly Toth and the other Vangaard are deeply concerned with the arrival of the Cruentus. The Black Council have not shown any concerns for the Vangaard and their numbers are still called upon for protection

There are no Cruentus Vangaard older than *age* 1 at this time. No one but Vangual knows what plans lie in store for them.

More information is available about the Cruentus Vangaard in **Darkness Rises**.

VANGAARD

WE ARE OLD. WE WERE BORN AT THE BEGINNING WHEN EVEN OUR HOME WAS JUST A HOLLOW OF BLACKNESS. MANY OF US ARE THE MOST ANCIENT OF CREATURES, OLDER THAN TREES, OLDER THAN CITIES, OLDER THAN THE OCEANS.

WE ARE DYING.

THERE ARE FEWER OF US NOW THAN EVER THERE WERE. PERHAPS THAT HAS SOMETHING TO DO WITH THE WORLD. WE FIND FEWER UPON WHOM WE WISH TO INFLICT THE *SACRED KISS*, FEWER THAT ARE FREE FROM THE CORRUPTION OF THE WORLD. WHEN WE FIND A CANDIDATE AND OUR HEARTS BURN TO BRING THEM INTO THE FOLD, OFTEN THE *SACRED KISS* FAILS AND THE MORTALS FALL INTO THE ETERNAL SLUMBER.

THE WORLD HAS CHANGED. GONE ARE MANY OF THE OLD WAYS. TIME HAS PASSED US BY.

AND WE ARE LESSENED BY IT.

WE ARE DYING.

THE NOBLE BLOOD THAT ONCE RAGED GROWS EVER COOLER. THE POWERS THAT GIVE US LIFE WANE. THE *GREAT SPIRIT* WITHIN HAS DIMINISHED.

WHERE ONCE WE NUMBERED THOUSANDS, NOW THERE ARE BUT A HANDFUL OF US. OUR CONCLAVE GATHERS, THE GREAT HALL FILLED WITH BUT A SCATTERING OF OUR KIND.

HAVE WE FAILED IN OUR *GREAT QUEST*? I CANNOT SAY. WE WERE SORELY OCCUPIED WITH OUR OWN WORLD FOR MANY LONG YEARS. OUR OWN INNER STRUGGLE ON THE *JOURNEY*. WE STILL CALLED THE LION WHEN IT WAS NEEDED. OUR SHADOW WAS ALWAYS THERE TO BANISH THE FIRE AND THE LIGHT.

OUR BATTLES WERE LEGENDARY. BUT NOW THE NEW LORDS HAVE NO NEED OF OUR PROTECTION. THEY HAVE FOUND OTHER TOOLS IN WHICH TO PLACE THEIR TRUST.

OUR STRENGTH WILL DIMINISH — BUT THE *GREAT JOURNEY* WILL TAKE US TO THE NEXT CYCLE.

VAMPIRE SCION

Vampire Scion are the most common vampire across the world. Many vampires desire to bring a mortal into unlife at least once during their long unlives and most choose to create Scion. Vampire Scion are locked in unlife at the moment of death, unchanging yet eternal. Slaves to their masters, most are created when a vampire bitten (*once touched*) mortal is slain before the effects of the first bite have worn off. These poor souls rise to become Vampire Scion, vampires in name alone, hunters of blood and bringers of death.

APPEARANCE

Vampire Scion are identical to Black Bloods in almost every way, except they vary greatly in their appearance. Some look far more like the living, with pale alabaster flesh, and even normal seeming eyes. Others are grotesque monstrosities with drooping features and gnarled, claw-like fingers.

THE BLACK KISS

Vampire Scion are created by a single draining of a mortal's blood (or levels) without following the ritualistic process of the *Black Kiss*. Devoid of the uniqueness of a true vampire, Vampire Scion have all the powers and abilities of a vampire, but do not gain any additional powers from age, remaining as they did the moment they arose from their *Second Waking*. They cannot gain new skills, feats, Dark Gifts, levels and/or experience points - they are simply unable to retain the knowledge. They can remember basic events, places, names and faces, but anything more is lost when they rise from sleeping. Vampire Scion are always chaotic evil, losing what remained of their mortal minds in the transformation process. Unless a force intervenes, a Vampire Scion will rise from the grave a feral and monstrous creation.

SOCIETY

Vampire Scion are under the absolute control of their master. They may despise him utterly, but they will obey his every command, even if it means their *Second Death* in the most barbaric way imaginable. They can never rise up against him: the necromantic forces prevent a Vampire Scion from attacking their master. A wise vampire will be precise about what his progeny can and cannot do.

A vampire can only create and control as many Vampire Scion as he has twice the total of his *age* and levels. When a vampire reaches his limit, the oldest Scion automatically become true vampires. Vampire masters are careful not to create too many Scion as they never fully know how many of their progeny are in the world. Those that become true vampires may return to exact revenge upon a particularly vindictive master.

A vampire normally creates Vampire Scion to act as bodyguards and warriors in his brood. Occasionally, a vampire will accidentally create Vampire Scion while travelling. By the time the Vampire Scion has awoken, the master can be long departed. Those that are not claimed by a master are condemned to remain near their coffins and places of death, devoid of any kind of instruction or leadership. They never outgrow their *ties to the grave* and are typically blood crazed and hungry - they may not even be aware of their entire range of vampiric powers. Vampire Scion that become free willed vampires immediately gain all physical bonuses as well as the ability to gain experience, skills and all the powers accessible to a standard vampire.

OUTLOOK

Vampire Scion mostly exist in isolated places. They are typical of the vampires in stories, shapechangers and bringers of fear and darkness. They arise from the crypts in which they were buried, spreading fear wherever they hunt, returning shortly before dawn. While they are easier to destroy than their vampiric brethren, they find it easier to create progeny (although this has its limits). Given free reign, Vampire Scion can be a plague upon the land.

ROLE-PLAYING A VAMPIRE SCION

You have been brought back from death to an unlife of eternal misery. You are bound to your master and must do his bidding - a pawn in his army. You may seem human, but in your heart lies a terrible darkness. The bitterness of slavery will sustain you until you can find a way to be free…

CREATING A VAMPIRE SCION

Vampire Scion is a template that can be added to any humanoid or monstrous humanoid creature. The creature's type changes to undead, and it uses all the base creature's abilities and special abilities except as noted here.

SPECIAL ATTACKS:

Blood Drain (Ex): As summarised on p. 30.

Charm (Su): Similar to vampire domination but the save is DC 14 and the effect is similar to charm person as cast by a 5th level sorcerer.

Create Spawn (Su): Vampire Scion cannot create true vampires. They can create other Scion, but these creations are two HD lower than themselves. One and two HD Vampire Scion cannot create progeny. Even if they follow the unholy resurrection procedure precisely, the necromantic forces within them simply are not powerful enough to bring a corpse back from the dead. Anyone slain by a Vampire Scion has a 1% chance of rising up as a Mock Vampire. Mostly, their necromantic energies are not strong enough to create progeny.

Energy Drain (Su): Living creatures hit by a Vampire Scion's slam attack suffer 1 negative level. The Fortitude save to remove the negative level has a DC of 14.

SPECIAL QUALITIES:

Advancement (Su): Vampire Scion can evolve to become true vampires, although the process is dangerous and involves either intervention by a lich, or the *Second Death* of their master. A Vampire Scion's necromantic energies are intrinsically linked to those of their master. If a vampire master is slain, all Vampire Scion under his control make a Will check DC 20. If they fail, they are forever slain, the negative energies that sustained them dissipating with their master. Success indicates they become fledgling vampires.

Damage Reduction (Su): A Vampire Scion gains damage reduction of 10/silver.

Fast Healing (Ex): So long as they have at least 1 hit point, Vampire Scion heal 2 hit points per round.

Gaseous Form (Su): Vampire Scion gain the Dark Gift, Gaseous Form.

Mirror of the Black Blood (Su): Vampire Scion gain ability modifiers and movement rate of an *age* 0 Black Blood.

Resistance (Su): Vampire Scion have cold and electricity resistance 10/+5 per *age*.

SKILLS

Vampire Scion receive a +4 racial bonus to Bluff, Hide, Listen, Move Silently, Search, Sense Motive and Spot checks. Otherwise same as the base creature.

VAMPIRIC WEAKNESSES

Allergy: Garlic, Allergy: Iron, Allergy: Silver, Cannot Cross Running Water, Cannot Enter Holy Ground, Cannot Enter without Invitation, Chill of the Grave, Fear of Fire, Fear of Sunlight, Gravebound, No Reflection, Stench of the Grave, Water Vulnerability

WEAKNESSES

Indomitable Command of the Maker: Vampire Scion are at the command of their master. They will obey his every word, even if it means their *Second Death.*

Stagnant Void: Vampire Scion cannot gain experience or learn new skills or spells until they become true vampires.

DEATH STATE

Vampire Scion turn to mist as per a standard vampire when they are reduced to 0 hit points or lower.

ADVANCED ENERGY DRAIN

Vampire Scion do not have an Advanced Energy Drain ability.

THE SLAVE

Trapped. This is a miserable existence.

It is barely an existence at all.

I hate this unlife.

Some days I can barely remember my own name.

I am a pawn, a fragment of memory, a vassal for my master's petty desires.

I hate him. He treats me with contempt, stealing away my first life and awaking me from death to this...

Whatever his command, I must obey. I have no will of my own. He leaves me in darkness when he has no use for me. Discarded, alone.

But I know a secret. It was whispered to me not long ago. I have struggled hard to remember it.

I can escape. Be free of this purgatory.

All I have to do is see my master destroyed.

I can wait.

Time is all I have...

Vampirica Anatomica

(excerpt from Black Cabal lesson)

Drinking Blood

A common misconception amongst new vampires is that we can feed upon any living thing.

This is wholly innaccurate.

We can only derive sustenance from red blood. Any other kind or color will sate our hunger but we cannot attune it to our magical energies

A good example is troll blood. Trolls have thick, appetising green blood and while it may taste delicious, we simply cannot distil it with our necromantic energies.

So if you are thinking of bingeing on a troll tonight, my advice is, don't.

You'll only regret it tomorrow.

And not only is some blood unpalatable, some blood is *even* poisonous and should be avoided altogether.

Demons and lower planar creatures, dragons and certain exotic monsters have highly toxic blood that can be exceedingly painful - even fatal to drink. So be careful when feeding on the non standard races.

You can find information on the most dangerous creatures in chapter nine of your textbooks.

Some creatures do not contain any of the vital energies needed to fuel our powers: Outsiders, summoned creatures and entities from Vangual's domain - while living, are devoid of life energy. So if you eat one, you'll feel like another an hour later.

But that said, it's mostly trial and error as there are some exceptions...

And to prove that point, I have here a rare treat - a bottle of ancient celestial blood that IS filled with compatible life-energy. It might give you a taste of what you've been missing.

It might also spur you on to seek out and destroy those damnable creatures of the *Powers of Light.*

Well don't just gawk at it. Pass it around.

I think you'll find it quite delicious...

DHAMPYRE

Dhampyre (Dham-Peer) or half-vampires are mortals touched by necromancy while still in the womb. While such encounters normally result in the death of both mother and child, occasionally the resulting progeny is a hybrid; a half-vampire creation that clings to life with tenacity greater than either realm. Dhampyres retain a fragment of their soul, while necromantic power swirls through their veins. Caught in a constant struggle between light and darkness, Dhampyre have many powers that set them above humans yet beneath vampires. They have great strength and speed, are able to walk in daylight and are almost totally impervious to the powers of necromancy. It is said that the Black Cabal have experimented with creating Dhampyre, but to this day all efforts have proved unsuccessful. The forces that create such creatures are fickle and cannot be controlled.

APPEARANCE

Dhampyre tend to be taller and more muscular than others of their race. They have dark eyes and a mysterious quality about them. Evil Dhampyre have eyes that gleam red in the dark, or have auras of glowering shadow, while goodly aligned Dhampyre have darker flesh and eyes that flicker with amber or even blue radiance.

THE CURSE

No one knows exactly how or why a Dhampyre is created. What *is* known is that mothers across the mortal realms have given birth to Dhampyre children for centuries. Whether bitten, *twice touched* or merely fed upon, a mother must have been influenced by a vampire in some way for a Dhampyre to be born. It is said that when a Dhampyre child enters the world, its eyes are filled with blood. While this quickly passes, it is considered a terrible omen in some cultures and a powerful prophecy for good in others.

Dhampyres live well beyond the life span of mortals, but they are rare. There are perhaps a handful in existence at any one time and those that will not ally with the powers of darkness are quickly slain. Dhampyre do not physically age as mortals; they reach adulthood then age very slowly. A human-born Dhampyre will reach middle age at around 175 and will only begin to look old at 250. Elves, Dwarves and other long lived races double or even triple their normal life spans.

A Dhampyre child is always 'different' from other children. They find it difficult fitting in until they find their 'calling'. Those that are not discovered by the forces of light and darkness are always outsiders, traditionally filled with anger or feelings of separation from those around them.

A Dhampyre does not exhibit their full range of powers until they come of age.

SOCIETY

Many Dhampyre sell their services to the undead or to the *Powers of Light* as seers or warriors. Some Dhampyre head the larger vampire hunter guilds across the realm. Others are leaders or clerics on the mortal side of the vampire cults. The *Church of the Immortal Corpus* is the evil clergy of Vangual and many Dhampyre are recruited into its ranks.

OUTLOOK

Dhampyre have no specific alignment restrictions. What Void festers in their souls does tend to force them toward chaos rather than law. Unlike vampires, Dhampyre are not fixed upon a path of alignment (although most are destined for evil). Some Dhampyre may walk the line toward good while others towards the blackest evil. The Black Cabal try to manipulate those they can toward their own dark desires. A Dhampyre that will not be manipulated is destroyed.

Dhampyre do not have Katharein although they may journey to the Arch where they can accompany a vampire on their Katharein (see p. 114).

ROLE-PLAYING A DHAMPYRE

You are Dhampyre, blessed by the *Powers of Light* and *Darkness*. You have always been stronger, faster and more powerful than other mortals (although you have not always known quite why). You are powerful, coveted by mortals and vampires alike. You are free to make your own choice, for good *or* ill, but the choice you make may mean you are hunted for the rest of your unnaturally long life...

CREATING A DHAMPYRE

Dhampyre is a race. Any of the mortal races can create Dhampyre offspring. Dhampyre can take any *age* 0 Dark Gift in place of any standard feat they gain as a result of their Character levels (as listed below). In addition, they automatically receive one Dark Gift when coming of age. When they have lived more than half their normal lifespan - Elder Dhampyre can buy *age* 1 Dark Gifts. They expend Constitution to power any Gifts that would otherwise require blood to work. Dhampyre are considered to be *age* 0 vampires (and Elder Dhampyre *age* 1) for the purposes of determining the effects of their Dark Gifts.

SPECIAL ATTACKS:

Blood Drain (Ex): A Dhampyre can drink the Constitution of the living to replenish his drained Constitution on a point per point basis. A Dhampyre recovers 1 point of Constitution per day as normal.

SPECIAL QUALITIES:

Ability Modifiers (Su): Dhampyre gain the following Ability modifiers: Str: +4, Dex: +4, Con: +4, Int: +2, Wis: +0, Char: +2.

Black Class: Dhampyre may convert their classes to black classes at any time, although once they make the change, they may not shift back.

Blood Potence (Su): A Dhampyre can drink mortal blood to enhance their physical abilities. For every point of Constitution or Blood they drink, they gain +1 to their Strength or Dexterity or Constitution (chosen on a point by point basis). Enhanced abilities last for 10 minutes per point drunk. A Dhampyre can enhance any ability he chooses but can allocate no more than a quarter of his level (round down) in points per day to each ability. Any excess blood drunk thereafter cannot be used to enhance abilities.

Example: A Dhampyre drains 3 points of Constitution from a mortal. He can choose to enhance his Strength by 3 points, or his Strength by 1 and his Constitution by 2, or any other permutation he desires. If he enhanced his Strength by 3 points, his Strength would be enhanced for 30 minutes.

Dark Aura (Su): As a free action Dhampyre can resist one necromantic spell per day at the expense of their hit points. They suffer twice the spell's level in hit points damage and the spell has no effect upon them. They gain +4 racial bonus to resist necromantic spells and are granted a save even if a spell would not normally allow one. Necromantic spells that affect them have only half effect and duration.

Dhampyre Mantle (Su): Dhampyre receive a +4 racial bonus against all vampire effects and powers and are wholly immune to vampiric charm in all of its forms.

Fast Healing (Ex): Providing they have at least 1 hit point, Dhampyre recover 1 hit point per round.

Favoured Class: Black Fighter. When determining whether a multiclass Dhampyre suffers an XP penalty, his highest-level black fighter class does not count.

Gifts: Dhampyre may choose from the following Dark Gifts in place of a standard character feat: Blood Agility, Blood Speed, Blood Strength, Darkvision 30 ft., Vampiric Senses. Evil Dhampyre may choose from these additional Gifts: Conjure Darkness, Darkvision 60ft., Domination, Gaseous Form, Vampire (Shadow) Step.

Immunity to Disease & Non-magical Poisons (Su): Dhampyre are fully immune to non-magical toxins and diseases. They gain a +4 racial bonus against magical toxins and diseases.

Low Light Vision (Su): Dhampyre have low light vision.

Resist the Void (Su): Dhampyre cannot become vampires. If they are slain by the *Black Kiss*, they do not rise up as vampires.

Sense (Su): Dhampyre can sense vampires as detailed below.

Vampiric Healing (Su): A Dhampyre can heal his wounds by drinking blood. A Dhampyre heals 1d8 points of damage per point of Constitution drained from a mortal. They can drink 1d3 points of Constitution per round.

Vampiric Resistance (Su): Dhampyre can absorb half their level in negative levels per day with no ill effect. Additionally, they gain a +4 racial bonus to their negative level check.

ECL: Dhampyre have an ECL of +2

Skills

Dhampyre gain a +4 racial bonus to Hide, Listen, Move Silently, Search and Spot checks, otherwise same as the base creature.

Vampiric Weaknesses

Dhampyre do not suffer from the traditional vampiric weaknesses.

Weaknesses

Blood Dependency: Dhampyre must eat and drink normally but they must also drink the blood of the living. Good Dhampyre must drink 1 point of blood per week, neutral Dhampyre 2 points of blood per week. Evil Dhampyre must drink 3 points of blood per week. Failure to ingest sufficient blood results in a loss of all ability bonuses and 1 point of Constitution per day after the first.

Delusion: Dhampyre are touched by the Void. As a result their mortal minds cannot handle such energies. Many go slowly insane. This madness manifests as megalomania in some, while others hear voices or are driven by a dark calling. Others become blood-crazed assassins or venture on wild crusades to destroy all manner of *imagined* evils.

Hunted: Dhampyre are hunted throughout their long lives. Vampires and other creatures greatly desire their magical blood for experiments, or simply to add to their army of darkness.

Sunlight Intolerance: Dhampyre are weakened during the day. They gain no ability modifiers and suffer a penalty of -1 to all of their actions in direct sunlight. They suffer an additional penalty of –1 against sunlight and divine/holy attacks.

Turning Vulnerability: Dhampyre *can* be turned but they cannot be destroyed.

Dhampyre Sense

Dhampyre have the innate power to sense vampiric energies. They can sense when a person has been *vampire touched* and can perceive all vampire-based illusions and abilities. Dhampyre can also sense potential corpses that may rise up as vampires as well as those who have been vampire charmed or otherwise manipulated. They must make a Sense Motive check to discern this (DC 15 + *age* of active vampire + active vampire's Charisma modifier).

Note: Active vampire is the vampire that has charmed, slain or otherwise affected a mortal or situation in some way.

Dhampyre can sense whether a vampire has crossed his path within the last 24 hours (DC as above). They can sense the presence of a vampire within 1000 yards (DC as above). Failure indicates they can sense the presence of a vampire, but not where.

Lastly, Dhampyre can sense a vampire in any of its forms, whether in animal, gaseous form or invisible. They must make a Sense Motive check (DC 20 + *age* of vampire) to see their exact form and location. A failure indicates the Dhampyre cannot directly sense the vampire, but will be aware of their presence.

Hunted

My life is misery
I am hunted, pursued by those who covet me
They desire my blood, my bones
My very soul.
Whenever the sun goes down, they are there,
lurking in the shadows, waiting for me to drop my guard.

I thought about my death. Taking my own life.
But I fear I will pass beyond the Veil and become like them.

I could not bear that. I shall live for as long as I can.

VAMPIRE TOUCHED

Drained of mortal essence on one or more separate nights, the *vampire touched* are mortals on the brink of vampirism. Necromancy flows through their veins lessening the divide between the realms of life and death. The *vampire touched* drift in a middle state, neither truly alive, nor dead. There are three stages to the *vampire touch*, each an integral part of the *Black Kiss*.

VAMPIRE BITTEN (ONCE TOUCHED)

SYMPTOMS

The *once touched* are those mortals bitten on one occasion by a vampire. They will have lost one or more points of Constitution and will be tired and devoid of appetite. They quickly grow weak when exerting themselves and will sleep long into the day.

The first bite causes a great weariness in the victim and on occasion, intolerance to bright light. The *once touched* are vulnerable to vampiric charm and other vampire powers. They suffer -2 to any saves against the vampire that has bitten them and -1 against all other vampires.

RECOVERY

A *once touched* mortal will recover after a good night's sleep. They will certainly recover any Constitution loss within a matter of days. Bruising will have healed within a week. The mystical effects of the bite wear off after 7 days +1 day for every *age* of the vampire.

TWICE TOUCHED

SYMPTOMS

Evidence of vampiric influence is strong in the *twice touched*. Weakness, shivers, pale and cold flesh, a terrible aversion to sunlight and disorientation are all symptoms of the second feeding. The victim will likely have been drained of one or more levels, for the vampire must drain them all if he is to create a true vampire. Additionally, the *twice touched* will have a desperate and unquenchable thirst and will feel sluggish and lethargic during the day. If not roused, they will certainly sleep until the sun goes down. Most are too drowsy to be aware of their condition. Making them understand the seriousness of their situation can prove difficult.

On the threshold of vampirism the *twice touched* may gain a semblance of a vampire's strengths and weaknesses - from their heightened senses to the ability to see in the dark. Some gain their prospective master's primary Dark Gift (such as *flight* or *gaseous form*). This uncontrolled power will manifest in a variety of different ways. Those *twice touched* with rudimentary vampire powers will certainly find themselves fearful of holy items and people. Garlic will cause a terrible reaction, vomiting, palpitations and nausea (-2 to all actions in its vicinity.)

The *twice touched* are especially vulnerable to vampiric charm and other vampire powers. They suffer -4 to any saves against the vampire that has twice bitten them and -2 against all other vampires.

RECOVERY

If a vampire is prevented from delivering the *Black Kiss*, recovery is possible. The worst of the effects typically wear off after a few nights of sleep, and preventative measures can be taken (using vampire lore) to ensure the *twice touched* recovers as swiftly as possible.

THRICE TOUCHED

SYMPTOMS

A vampire will *thrice touch* a mortal if he wishes to make the bond between them more permanent. This involves a vampire draining a chosen or favoured mortal almost to the point of death and then allowing them to heal, after giving them a single drop of their blood. If the mortal does not die (becoming a Vampire Scion), they will recover to become *thrice touched*. If a vampire drains all of their Constitution and levels (the *Black Kiss*), they will rise as a true vampire 1d4 nights later.

The *thrice touched* are mortal clerics or necromancers or those who have gained favour with the Children of Vangual. They are touched by vampirism, gaining permanent vampiric abilities, yet losing a fragment of their mortality. They have at least one Dark Gift, but lose 1 point of Constitution per *age* category of their patron vampire. They enjoy enhanced strength, but rely on their vampiric patron to regularly fuel their powers. They require a drop of vampiric blood once per month or begin to recover from their *thrice touched* state.

The *thrice touched* are typically very pale, and quickly grow weak when exerting themselves. They grow out of breath easily and do not like the sun or holy places. Some have eyes that glow in darkness, fangs or claws. They have increased resistance to disease and poisons and rarely grow sick. They suffer -6 to their saves against the domination attempts of their master, and -4 against all other vampires. So long as they are continually fed vampire blood, they will benefit from extended lives, living for a number of additional mortal lifetimes equal to the *age* of their master.

RECOVERY

After one full month of being without vampire blood, the *thrice touched* loses his Dark Gifts and abilities. He then recovers 1 Constitution per month until he is fully restored. He retains his aversion to sunlight throughout the recovery period. A *thrice bitten* mortal forever suffers -2 to their saves against that vampire and -1 against all other vampires.

SPECIAL QUALITIES:

Dark Gift (Su): The *thrice touched* can buy any one *age* 0 Dark Gift that their master knows. They can use this Gift once per day. Additional uses cost 1 point of Constitution.

Darkvision (Su): The *thrice touched* gain darkvision 30 ft.

Immunity to Disease & Non magical Poisons (Su): The *thrice touched* are immune to non-magical diseases. They gain a +4 bonus against magical diseases and poisons.

Ability Modifiers (Su): The *thrice touched* gain the following ability modifiers: Str: +2, Dex: +2, Con: -*, Int: +1, Wis: +1, Char: +2.

*Con is reduced by the *age* category of the vampire master.

WEAKNESSES

Light Vulnerability: The *thrice touched* detect as necromantic creatures and suffer -2 to their actions in daylight.

> *"I am neither dead or alive, but stuck somewhere in between."*
> Drellius, *Thrice Touched* Cleric of Vangual

CHAPTER THREE: VAMPIRE RULES

Vampires are undead. They are immune to poison, sleep, paralysis, stunning, disease, death and necromantic effects, and they ignore mind-influencing effects (except for vampiric domination). Vampires are not subject to critical hits, subdual damage, ability damage, ability drain, or energy drain. They have no Constitution scores and are therefore immune to any effect requiring a Fortitude save (unless it affects objects). An undead spellcaster uses its Charisma modifier when making Concentration checks. A vampire is not at risk of death from massive damage.

ADDITIONAL NOTES

* Negative energy spells (such as *inflict light wounds*) heal vampires.
* A vampire is immune to magical ageing. They cannot be advanced beyond their *age* category by any means (other than through specific vampiric spells).
* All vampires have darkvision with a range of 60 feet.
* Saves against a vampire's powers have a DC of 10 + 1/2 vampire's HD + *age* category + Charisma modifier unless noted otherwise.

AGE

As a vampire ages, the powers of darkness ferment within them, increasing their physical and supernatural abilities. The Vampire *Age* Table (below) details the *age* thresholds, names, Blood, Dark Gifts and Vampiric Traits a vampire gains as they age. The Master *Age* Chart (detailing ability modifiers) is on p. 127.

THE BLACK KISS: CREATING PROGENY

A vampire must come to a mortal three times if he wants to make a true vampire. The reasons are subtle, but important. A Vampire Scion is a static creature, they lose much of their minds in the transformation to undeath. Many vampire masters desire much more than this from their progeny, and so they create true vampires.

THE VISITATION

To create a true vampire, a vampire must drain all of the blood from a mortal and **all** of their levels. He must do this on three separate encounters on three or more nights. The vampire must drink carefully, for should his victim die before the third *visitation*, they will rise up as a Vampire Scion a few nights later. There can be interruptions in the process, but any vampire wishing to cement a full and complete relationship with their progeny must follow this procedure. The vampire must perform the *Black Kiss* within one month of his first *visitation* or he must begin the whole process anew.

PROGENY

A master vampire has greater control over his own progeny. The DC of his domination attempts rises by +4 when attempting to charm vampires he has created.

Additionally, an older vampire gains a bonus to the DC of his charming attempts when attempting to dominate a lower age category vampire. The DC is increased by the difference in their ages. The reverse of this is also true, the DC of a younger vampire's attempt to charm an older vampire is reduced by the difference in their ages.

Example: An age 4 vampire attempting to dominate an age 1 vampire has his domination DC increased by +3. The age 1 vampire's DC to charm the elder vampire would be lowered by 3.

THE BITE

A vampire can bend a previously bitten mortal far easier to his will. Any character previously bitten by a vampire suffers – 2 to all saves for each biting attempt (maximum of -6). This biting lasts the vampire's *age* in days. A vampire can only bite a single mortal (with regard to *touching* them) once per day (see vampire touched p. 28).

TELLTALE SIGNS

It is not always easy to tell if a mortal has been bitten by the undead. A wise vampire will choose the location from which they draw blood very carefully. Few drink from the throat unless they wish to draw attention to themselves. Unless someone has the skill or foresight to look, the bite wounds will be small (but evident).

Most vampire wounds ache and swiftly become black and discolored. Unless a mortal is 'charmed' by a vampire, they may alert others to the presence of their bites (drained of blood the *vampire touched* are typically sickly and pale individuals). A successful healing check will diagnose the presence of a vampire bite. Most careful vampires will dominate their victims to 'overlook' their injuries or at least so that they cannot alert others to their condition. They will grow steadily weaker as their vampire continues to visit them, bringing them slowly, night after night, one bite closer to undeath...

"Rumors of my undeath have been greatly exaggerated!"
Mark Twain, Black Bard

VAMPIRE AGE TABLE

Age	Age Years	Powers/Title	Blood	Dark Gifts	Traits
0	0 - 1	Fledgling	+0	+3	+0
1	1 - 10	Youth	+1	+6	+0
2	10 - 100	Mature	+2	+9	+0
3	100 - 500	Aged	+3	+12	+1
4	500 - 1000	Elder	+4	+15	+2
5	1000+	Venerable	+5	+18	+3

BLOOD

Blood is the source of a vampire's strength and fuels all of their mystical powers. The Blood score is the amount of blood a vampire can hold at any one time. A point of Blood generally equals a point of mortal Constitution.

A vampire's Blood score is converted from and replaces a character's mortal Constitution. It is used to calculate any Fortitude saves a vampire must make (if any). For the purpose of these game rules, blood refers to any blood, mortal or otherwise. Capitalised 'Blood' refers to attuned vampire blood or the ability score, Blood.

Additional Notes

* A vampire adds 1 to their Blood score for every *age* category they advance. If they gain an ability increase, they can use this to raise their Blood score by +1 (if they so choose).
* Magical items and spells that augment Constitution do **not** affect a vampire's Blood score.
* A vampire burns 1 point of Blood while sleeping (or at dusk). If their Blood score falls to 0 they will pass into the *eternal quiescence* when they next sleep (or at dawn).
* A vampire that uses *all* of their Blood resources is considerably weakened. They lose any ability modifiers they may have until they attune further blood to their necromantic energies.

Feeding

A vampire can drink up to his Blood score + his *age* in Constitution per day. Surplus blood serves no purpose (and cannot be used to replace expended blood). It is merely for use in performing the *Black Kiss* on a victim.

Blood Drain

A vampire can suck blood from a living victim with its fangs by making a successful grapple check. If it pins the foe, it drains blood, inflicting 1d4 points of Constitution drain each round the pin is maintained (or if the target is unwilling to resist).

Note: The Children of Vangual do not normally drain permanent Constitution. Constitution is recovered at one point per day of rest.

A *once-touched* mortal will be pale seeming for about a day. After that they will slowly recover, regaining their color and looking healthy again. A twice-touched mortal will take considerably longer to recover, as their blood levels have been considerably depleted.

Drinking Blood

Blood must be taken from the living, a corpse loses its life force after one hour and becomes indigestible.

Blood only stays fresh outside of the mortal body for a few short minutes. After that it quickly cools and loses its vitality. A vampire cannot derive any sustenance from cold blood.

Note: Any mortal that drinks the blood of a vampire suffers -8 to their Will saves against that vampire's domination attempts. This lasts for 24 hours or until sunrise. A clever vampire will ensure some of his blood is added to food (which is on the wrong side of rare), or put into wine - it only takes a single sip.

Attunement

Newly ingested blood has no mystical powers of its own. It must be attuned before it can be used to fuel a vampire's Dark Gifts. A vampire must sleep (or 24 hours must have passed) before newly ingested blood is fully attuned to his necromantic energies (consider it digestion if you will). A vampire cannot use any unattuned blood until that time (although he can use previously attuned Blood).

Example: A vampire with a Blood score of 12 uses 6 Blood on his Dark Gifts, then immediately feeds back up to his full quota. Although he has 12 blood, he only has 6 Blood points that he can use to fuel his Dark Gifts. He must wait until he has attuned the other 6 Blood before he can use them.

Elder Blood

Any vampire can drink any other vampire's Blood. An elder vampire's blood is much more potent than a younger vampire's. Using Blood from an elder vampire grants the vampire *age* equal to the elder vampire's *age* category while using that Blood to fuel any of his abilities.

Example: An age 1 vampire is given a single point of age 5 vampire Blood. When he uses that Blood to fuel one of his Dark Gifts , he is considered age 5 (for the single use of that Dark Gift only).

Note: An elder vampire can re-attune a younger vampire's blood to their new *age* category by the same Attunement process. As blood can be used for many magical purposes (the least of all to greatly influence a domination attempt), wise vampires do not willingly share their blood with other vampires not of their brood.

Damage and Death States

If reduced to 0 hit points or lower, a vampire automatically assumes its death state (see racial descriptions) and attempts to escape. It must reach its *place of rest* within 2 hours or be utterly destroyed. Once at its *place of rest*, it rises to 1 hit point after 1 hour (minus ten minutes per *age* category), then resumes healing at its standard rate.

Note: A vampire cannot heal true sunlight or Holy damage in the same way as standard damage (see below).

Destruction of the Corpse

When destroyed, a slain vampire that has lived out their mortal years turns to dust in 1 round plus 1 round per *age*. All that remains are their fangs that will not turn to dust unless they are exposed to bright sunlight for 10 full minutes at which time they will disintergrate.

A vampire that has not lived out their mortal years does not turn to dust, instead turning into a greyish corpse from which their stores of blood and ichor slowly seep slowly out around them.

Places of Rest

The *place of rest* is the location in which a vampire was buried or where it was created. This is typically a crypt, grave or coffin. A vampire has greater power to heal his wounds at his *place of rest* - even if he is unbound (see Unbound Healing, below).

If a vampire was buried in a coffin, he must return to it every morning without fail. A coffin can be moved anywhere, but if destroyed the vampire must return to their *place of rest* to sleep or they derive no benefit from sleeping that night (see Penalties for Not Sleeping, p. 32). If *all* of a vampire's coffins are destroyed, it takes a year and a day to bind a new coffin to their necromantic energies.

Healing

Fuelled by the Void, a vampire has an incredible ability to heal their wounds. A vampire's fast healing ability applies to **all** damage except that done by sunlight, true sun-based spells and Holy magic.

Unbound Healing

When an Unbound vampire (see Gravebound, Vampiric Weaknesses p. 35) is reduced to 0 hit points or less, they assume their death state and can flee to *any* place to restore themselves.

However they are *not* bolstered by the grave and must use Blood to bring their hit point total back to 1 or greater (at which point they begin to heal naturally). Each Blood point they expend (one per round) restores 1d4 (plus their *age*) hit points. An Unbound vampire that returns to their grave or *place of rest* heals as though they were *gravebound.*

- ❋ A vampire that cannot (or will not) expend Blood to heal sleeps until their hit point total reaches 1 at which point they awaken (unless they are slain in the meantime or run out of blood).
- ❋ While sleeping a vampire heals 1 + *age* category hit points per night and burn 1 point of Blood every *other* day.
- ❋ A sleeping vampire can be given blood by minions (to prevent it falling into the *eternal quiescence).*

Hit Points

The Children of Vangual gain hit points in different ways depending on their alignment. The Servants of the Void (see p 112) always gain d12 for their hit points. Other characters retain the hit points they had in life and gain a bonus to their hit point total based on their Blood score for each new level that they gain.

A vampire does not gain or lose hit points from modifications to their Blood score. A vampire that loses 5 points of permanent Blood does not suffer any hit point loss (but will gain a reduced number of hit points when they next advance a level).

Notes: A vampire buys the Dark Gift, Blood Vault. This raises his Blood score by +3. When he next gains a level, he benefits from his increased Blood score by adding additional hit points to his hit point total (as he would have done with his mortal Constitution). He does **not** *retrospectively gain additional hit points for all of his previous levels (as he would with his mortal Constitution), only a benefit for every level he advances after increasing his Blood score.*

Holy

Holy refers to the abilities of the *Powers of Light*. A Holy power is described as Holy and is not considered damage that a vampire can easily heal. Unless a spell *specifically states* that it is Holy it is not Holy and does not have the same debilitating effect on a vampire (just because a spell comes from a good deity does not qualify it as Holy). Holy incorporates all the qualities of holy (see below).

Example: Although the spell sunray may be cast as a Holy spell (see Devotion, **Powers of Light***) it is not in itself Holy and vampires can heal the damage caused by it normally. The spell aura of light is a Holy spell and causes damage to a vampire that can not be healed by their fast healing ability.*

Holy Ground

Holy ground is considered any permanent site of lawful and good divine magic. The temple to the sun god Auraran is considered blessed and holy. Although temples to neutral gods are considered blessed, only those places of alignment opposite to the Void are considered harmful to a vampire. This means Lawful Good temples only (although other locations do exist - on a god by god basis).

A vampire cannot easily enter holy ground. It causes them great pain and they will slowly burn, taking 1 hit point per round damage.

A vampire suffers many of the same effects when standing on holy ground as they do in sunlight. They lose all benefits of their unnatural Strength and Dexterity, can only take partial actions and suffer -4 to any actions they do take. In addition the costs of any Dark Gifts they use are increased by +1 Blood.

Note: A vampire's Fast Healing ability does not work on holy ground. Vampires heal damage from walking on holy ground in the same way as sunlight damage (see page 31).

Holy Water

Holy water does 2d4 points of damage to the Children of Vangual or 2 points of damage on a splash. If the holy water is Holy water, then the damage is not subject to a vampire's Fast Healing ability and must be healed in the same way as Sunlight Damage.

SLEEPING

"Sleep. How I loathe those tiny slices of undeath..."
Alfred Hitchcock, Devoted Incarnate

Vampires are nearly powerless while the sun is in the sky. A great lethargy fills them in the moments before dawn and as the sun rises, they fall into a deep and deathlike state. While they are forced to sleep during the day, vampires can awaken with exceptional effort, although they are drowsy and weak. A vampire acting during the day (even while underground) suffers -4 to all of his actions (unless previously stated due to other powers or Gifts) and burns 1 point of Blood per round. Additionally he suffers a penalty of -2 to each of his abilities. This ability penalty rises in sunlight (see Sunlight Damage Table page. 33).

WAKING CHECKS

To be roused from sleep, a vampire must make a Waking (Will) check. This is made at the end of every round in which something disturbs them in some way. Merely wandering around their crypt (or even opening their coffin will not rouse a sleeping vampire. Successful melee attacks and offensive spellcasting will invoke a Waking check (DC 20 minus the cumulative amount of damage done in a single round).

Example: A party of adventurers open a vampire's tomb (no Waking check required) and attack him with magic weapons. He suffers a total of 5 points of damage in the first round. At the end of the round, the vampire gets a Waking check DC 15 (he suffers a -4 penalty to his Waking check due to it being daytime). On the second round, he is attacked twice, once for 8 points of damage and a second for 10. His Waking check is DC 2 (almost certain that he will awaken - despite his -4 penalty due to it being daytime).

PENALTY FOR NOT SLEEPING

A vampire that does not (or can not) sleep during the day suffers greatly. They lose all of their supernatural ability bonuses, cannot attune blood and all Dark Gifts cost double the normal amount to use, or 1 Blood if they do not already have a cost.

In addition, their damage resistance and fast healing abilities are halved (round down) in effectiveness until they again manage to sleep for their full daily quota.

DAYTIME DISCOVERY

Unless they have a reason to suspect otherwise, adventurers discovering a sleeping vampire will not immediately be aware that the corpse is one of the undead. There are no visible signs to indicate that the body is a vampire, it looks exactly like a corpse; cold, pale and dead.

A cleric may be able to sense the undead if he has the ability (see Sense, **Powers of Light**), or a *detect magic* spell *may* determine some residual necromantic energies around the corpse.

Of course if the PCs do not have these luxuries, a good adventurer can devise all kinds of ways to seek out sleeping vampires. Failing that, the only way to tell if a corpse is really a vampire is to wait until nightfall...

THE ETERNAL QUIESCENCE

The *black sleep* or the *slumbering death*. When a vampire runs out of blood, their necromantic energies are no longer able to sustain them. They automatically fall into a deep slumber from which they may never awaken. While they are not dead, they assume the appearance of a long dead and desiccated corpse. They are vulnerable and easily slain in this form.

Vampires do not expend any of their remaining Blood resources while in the *black sleep*. Many lie sleeping in crypts, hiding amongst the dead for thousands of years, never again to open their eyes.

A vampire will only waken from the *black sleep* when something stirs them. To awaken, they must make a Waking check for every day that they have reason to wake. A failure indicates that they keep on sleeping and may do so forever. A vampire can only make one Waking Check per night to rouse themselves from the *black sleep*. Even the most enticing mortal blood will not wake a vampire who has already failed their Waking Check for that night.

ENCOUNTER	WAKING CHECK
When within 10 ft. of mortals	DC 30
Physical contact with mortals	DC 25
Fed same age or younger vampire blood	DC 20
Fed older vampire blood	DC 15
Fed/contact with fresh mortal blood	DC 15

DARK GIFTS

Dark Gifts are magical abilities, strengths and powers given to a vampire through the energies of undeath. Necromantic in nature, they are grouped into *age* ranks.

A vampire can use their Dark Gifts as spell-like abilities. Unless stated, a Dark Gift requires a standard action to activate. If a Dark Gift has no activation cost (Blood) the vampire can use that Dark Gift at will.

All Dark Gifts are fuelled by attuned Blood. If a vampire has used all of their Blood resources, they cannot use any of their Dark Gifts until they have attuned a fresh supply of blood.

GAINING DARK GIFTS

A vampire gains 1 additional Dark Gift for every 3 levels he gains *after* becoming a vampire. In addition, all vampires gain a Dark Gift at 10th level and every 10 levels thereafter. A vampire can use a standard character feat to buy a Dark Gift.

FEATS

Assuming the base creature meets the prerequisites and does not already have them, the Children of Vangual gain the following feats:

Alertness, Combat Reflexes, Dodge, Improved Initiative, and Lightning Reflexes.

"What is life, except excuse for death, or death but an escape from life?"
Maximillian Aranais, Black Blood

Sunlight

A vampire takes damage per round dependant on the intensity of sunlight and the number of rounds they are exposed to it. Regardless of damage taken, vampires can only withstand a certain number of rounds of sunlight before they are forever destroyed (see Sunlight Damage Table, below).

Example: An age 1 vampire can survive for just 2 rounds in bright sunlight before being destroyed. If he finds sanctuary before the end of the second round he suffers 16d6 points of damage (which may still destroy him).

Additional Sunlight Notes

❋ The penalties listed here are cumulative with any other a vampire may suffer for being awoken during the day. A vampire in bright sunlight suffers a -10 penalty to his actions.

❋ A vampire can only take partial actions while exposed to any form of bright or overcast/cloudy sunlight.

❋ Use of a vampire's Dark Gifts costs *double* the normal amount of Blood or 1 Blood point if no cost is stated.

❋ A vampire's Fast Healing ability does not work in sunlight.

❋ A vampire's Damage Resistance ability is halved in sunlight (round down).

❋ A vampire reduced to 0 hit points by sunlight is forever destroyed (see race description for more information).

❋ A vampire suffers a penalty to their Strength and Dexterity while awake during the day (see Sunlight Damage Table, below).

❋ Shielded is a considered minimum of thick clothing (several layers of heavy blankets or leathers) and heavy facial cover. Even under these conditions a vampire's eyes will still fill with blood and seeing will be very painful.

❋ A vampire is considered to be *indoors* if they do not have at least ten feet of solid rock between them and the sun.

Sunlight Damage

Sunlight (and Holy) damage cannot be healed naturally and is restored at a rate of 1 plus the vampire's *age* category hit points per night. A vampire can further accelerate this healing by expending Blood to restore damage at a rate of 1 hit point per point of Blood expended. A vampire can only spend Blood equal to his *age* category in this way per night.

Example: An age 3 Black Blood suffers 40 points of sunlight damage. He cannot heal this wound with his fast healing ability, and notes the damage separately on his character sheet. He automatically heals 4 points of sunlight damage upon waking each night and can choose to expend up to 3 points of Blood per night to restore 3 further hit points of damage. If the vampire has lower than 0 hit points, he cannot consciously expend blood to heal himself.

Recovering from Sunlight

It can take a *long* time for a vampire to recover from an encounter with sunlight. Until they are healed, they will appear black and blistered with heavily charred and still-smouldering flesh. They suffer no penalties to their actions while burned and can act normally, despite the terrible pain they feel from their wounds.

Stakes

A stake in the heart will utterly incapacitate a vampire, forcing it into a deathlike state similar to the *eternal quiescence* (but with no chance of waking). Should the stake be removed, the vampire will immediately assume its death state and reform in 1d4 rounds on whatever hit point total it was on when it was staked. A vampire has no awareness while staked and can use none of its powers or Dark Gifts.

Note: Other implements (swords, broken wood, arrows) can also serve the same function as a stake. However, the Children of Vangual are tough; staking a vampire in the heart is a very difficult task indeed…

Strength of the Grave

A newly created vampire has Strength +10 until they feed or sleep or until dawn. This *Strength of the Grave* allows them to break free from their tomb or crypt and reach freedom. It also gives them the strength to be able to find food quickly, by overpowering any mortal opponent they may encounter.

Turn Resistance

As a vampire ages they are more difficult to turn. They gain a bonus to their effective turning level as detailed on the Master Age Chart (see p. 127).

Vampiric Age Modifier

The Children of Vangual add their *age* category to any saving throws they make. They also add their *age* category to any vampiric specific powers and abilities they use (see p. 29 for more details).

Example 1: An age 2 vampire adds +2 to the DC required to resist his energy drain attacks. An age 0 vampire gains no modifier.

Example 2: The DC to resist an age 3 vampire's domination attempt is increased by +3.

Clarification: This age bonus is only applied to vampiric actions. A vampire does not gain a bonus to his attack rolls, or to the DC of his spellcasting attempts, no matter what age he is.

Sunlight Damage Table

Sunlight	Damage	Rounds before Destruction	Penalty to Actions	Ability Penalty
Bright Sunlight	8d6	1 round + *age*	-10	-8
Overcast/Cloudy	6d6	5 rounds + *age* rounds	-8	-6
Dawn/Dusk	4d6	1 minute + *age* minutes	-6	-4
Shielded	2d6	2 minutes + *age* minutes	-6	-4
Indoors	None	None	-4	-2
Underground	None	None	-4	- -

VAMPIRIC TRAITS

When a vampire reaches *age* 3 he must take a vampiric trait for every age category he advances thereafter. These traits are an indication of a vampire's alienation from mortality and their growing ties to the Void. Vampiric Traits cannot be reduced, negated or otherwise avoided.

CLAWS/FANGS

The vampire has permanent claws or fangs that cannot be retracted. They must have the Dark Gift, Claws before they can choose this Vampiric Trait.

ENERGY DRAIN

The vampire permanently drains life energy. This can be temporarily reduced with the Dark Gift, Stifle the Chill but the vampire cannot come into contact with any living being or risk destroying it. The *Chill* around a vampire with this vampiric trait is greatly increased and a palpable aura follows them wherever they go.

GLOWERING DARKNESS

An aura of blackness surrounds the vampire. This has no benefit but is simply another indication of the vampire's great *age* and his bond to the Void.

SHADOW MONSTER

The vampire's shadow is forever stuck in a bestial or demonic form. It could dance or move about of its own accord. This can not be negated except by powerful magic.

STRANGE SENSE

Something accompanies the vampire when he travels, whether a high pitched whine or a terrible hush. Plants could die or milk curdle, the temperature could fall, or a strange smell could fill the air (like flowers, blood or cinnamon).

UNMISTAKABLE EYES

The vampire's eyes are unnatural, whether they are all black, catlike or blood filled. They could have the appearance of dragon eyes, blaze when angry, or have no pupils.

UNNATURAL SKIN

The vampire's flesh is different in some way. Whether it is simply an odd color (blue, gold or green), or thick and leathery, like vellum.

WINGS

The vampire has leathery wings. If he does not have the flight power, these wings are useless.

OTHER

This can be a trait of your choosing. Vampires are unique; one can not predict how the necromantic energies will affect them.

VAMPIRE SIZE

In addition to gaining Vampire Traits, all vampires grows as they age. The Void twists them into new forms, removing their mortality and transforming them into near giants. The Children of Vangual add 10% to their size with every *age* they advance beyond *age* 2.

A vampire that grows to more than 8 ft. in height gains the trait Large (and all the additional benefits and disadvantages associated with their new size). When shapechanged their new forms are always larger than normal.

> *"When we are young, wandering the face of the Earth, wondering what our dreams might be worth,*
> *learning that we're only immortal; For a limited time."*
> Dreamline, Black Cabal

VAMPIRE WEAKNESSES

Every vampire has a number of weaknesses as listed in their race description. A vampire may buy off one Vampiric Weakness at *age* 1 and with every *age* category they gain thereafter. Additionally they can buy off a Vampiric Weakness at the expense of a character feat.

Allergy - Garlic

Vampires are repulsed by garlic. They must make a Will save DC 15 to enter a building where fresh garlic is hanging or presented. Vampires acting in areas filled with the stench of garlic suffer a penalty of −2 to all of their actions.

Allergy - Iron

Iron bites deeply into vampire flesh. It passes through their damage resistance.

Allergy - Silver

Silver bites deeply into vampire flesh. It passes through their damage resistance.

Cannot Cross Running Water

Vampires cannot cross running water unless they are asleep in their coffins. Running water is defined as any free flowing water, stream, lake or river of more than 12" in width. Moats or mortal made structures (such as sewers) do not count. A stream or river must have been in existence for over 100 years for it to be effective against a vampire.

Cannot Enter Holy Ground

A vampire is unable to cross holy ground; places blessed by the *Powers of Light*. These are usually locations of great spiritual power and range from majestic cathedrals to humble chapels to the gods of goodness.

Cannot Enter without Invitation

A vampire cannot enter a private dwelling without permission. Once given permission by anyone who permanently lives in that dwelling (or if the sole owner dies), they can freely enter at will. Once invited, they cannot be refused entry. The 'necrotic threshold' must be replaced (see *replace the necrotic threshold* in **Powers of Light**).

Chill of the Grave

An aura of frigid cold surrounds all vampires. This is the chill of death, the icy aura of negativity. Their very bodies swirl with necromancy. Anyone standing within 10 ft. of a vampire will feel the *Chill* washing over them. The *Chill* permeates clothing, armor and is noticeable on even the warmest of days. It is the touch of death and only the most powerful magic can stave its effects – and then only temporarily. The *Chill* strikes unease into mortals and terror into animals. The extent of this weakness is dependent on the vampire and his *age*. **A vampire cannot buy off this weakness.**

Fear of Fire

Vampires hate fire. When forcibly presented with fire they must make a Will save DC 15 or flee from it as per the spell *cause fear*.

Fear of Sunlight

Sunlight strikes terror into a vampire. They must make a Will save DC 20 or recoil from it as per the spell *cause fear*.

Gravebound

A vampire must return to their *place of rest* when they sleep. They must sleep in their coffins, or in the ground in which they were buried. A vampire that does not have this weakness is said to be *unbound* and can sleep anywhere they choose.

No Reflection

A vampire has no reflection and cannot see themselves in any reflective surface.

Stench of the Grave

This smell is the stench of death, decay and rot. Animals find it intolerable and humans will be unnerved by it. Although there are no penalties attached to this weakness, the 'aura of death' will reveal a vampire's presence long before a vampire chooses to reveal themselves. Everyone will sense something amiss about the 'stranger' - the smell of death. A vampire automatically loses this weakness at *age* 3.

Water Vulnerability

Immersing a vampire in running water robs it of one-third of its hit points each round until it is destroyed at the end of the third round.

CHAPTER FOUR: BLACK CLASSES

The black classes are powerful. Derived from necromancy and fuelled by the Void, they are wreathed in darkness and the blackest sorcery. Only vampire characters can pick up a black class. They are a reward from Vangual for his favoured. When a mortal becomes a vampire, the dark energies of necromancy transform their abilities. For some, these changes are minor, yet for others, the transformation can be dramatic. Most affected are the holy classes: clerics, paladins and druids.

A black class is similar to a character's mortal class, but has a new name (like black fighter or black wizard) and new powers. The necromantic forces bolster existing abilities and create completely new ones.

Black classes are more powerful than their mortal equivalents. At their heart lies the Void - the source of all vampiric malevolence. A character will find himself moving far more quickly towards evil in a black class than he would remaining with his mortal classes. A good character must outweigh the balance; gain great power and risk falling to darkness, or remain true to mortality and sacrifice the greatest powers of the vampire kingdom.

MAINTAINING TRADITIONAL CLASSES

A character may only cling to any mortal character class for as long as they can continue to meet the alignment restrictions of that class. As they use their powers, the Void will drag them steadily towards evil. A character who can no longer maintain the alignment restrictions of his class can no longer maintain that class and suffers any penalties (as listed in the class section of the PHB).

CONVERSION TO BLACK CLASSES

When a character becomes a vampire, he can transfer his mortal classes to their black class variants during any Katharein (see p. 114). This is typically a permanent choice - once a character picks up a black class, few can go back. They have made a conscious choice to accept the gifts of Vangual.

When a character converts their mortal classes to black classes, all levels are transformed.

Example: A 6ᵗʰ level character with three levels in cleric, two in bard and one in wizard would convert all levels to their black class variants. These changes are made retrospectively, so a 10ᵗʰ level sorcerer vampire would gain all the benefits of his 10 black sorcerer levels, including all Dark Gifts and powers therein.

POSITIVE ENERGY

As long as a cleric matches the alignment restrictions of his faith, his deity will continue to grant his spells and divine powers. The vampire cleric may retain his mortal class and can still cast positive energy spells (see below). He may even turn the undead. But without powerful intervention, darkness calls and the Void ever twists the mind of a vampire…

Positive Energy: If a cleric channelled positive energy in life, they can continue to do so in undeath (providing their alignment permits it). A cleric can cast positive energy based spells, although such magic is harmful to their necromantic forces. A vampire suffers 1d6 points

of damage for every level of positive energy spell he casts. He can make a Will save for half damage (DC 10 + spell level). Examples of such spells are: *cure light wounds, light, flame strike* (most good spells and **all** spells from the Holy domain).

Falling: As soon as a cleric slips from the alignment path of his deity, he will lose all powers, retaining only his base attack bonus and saving throws. Clerics abandoned by their god must either choose a more suitable deity or transfer to black cleric.

Changing Faith: Many evil gods will eagerly pick up the faith of a cleric that has fallen from the light. However, this is a huge shift in belief on the part of the vampire cleric. Changes of faith and alignment can take years, or a Katharein can change a cleric's beliefs overnight (see Katharein p. 114).

Note: Some deities will not allow vampire followers of any description. In such instances, vampire clerics immediately lose all powers, even if they are in good or better standing with their god.

TURNING THE UNDEAD

If a vampire cleric retains their mortal cleric class, they may continue to turn the undead as long as their alignment permits this (and they have chosen to channel positive energy). This positive energy is harmful to their existence and causes them 1d6 points of damage for their effective turning level. Evil vampires cannot channel positive energy and lose their turning powers should they fall to evil.

Example: An 11ᵗʰ level black cleric with an effective turning level of 13ᵗʰ level suffers 13d6 points of damage as positive energy surges through him. He can make a Will save (DC 13) for half damage. If this damage is Holy damage, the vampire cannot restore it with his fast healing ability.

SPECIAL ABILITIES

A special ability is identical to that in the PHB unless otherwise noted in the black class description.

The Void

As we age, the Void reaches out and envelops our dark hearts. It stares into our souls, learning our ways and knowing our minds. It understands how to beguile us. It is tricky and trecherous, the ultimate manipulator. Many are lost to its wiles. Although it offers great power, it takes much in return. We begin to take on its shape, growing larger and more twisted turning into monstrous creations of our former selves.

I can but wonder as to the true form of the Void, but I would imagine that it is terrible beyond belief, a shape that would shatter fragile mortal minds were they to gaze upon it…

I fully intend to look upon the Void with my own eyes.

It is a good thing then I am **not** mortal…

Agoravaal on Musings of the Void

BLACK BARBARIAN

The black barbarian remains much the same as they did in life, but the Void transforms them in subtle ways. They gain greater control over their bodies and the rage that once sapped their strength is transformed by darkness. They are deadly foes and powerful allies.

Adventures: Free from the limitations of mortal flesh, black barbarians find their skills and abilities are greatly enhanced. Many seek solitude where they can meditate and learn the secrets of their new bodies free from the distractions of civilisation. Others seek out increasingly difficult battles in order to prove their superiority and skill in melee.

Characteristics: Necromantic energy turns a barbarian's rage into a cold frenzy of blood enhanced attacks. They are fearsome warriors, ceaseless in battle and filled with darkness. They like to collect tokens of their battles and wear them as trophies. Where once a barbarian may have worn animal skins, many black barbarians choose to wear the skins of slain enemies. A black barbarian is no longer hindered by the frailties of the flesh and can become a powerful force for darkness. Barbarians typically handle the transformation to undeath well, as their chaotic nature is at least partially aligned with the vampiric existence.

Religion: Black barbarians follow many religions, following the shamanistic beliefs of their people. Many believe that life is a journey and that even in undeath, a soul is still on the path of life. This tends to make them arrogant, as they believe they have been chosen by the fates for a superior destiny.

Background: The greatest mortal barbarians are singled out by black barbarians for their skill and battle prowess. These barbarians are taken (often by the Vangaard) to become the new generation of black barbarians. Many barbarian tribes are controlled by powerful vampire masters who rule with an iron grip. Few are even aware that their chieftains are undead, only that they are powerful masters of earth and darkness.

GAME RULE INFORMATION

A black barbarian's class skills (and the key ability for each skill) are the same as a standard barbarian in the PHB. They retain the same Base Attack Bonus, Fortitude, Reflex and Will saves.

THE BLACK BARBARIAN

Level	Special Ability
1	Blood Rage 1/day, Fast Movement
2	Uncanny Dodge (Dexterity bonus to AC)
3	Beastform
4	Blood Rage 2/day
5	Uncanny Dodge (can't be flanked), Cold Frenzy
8	Blood Rage 3/day
12	Blood Rage 4/day
13	Uncanny Dodge (+2 against traps)
15	Greater Blood Rage
16	Blood Rage 5/day; Uncanny Dodge (+3 against traps)
19	Uncanny Dodge (+4 against traps)
20	Blood Rage 6/day

CLASS FEATURES

All of the following are class features of the black barbarian.

Blood Rage: As the original barbarian's rage except the black barbarian gains +6 to Strength and an additional 2 Hit Points for each of the black barbarian's levels. When the black barbarian ends the rage, he is not winded but instead loses 1 Blood point.

Fast Movement: The black barbarian's speed is +10 regardless of weight or armor carried.

Beastform: At 3rd level, the black barbarian gains the ability to shapechange into a single animal (or dire animal) in addition to any creatures he can already assume (if any). This creature is chosen at the time of the first transformation and is typically a Winter Wolf (although other creatures are acceptable depending on the barbarian's background). This power is otherwise identical to the Dark Gift, Beastform.

Cold Frenzy: While raging, a black barbarian may choose to spend a point of Blood to gain an additional attack per round. This is at his full attack bonus and occurs before any of his other attacks.

Greater Blood Rage: At 15th level, the Blood Rage increases to a bonus of +8 to Strength and +4 Hit Points per level.

BLACK BARD

Black bards quickly discover there is music in darkness, that the powers of necromancy have their own song. The flow of shadow seeps through them, bringing a new tune to their dead hearts. The old tales are forgotten in favour of the ability to greater utilise the vampiric powers of charm and command.

Adventurers: When chance presents itself, black bards will stop at nothing to influence those around them, to instil strife and pain, fear and hopelessness. Black bards are amongst the most capricious of the vampire classes, taking pleasure in destroying faith and shattering trust whenever they can. They do not lean towards violence, but instead are the passive dissidents, those who instil mistrust in others. Their songs are designed to beguile and to mislead. They can be found in taverns across Avystervan, singing of their dark tales and evil exploits. Black bards are the information gatherers for the Black Council. They move across the mortal realms, hiding in plain sight, using illusion and charms to conceal their true visage and learning all that they can. This they take back to their dark masters, in exchange for rewards and ever-greater power.

Characteristics: Black bards are charmers and manipulators. In addition to spells, a black bard works magic with music or poetry. They can cause fear in their opponents, captivate their enemies, and counter magical effects that rely on speech or sound. They can entrance a crowd with their words, or cause agony with a single discordant note.

Religion: Black bards most commonly revere gods of darkness, shadows or night. A few are attracted to Vangual but most black bards do not seek any kind of deity, believing solely in their own necromantic talents.

Background: Only those with the best voices, artistic talents or exceptional beauty are chosen to become black bards. Those black bards that are created discover a sinister beauty to the night. They know their talents will last forever, and are prized the realm over. Black bards have centuries to perfect their skills and many have incredible musical ability forged from centuries of practice.

The greatest mortal performers are approached at least once in their careers by vampires wishing to bring their talents into the eternal fold of House *Mnemosyne*.

Lastly, House *Sonoruus* in Avystervan is home to many of the most powerful, genius and influential black bards the mortal realms have ever seen.

GAME RULE INFORMATION

A black bard's class skills (and the key ability for each skill) are the same as a standard bard in the PHB. They retain the same Base Attack Bonus, Fortitude, Reflex and Will saves.

THE BLACK BARD

Level	Special Ability
1	Bardic Charm; Bardic Lore, Bardic Song
3	Sound Burst
11	Mass Suggestion 1/week
20	Wail of the Banshee 1/week

CLASS FEATURES

All of the following are class features of the black bard.

Bardic Charm: For every round a black bard plays an instrument or sings, those listening suffer -1 to their saves against his charm powers (max penalty the black bard's *age* +1). This lasts for a number of rounds equal to the black bard's *age* +1 after the black bard stops playing or singing. Additionally, if a black bard plays a musical instrument or sings while using his vampiric charm powers, all listening suffer -2 to their saves. These effects are cumulative.

Bardic Lore: This works as the bardic lore ability in the PHB.

Bardic Song: This works exactly as the bardic song ability in the PHB, with the following changes:

* **Cause Fear:** A black bard with 3 or more ranks in Perform can cause fear as per the spell *cause fear*. The effect lasts as long as the black bard sings and for 5 rounds after the black bard has stopped singing (or for 5 rounds after the enemy can no longer hear the black bard).

* **Countersong:** A black bard with 3 or more ranks in Perform can perform a counter song as per the standard bard power.

* **Fascinate:** A black bard with 3 or more ranks in Perform can use *fascinate* as per the standard bard power.

* **Despair:** A black bard with 6 or more ranks in Perform can cause despair as per the spell *emotion*.

* **Suggestion:** A black bard with 9 or more ranks in Perform can influence their targets as per the spell *suggestion*.

* **Cause Agony:** Black bards with 12 or more ranks in Perform can sing a screeching note that causes agony to all living beings within 30 ft. of the bard. The song inflicts 1d8 points of damage per round while the bard sings. Characters may make a Will save to resist the effects (DC Black Bard's level + *age* category).

Sound Burst: As per the spell *sonic burst*. The black bard can do this once per day for every three of their black bard levels.

Mass Suggestion: The black bard can use their Perform skill to cast the spell *mass suggestion* once per week as a sorcerer of their black bard level.

Wail of the Banshee: The black bard can use their Perform skill to cast the spell *wail of the banshee* once per week as a sorcerer of their black bard level.

> *"One can survive everything, nowadays, except death, and live down everything except a good reputation.*
> *Who wants a good reputation?"*
> Oscar Wilde, House *Sonoruus*

BLACK CLERIC

Of all the black classes, the cleric is most affected by the transformation into undeath. An evil cleric has the most to gain while a good cleric has furthest to fall. Those evil clerics that were already aligned with negativity will find their powers greatly enhanced. Those of goodly alignments will be sorely pressed to keep their faith, their deity and their sanity.

Adventures: With blackness driving them, a black cleric primarily seeks advancement in the eyes of their god. Many seek revenge on the *Powers of Light*, some because the *Powers* failed to protect them from the curse of undeath, others simply because the Void desires their absolute destruction. Many black clerics are given quests that involve causing harm to the *Powers of Light* in some way. There are very few good black clerics and those that survive their *Second Waking* typically do not survive for very long in undeath.

Characteristics: A black cleric's transformation is fully dependent on their god. Some gods will ignore their vampire followers, while others will fully embrace their undead vassals. Most black clerics will find their powers greatly enhanced by the change to vampire. They are the champions of the Void, bringers of darkness and servants of death. Those that remain true to their mortality find their resolve greatly tested.

Religion: Any (special).

Background: Black clerics are indeed the chosen of Vangual. Dragged into shadow, they revel in bringing clerics of light into darkness. Many become worshippers of Vangual, god of vampires and blood, although a great number seek patronage under other gods of shadow and night. The Devoted Incarnate, the ancient order of vampire clerics is one of the most powerful religious organisations in the world.

GAME RULE INFORMATION

A black cleric's skills (and the key ability for each skill) are the same as a standard cleric in the PHB. They retain the same Base Attack Bonus and spellcasting abilities, as well as identical Fortitude, Reflex and Will saves.

THE BLACK CLERIC

Level	Special Ability
1	Bolster undead, Turn holy

CLASS FEATURES

All of the following are class features of the black cleric.

Bolster the Undead: Black clerics can no longer turn the undead. They can bolster or command them instead. Black clerics can also bolster other vampires, further protecting their allies against the *Powers of Light*.

Turn Holy: A black cleric gains the ability to turn good clerics and paladins. Mortals that would be slain are instead put into a deep slumber and will awaken 1d4 turns later. They cannot be woken during this period except by the use of powerful restorative magic. Additionally, a black cleric is able to buy the Extra Turning feat.

Spell Transformation: Black clerics can only channel neutral and evil spells. Black clerics gain domains as per any evil cleric. Black clerics of Vangual gain access to the Blood, Faithful Undead and Harm domains.

BLACK DRUID

Druids are amongst the most changed by the transformation into undeath. Separated from the life-force of the earth, they have become the antithesis of all in which they once believed. Known as anti-druids, black druids are opposite to the powers of the earth in every way. They devote themselves not to the destruction of the earth, but to its utter corruption. They pride themselves on tainting the land, taking what was once beautiful and transforming it into a nightmarish shadow of its former glory.

Adventure: Black druids are highly capricious. What they do, they do for themselves. They often seek destruction of all things living, yet many seek to establish themselves in the mortal realms, experimenting with undeath and vampirism, exploring the possibilities of twisted abominations and monster vampires. Their creations can be found the realm across, as can their homes, foul forests and groves - places of darkness and terrible evil. Black druids seek to undo what was created by mortal druids and woodland folk, while clashing with the powers of nature at every opportunity.

Characteristics: Black druids no longer gain their powers from the earth. Necromancy now fuel their magic. They become inimical to the forces of nature, but still retain some of their former powers, which are twisted by the blackness of the Void. A black druid's grove is typically filled with rotting vegetation and covered with thick blankets of fog that utterly occlude the sun. Everything takes on an unhealthy sheen as the druid's blood corrupts the plants, animals and even the soil itself. They are fond of oozes and slimes and other creatures that detest the day.

Religion: Black druids are no longer neutral. The Void strips them of their dispassion, twisting their hearts until darkness is all that remains. They typically find employ with the darker powers, although many find solace with others of their kind. Gods revered are those who corrupt or have contempt for all living things. Anti-druids are wholly opposite to mortal druids. To a mortal druid, there is nothing more horrifying than seeing healthy flora defiled by a black druid.

Background: Black druids are strange creatures indeed. They take delight in creating evil monsters bound by necromancy and twisted by blood. Separated from the earth they once tended, they now seek to twist and defile, poison and corrupt. While they do not typically have a society, they can be found gathering in swamps, deep forests and caves across the realm where the sun never shines.

GAME RULE INFORMATION

A black druid's class skills (and the key ability for each skill) are the same as a standard druid in the PHB. They retain the same Base Attack Bonus and spellcasting abilities, as well as identical Fortitude, Reflex and Will saves.

THE BLACK DRUID

Level	Special Ability
1	Black Companion, Stricken
3	Children of the Night
5	Beastform, Stricken x 2/day
7	Shapechange
9	Control Weather
13	A Thousand Faces
15	Stricken x 3/day
16	Blood Form
20	Stricken x 4/day

CLASS FEATURES

All of the following are class features of the black druid.

Black Companion: The black druid can summon and bind an animal creature to him. This animal can be of no more than 2 HD, but will grow with the druid as he feeds it blood and infuses it with necromancy (see below).

Stricken: A black druid drains the vitality from the land around him. While this does not destroy - it corrupts utterly. Plants will blacken, growing thorns and bloody barbs. Trees and lush foliage will fester and rot. Decay will abound. While this power is always active, blackening the grass at his feet, active use will give him strength.

Use: Once per day, a black druid can draw life energy from the wilderness. Flora in a 5 ft. radius per level of the druid is afflicted by the stricken effect. It withers and rots - a foul abomination to a mundane druid. If there is no 'vital' energy in the area of effect, this power has no effect. This power grants the black druid +1 to hit, saves and AC and restores 1d4 hit points for every 10 ft. drained. This effect lasts for 1 round per level. If there are sentient plants in the area, this effect is doubled as the plants are afflicted with the stricken effect. They gain a Will save against the black druid's level or are immediately transformed into evil and twisted blood-afflicted creatures under the command of the black druid.

Children of the Night: The black druid can command the lesser creatures of the world and once per day can call forth a pack of 4d8 dire rats, a swarm of 10d10 bats or a pack of 3d6 wolves as a standard action. These creatures arrive in 2d6 rounds and will serve the druid for up to 1 hour. If the black druid already has this Gift or ability, he can summon double the normal number of creatures of the night.

Beastform: At 5th level, the black druid gains the Dark Gift, Beastform. If he already has the Beastform Gift, he can assume one additional form for every *age* he advances.

Shapechange: At 7th level, the black druid can shapechange as per the druid power *Wild Shape*. He can also assume the form of any dire animal. The black druid regains hit points equal to his druid levels per transformation. Each transformation costs 1 Blood.

Control Weather: At 9th level, a black druid gains the Dark Gift, Control Weather.

A Thousand Faces: At 13th level, a black druid gains the ability to change his appearance at will, as if using the spell *alter self*.

Blood Form: At 16th level, a black druid can transform into a small or medium-size blood elemental once per day.

BLACK COMPANION

A black druid can bind a creature to his dark powers by *vampire touching* it (feeding it 1 point of Blood per week). Any sort of evil creature can be chosen: an animal, a dire animal, lesser shambling mound, jelly, ooze, slime or even blood elemental. His companion will live for as long as he feeds it blood and will grow ever more wicked. The druid can communicate telepathically with his companion at any time.

The companion will gain 1 point of Intelligence with every HD it advances, up to the maximum HD for that creature plus the Black Druid's *age* category. If it gains sufficient HD, it becomes a dire animal.

Example: A wolf can advance up to its maximum HD 5 (Large). Thereafter it can gain additional HD equal to the Black Druid's age. If the Black Druid was age 2 or older, the companion could evolve into a dire wolf with 7 HD. It could then follow that creature's advancement progression.

BLACK FIGHTER

An undead warrior is about as fearsome as they come. Relentless, powerful, strong beyond mortal measure, a vampire fighter can withstand terrible blows that would fell a living being, as well as gaining an ever-greater insight into the skills and knowledge that makes up a warrior. They literally have all the time in the world to become the best fighter they can.

Adventures: Black fighters spend their days honing their skills or using their battle prowess to protect the denizens of Avystervan. High level black fighters offer their services in many ways: as bodyguards, hunters, even assassins. Many black fighters choose to form broods in cities where they can feast upon the rich blood of the living. There they use a variety of nefarious methods from extortion to protection rackets to gain money, power and riches. Avystervan's guild of black fighters is called the Blood Guard who pledge their unlives to protecting the *City of Graves* and its inhabitants from harm.

Characteristics: Darkness supports the vampire fighter. They gain increased powers from their blood, as well as being able to attune a weapon to their own mystical darkness. They are merciless killers, the devourers of virgin flesh and the gore of children. They seek out mortal warriors with whom to prove their physical superiority.

Religion: Black fighters rarely take on a religion, although they are frequently hired for assignments involving clerics of various black churches. They tend to believe in their own powers and not in the belief of any one god (although they are free to choose whichever deity they see fit).

Background: Black fighters are created for many reasons. The best warriors are singled out and given unlife, added to the army of fighters in Avystervan. Many are made by fledgling broods in cities, vampires taking the town guard or the young warrior that shows great promise for their ranks. These recruits form the staple of their defences.

VAMPIRIC BLOOD WEAPONS

A Blood Weapon is a mystical item that a black fighter alone may create. The warrior instinct lies heavily within their nature, allowing them to attune a single weapon to their vampiric energies.

CREATION

Any weapon the black fighter has used for at least one full month can be made into a Blood Weapon. The weapon must have taken no less than 10 times the black fighter's level in hit points damage from mortal opponents during that time. To attune the weapon, the black fighter must spend one full night in ritual meditation. They must end the process with the death of a mortal (of no lower than half the black fighter's level) in single combat with the weapon to be attuned. The weapon must then be anointed with necromantic oils worth 500gp. It costs 500 XP to create a Blood Weapon and 1000 XP to create a Greater Blood Weapon. Once attuned the weapon takes on a liquid, bloody hue and becomes attuned to the vampire. A Blood Weapon has no powers in the hands of another (even another vampire).

A black fighter may only possess one Blood Weapon at any one time and if the weapon is destroyed, he must wait a full month before he can begin to attune another one. If the black fighter is slain, his Blood Weapon immediately reverts to a pool of blood and rusted metal. A Blood Weapon corrodes in sunlight in 1 round.

A Greater Blood Weapon can be made from a standard Blood Weapon but requires two nights of meditation and oils that cost 1000gp.

A vampire must feed their Blood Weapon 1 point of attuned Blood every seven days to keep it in perfect condition. A Greater Blood Weapon must be fed 2 points of attuned Blood per week. Failure to give it the required amount of Blood causes the weapon to become non-magical until it is given Blood. If the weapon is denied Blood for two full weeks it immediately corrodes and becomes useless.

VAMPIRIC BLOOD WEAPON

Attuned Vampiric Weaponry: A black fighter can drain levels as though he had personally scored a Slam Attack on his victim. Additionally, he gains all the benefits as though he had personally drained a level from his target although he can only drain 1 level per attack in this way. Every level he drains through his weapon costs him 1 Blood point.

Drain Blood: The Blood Weapon can drink the blood of those it strikes. For every 12 hit points of damage it deals in a single attack, the vampire can absorb 1 point of blood from that victim (a mortal target loses one point of Constitution).

Keen: The Blood Weapon becomes a Keen weapon (if it was not already Keen).

GREATER BLOOD WEAPON

Call to Arms: Black fighters can summon their Blood Weapon to their hand as a move-equivalent action. The weapon can be called across any distance (but not across planes or through magically warded areas). It costs the vampire 1 point of Blood to do so and the weapon materialises on the same round as the Call.

Cannot be Disarmed: While using their Blood Weapon, a black fighter can spend 1 point of Blood to avoid being disarmed at any time (as a Free Action).

Magical Weapon: A vampire may expend a point of Blood to use the Magical Weapon ability without having to physically coat his weapon. He must still expend Blood to power the ability. This is a free action.

GAME RULE INFORMATION

A black fighter's class skills (and the key ability for each skill) are the same as a standard fighter in the PHB. They retain the same Base Attack Bonus, Fortitude, Reflex and Will saves.

THE BLACK FIGHTER

Level	Special Ability
5	Magical Weapon +1
10	Attune Blood Weapon, Magical Weapon +2
12	Dual Wielding
15	Attune Greater Blood Weapon, Magical Weapon +3
20	Magical Weapon +4

CLASS FEATURES

All of the following are class features of the black fighter.

Bonus Feats: As a standard fighter, a black fighter gains a bonus feat in addition to the feat that any 1st level character gets, and gains an additional feat at 2nd level and every two levels thereafter. As in the PHB, black fighters gain access to the standard list of feats available to all fighters.

Magical Weapon: A black fighter can coat any weapon with a point of his own Blood to make that weapon +1 for one round plus one round per *age* category. This increases to +2 at 10th level, +3 at 15th level and finally, +4 at 20th level. It takes a full round action to coat a weapon in blood (although if a vampire has Blinding Speed, he can do this at the end of his round as a move-equivalent action at an additional cost of 1 Blood point).

Attune Blood Weapon: A black fighter can create a Blood Weapon from any weapon he has used for one full month in battle (see previous page for details).

Dual Wielding: The black fighter can wield two weapons of the same length with only the traditional penalties (as if one were light). They must have the feats Ambidexterity and Two-Weapon Fighting.

BLACK MONK

Perhaps the most feared of all the classes, black monks are terrifying creatures to behold. They are evil and wicked monsters who have learned to harness the dark energies of necromancy. Their *ki* becomes necromatically charged black *ki*, and is a source of ruthless destruction and cold strength. Black monks are known for their ability to drain multiple levels in a single attack and their terrible power to launch a silent attack at an enemy, then vanish back into the shadows without a trace. They are the assassins and murderers, the elite killers of the Black Council.

Adventures: Black monks adventure to gain further insight into their black psyche. The Void burns at their core, driving them on to ever-greater heights of black enlightenment. Black monks seek to further understand this relationship, to enhance the bond between mortal soul and vampiric body. Some adventure to test their skills, while others to prove their battle prowess. Others adventure for the hunt or to gain experiences in the world to further test and enhance their already considerable abilities. Many seek out mortal monks, some to learn, some to bring into unlife, but most, simply to destroy.

> *"Fear not death, for the sooner we die the longer we shall be immortal."*
> Benjamin Franklin, Black Monk

Characteristics: Black monks are driven by their black *ki*. This was once a force of harmony and balance, but black *ki* is pure darkness, a force of silent vengeance. It is the stillness of death combined with the cold fury of vampirism. Black monks and mortal monks are terrible enemies. Even those monks who retain their good nature in undeath are still considered abominations by mortal monks. The black *ki* burns within them, an anathema to the shining purity of the mortal monk.

Alignment: Black monks are dedicated to a discipline of absolute control over their vampiric forms. The teachings of their order allow them to stave off the worst of the Void, granting them greater command over their black *ki*. That they are so controlled only makes them that much more evil, as what they do they do of their own volition and not because the Void compels them.

Background: Evil monks brought into the fold do so eagerly, knowing that they will no longer suffer from the flaws of age. Their bodies will no longer betray them, become tired or sick, and they will be able to spend forever honing their art. Silent, evil, blood thirsty, black monks are a terrible enemy. Attacking with blinding speed, looming out of the night and vanishing just as quickly, they have powers and skills far in excess of any mortal. Hoarded jealously by the Black Council, the order of black monks, the Black Rain is treated exceptionally well.

MORTAL MONKS AND VAMPIRISM

A mortal monk relies on the inner calm and balance of their *ki*. This is wholly shattered in the transition to undeath. A newly created vampire monk suffers many problems; their powers are opposite to those of their mortal lives. They must weave a new path, learning to harness their black *ki*. This is both difficult and demanding, and many monks fall prey to the Void before they achieve a new balance within their dead hearts.

Unless a vampire monk changes their mortal monk class to their black monk variant, they suffer -2 to **all** of their monk-based actions and lose 2 from their monk levels (for the determination of which skills they gain) until they gain a full level in their monk class. This is specific to their monk skills; attack bonuses, saving throws and general abilities are unaffected.

GAME RULE INFORMATION

A black monk's class skills (and the key ability for each skill) are the same as a standard monk in the PHB. They retain the same Base Attack Bonus, Fortitude, Reflex and Will saves.

THE BLACK MONK

Level	Special Ability
1	Unarmed Strike, Stunning Attack, Evasion
2	Deflect Arrows Feat, Invisibility
5	Black Ki Strike (+1)
7	Wholeness of Body, Leap of the Clouds
9	Improved Evasion
10	Black Ki Strike (+2)
12	Abundant Step
13	Diamond Soul,
15	Black Ki Strike (+3), Quivering Palm
19	Empty Body
20	Black Ki Strike (+4)

CLASS FEATURES

All of the following are class features of the black monk.

Invisibility: Black Monks gain the Dark Gift, Invisibility.

Bonus Gifts: Once every three levels, a black monk gains a free Dark Gift from which they can choose one of the following: Alternate Form, Beastform, Blinding Speed, Blood Agility, Flight, Gaseous Form, Vampire Step, Vampiric Senses.

Black Ki Strike: As a Free Action a Black Monk can expend a point of Blood to make his unarmed attacks +1 for one round per *age* category. This bonus increases to +2 at 10th level, +3 at 15th level and finally, +4 at 20th level.

BLACK PALADIN

Of all the vampiric classes, the black paladin is the rarest, and most evil. They have the blackest, most corrupted hearts, turned away from all they once held dear. Where they were once a shining beacon of virtue, they have become a glowering force of evil, filled with treachery and brooding shadows.

Adventures: Black paladins strive to spread darkness and to fulfil their own evil ends. They delight in destroying good and thwarting the efforts of the *Powers of Light*. They revel in proving their superiority in melee, especially in slaying vampire hunters and those who would cast back the minions of the night.

Characteristics: Darkness lingers close to the surface in black paladins. They take what they want, seeing no one their peers. They think nothing of invoking their curse power at every opportunity, spreading death and disaster wherever they go.

Religion: Black paladins need not devote themselves to a single deity. The path of darkness is enough for most. Those who align themselves with a particular religion prefer those of death, or in particular, Vangual, god of blood and vampires.

Background: Black paladins are carefully selected by the dark powers. Fallen, they are an example of nobility and honor turned to darkness. They have dark hearts, filled with hatred for all life. No paladin of light can become a vampire. The *Powers of Light* simply do not allow it. A paladin cannot allow even a sliver of malice in their hearts, and the Void is a terrible companion. A newly created vampire paladin gains a choice; succumb to the Void and fall from grace, or death. Either way, a paladin will lose his divine abilities. Only when he is ready to accept his new destiny is he approached by the dark powers who reinstate his black status. Many black paladins embrace their new purpose, given a second chance to be amongst the faithful of the gods, even if those gods are opposite to all they once held dear. A paladin who drinks the blood of the living immediately falls.

GAME RULE INFORMATION

A black paladin's class skills (and the key ability for each skill) are the same as a standard paladin in the PHB. They retain the same Base Attack Bonus and spellcasting abilities, as well as identical Fortitude, Reflex and Will saves.

CLASS FEATURES

All of the following are class features of the black paladin.

Detect Good: At will, the black paladin can *detect good* as a spell-like ability. This ability duplicates the effects of the spell *detect good*.

Vampiric Boon: This works as the paladin power of *Divine Grace*.

Black Touch: A black paladin can cause wounds by touch. Each

night he can inflict wounds equal to a number of hit points equal to his Charisma bonus (if any) times his level. This power works in exactly the same way as the paladin *lay on hands* ability. This negative energy power heals the undead.

Cause Fear: The black paladin can cause fear as per the spell *Cause Fear* on touch.

Smite Good: As the paladin ability, *Smite Evil*, but works solely against Good opponents.

Turn Holy: When a black paladin reaches 3rd level he gains the ability to turn good clerics and paladins as a black cleric of two levels lower. Mortals that would be slain are instead put into a deep slumber and will awaken 1d4 turns later. They cannot be woken during this period except for the use of powerful restorative magic. Additionally, a black paladin is able to buy the Extra Turning feat.

Blood Curse: Beginning at 5th level, a black paladin can curse his opponents as per the spell *blood curse* (except the power only works for 1 hour per level). He can use this power more often as he rises in levels (as detailed below).

Special Mount: Upon or after reaching 5th level, the black powers pair the paladin with an undead Mount (see below). Should the black paladin's mount be destroyed, he may call for another one after a year and a day. The new mount has all the accumulated abilities due to a black paladin of the black paladin's level.

Aura of Fear: At 20th level, a black paladin is surrounded by an *aura of fear* as per the Dark Gift of the same name.

Code of Conduct: A black paladin must have a despicable heart. Although they do not have to go around committing acts of darkness that would ruin their long-term plans, black paladins whose souls are not filled with evil are quickly discovered and destroyed.

Associates: Black paladins are not restricted in with whom they can associate as long as they are serving the *Powers of Darkness*.

THE BLACK PALADIN

Level	Special Ability
1	Detect Good, Vampiric Boon, Black Touch
2	Cause Fear, Smite Good
3	Turn Holy
5	Blood Curse, Special Mount
10	Blood Curse 2/week
15	Blood Curse 3/week
20	Aura of Fear, Blood Curse 4/week

THE BLACK PALADIN'S MOUNT

The powers of darkness grant the black paladin an undead mount. This creature is utterly obedient to its master and will come at his bidding. The Mount has all the abilities as detailed in the PHB except that it is also undead. If the black paladin can turn to mist or shadow, his mount can do the same. It has darkvision. Some mounts are skeletal figures, while others are black steeds draped in mist and freezing darkness. Much depends on the character of the paladin as to the kind of mount he will receive from the dark powers.

EX-BLACK PALADINS

It is unknown for a black paladin to fall. Their hearts are filled with absolute darkness. Those who join the order remain faithful until they are destroyed. There have been a few cases where a black paladin has been reclaimed by the *Powers of Light* and restored to mortality, yet those isolated few do not return to their holy orders. They are simply too corrupted by necromancy, their minds and souls shattered by the journey into undeath and the blackest of evils.

Like a member of any other class, a black paladin may be a multiclass character, but faces a special restriction. A black paladin who gains a new class or (if already multiclass) raises another class by a level may never again raise his black paladin level, though he retains all of his black paladin abilities. The dark path of a black paladin requires a diabolical heart. Once you undertake the path, you must pursue it to the exclusion of all other careers. Once you have turned off the path, you may never return.

BLACK RANGER

Black rangers are the scouts and trackers, the senses of the Black Council. Where others may keep a watch on the mortal realms, black rangers are those who track down rogue vampires, their abilities to sense blood heightened. It is they who control the Blood Hounds and who spend much time travelling the world, seeking out knowledge and information. They have a guild home in Avystervan, the Crimson Heart, which is a place of information and dark purpose.

Adventures: Rangers take on the roles of hunters and trackers for the Black Council. Based in Avystervan, they are the information gatherers and the seekers of knowledge. They can be found in cities or far away from civilisation, searching out elusive information or secrets for the vampires of Avystervan. They also catalogue the whereabouts of known vampires unaffiliated with the Black Council.

Characteristics: Black rangers have heightened senses far beyond those of normal vampires. They can smell blood, attack when blinded and have the ability to go without feeding for long periods of time. As they spend much time travelling far from civilisation, the Void has adapted them, allowing them to spread their blood reserves over a longer period.

Religion: Black rangers typically do not follow any religion.

Background: Black rangers are taken from those mortals who show great promise in the arts of tracking and hunting. They are skilled warriors who excel at the woodland arts. Those who are adept in gathering information are often taken.

GAME RULE INFORMATION

A black ranger's class skills (and the key ability for each skill) are the same as a standard ranger in the PHB. They retain the same Base Attack Bonus, Fortitude, Reflex and Will saves.

THE BLACK RANGER

Level	Special Ability
1	Track, Favoured Enemy, Speed +5, Vampiric Senses
3	Blood Thrift
5	Enhanced Senses, Speed + 10
10	Bind Blood Hound, Speed +15
15	Speed +20

CLASS FEATURES

All of the following are class features of the black ranger.

Track: Black rangers gain the Tracking feat.

Favored Enemy: Black rangers must choose humanoids as their Favoured Enemy

Speed: A black ranger gains a bonus of +5 to their base speed. This rises to +10 at 5th level, +15 at 10th level and +20 at 15th level.

Vampiric Senses: Black rangers gain the Dark Gift, Vampiric Senses.

Two-Weapon Fighting: As per the PHB except a black ranger can gain the benefits of dual-wield while wearing any type of armor.

Bind Blood Hound: A black ranger can permanently expend 3 points of Blood to bind a Blood Hound to himself. This creature must be fed a point of Blood every week. The black ranger can expend a point of Blood to conjure the Blood Hound at any time as a standard action. If destroyed, the black ranger recovers the lost 3 Blood after one full month and must wait another month to bind and create a new Blood Hound. The Blood Hound and black ranger always know the others' location and the Blood Hound can store up to 6 points of Blood for the ranger at any one time (the ranger cannot remove the 6th point or the Blood Hound will be instantly destroyed). See Blood Hounds p. 98.

Enhanced Senses: At 5th level, a black ranger gains a bonus of half his black ranger levels to his Listen, Spot, Search, Sense Motive and Tracking checks.

Blood Thrift: A black ranger can reduce the Void's drain on his Blood reserves. He can at any time expend Blood up to his black ranger level to suffer no daily blood drain for a total number of days equal to twice the amount of Blood spent. He suffers a penalty of -1 to his abilities for every day beyond his *age* category +1. Failure to feed at the end of the elapsed period means the vampire loses double the amount of Blood and must make a Will save (DC 10+ number of days spent on Blood) or fall into the *eternal quiescence*.

Example: A 10th level, age 3 black ranger expends 5 points of Blood. He can go for 10 full days without losing any blood while sleeping. At the end of the fifth day, he loses -1 to each of his physical abilities. At the end of the sixth day, he suffers a penalty of -2 to his abilities. A vampire cannot fall below 1 in any ability. On the 11th day and every subsequent evening thereafter, he loses 10 Blood amd must feed or make a Will save DC 20 or fall into the eternal quiescence. He continues to lose 1 from his abilities each day until he either feeds or falls into the eternal quiescence.

BLACK ROGUE

Of all the classes, perhaps the rogue makes the best transition to undeath. Already a part of the shadows, the black rogue is granted powers far in excess of those he could ever normally attain, and many rogues jump at the chance for eternal life and the abilities granted to a vampire.

Adventures: Black rogues use their powers to gain riches and to further their own ends. Some seek revenge on those who wronged them in life, while others are content to hone their skills, spending the long years learning their craft.

Characteristics: Black rogues have many advantages. Being dead, they do not suffer from shakes or trembles when picking locks and can move without a sound when they choose to. They can see in the dark and are perfectly at home in sheer blackness. Black rogues are confident and powerful, utilising their Dark Gifts and abilities to their greatest potential. Few places are safe from their reach; they can turn to mist, change shape and even melt into darkness.

Background: Black rogues are often taken from promising rogues on the street. Black rogues form guilds in great cities, where the master vampire thieves watch for promising candidates. Those with talent are spirited away to Avystervan where they are given eternal life, so long as they swear their absolute allegiance to the Black Council and the Black Eye (the guild of vampire rogues).

GAME RULE INFORMATION

A black rogue's class skills (and the key ability for each skill) are the same as a standard rogue in the PHB. They retain the same Base Attack Bonus, Fortitude, Reflex and Will saves.

THE BLACK ROGUE

Level	Special Ability
1	Blood Grace, Friend of the Shadows, Sneak Attack +1d6
2	Evasion
3	Uncanny Dodge (Dex bonus to AC), sneak attack +2d6
4	Hidden Weapon
5	Sneak attack +3d6
6	Uncanny dodge (can't be flanked)
7	Sneak attack +4d6
9	Sneak attack +5d6
10	Special Ability
11	Uncanny dodge (+1 against traps), sneak attack +6d6
13	Sneak attack +7d6, special ability.
14	Uncanny dodge (+2 against traps)
15	Sneak attack +8d6
16	Special ability
17	Uncanny dodge (+3 against traps), sneak attack +9d6
19	Sneak attack +10d6, special ability
20	Uncanny dodge (+4 against traps)

CLASS FEATURES

All of the following are class features of the black rogue.

Blood Grace: A black rogue can increase his Dexterity at the cost of Blood. He can increase his Dexterity to a maximum total of his black rogue levels per day at a cost of 1 Blood per point. Each point of Dexterity lasts for 1 minute.

Example: a 15th level black rogue could expend up to 15 points of Blood per day to increase his Dexterity. He could spend five Blood one round, and then an hour later, expend 10 Blood to increase his Dexterity by 10 points for 1 minute.

Friend of the Shadows: A black rogue's abilities are greatly enhanced by the change to undeath. They gain a +4 bonus to Balance, Climb, Jump, Tumble, Hide and Move Silently. These bonuses are in addition to any they may receive from being a vampire and/or their original race.

Hidden Weapon: Black rogues can conceal a small weapon within their bodies. They can remove this at any time as a full round action. Insertion of a weapon into their flesh takes a single minute and costs 1 Blood point to insert and to remove.

Special Ability: A black rogue can choose from the following Dark Gifts instead of choosing a special ability (as listed above): Blinding Speed, Blood Agility, Conjure Darkness, Gaseous Form, Invisibility, Shadow Form, Spider Climb.

BLACK SORCERER

The flows of necromancy focus a sorcerer's powers in undeath, granting them the ability to fuel their magic with blood. Their looks darken and they become if anything, more intriguing; that exotic quality about them mixed with the strangeness of the undead.

Adventurers: Black sorcerers do not lose the drives they had in life, at least not the selfish desires that lead them on to greatness, power and wealth. Granted further abilities, sorcerers seek to elevate themselves, to shatter their rivals and to do harm to those who would have done them wrong. Black sorcerers are free without restriction.

They can go where they will without being tied to books or halls of learning. They can seek riches or knowledge or power. Many work for the Black Council on missions that require their unique talents.

Characteristics: Most black sorcerers do not consider being dead a disadvantage. As the wells of necromancy focus, they see undeath as a means to unlock ever greater mysteries, to harness ever increasing sources of power and to have unlimited potential. They are the most charismatic of the black classes, charming and mysterious and have a great affinity with the mortal races - treating them as objects of intellectual stimulation or pets - depending on the sorcerer. Black sorcerers are wild, untamed spirits. With thoughts only for themselves, they are wilful, arrogant and free with their magic.

Religion: Those sorcerers that do not consider religion a waste of time revere either gods of magic or Vangual, who is always willing to bring another sorcerer into the fold.

Background: Black sorcerers are chosen by the Black Council for exceptional style or magical ability. Powerful sorcerers are in high demand and their services command a high price in Avystervan.

GAME RULE INFORMATION

A black sorcerer's class skills (and the key ability for each skill) are the same as a standard sorcerer in the PHB). They retain the same Base Attack Bonus and spellcasting abilities, as well as identical Fortitude, Reflex and Will saves.

THE BLACK SORCERER

Level	Special Ability
1	Summon Vampiric Familiar, Restore the Arcane
2	Revive the Arcane I
3	Revive the Arcane II
5	Revive the Arcane III
7	Revive the Arcane IV
9	Revive the Arcane V
12	Revive the Arcane VI
14	Revive the Arcane VII
16	Revive the Arcane VIII
18	Revive the Arcane IX

CLASS FEATURES

All of the following are class features of the black sorcerer.

Summon Vampiric Familiar: A black sorcerer can summon a vampiric familiar as detailed below.

Restore the Arcane: The basic ability of the black sorcerer is to rekindle used spell energy at the cost of Blood. This power works as Revive the Arcane I to IX except the sorcerer can restore *any* one spell slot per night at the cost of 1 Blood plus the level of the spell.

Revive the Arcane: The sorcerer can rekindle his ability to cast spells by expending blood. Once per night he can expend blood to regenerate any spell slot of his choice. This requires a full round action and costs an amount of Blood equal to the level of the Revive the Arcane. A sorcerer can use a higher level Revive to restore a lower level spell, but it still costs the level of the Revive to do so.

Example: At 1st level, a sorcerer can use Restore the Arcane I to restore one 1st level spell slot per night at the cost of 1 point of Blood. At 7th level, he has Revive the Arcane I to IV. He can use each of them once per night to revive any spell level equal to or lower than the Revive the Arcane level. To restore a 3rd level spell with Revive the Arcane IV costs 4 Blood points.

BLACK WIZARD

Necromantic energies ferment within a black wizard, greatly increasing their powers. No longer restricted by their weak nature or fragile bodies, the transformation to undeath has heightened their intellect and greatened their physical abilities. Black wizards are truly fearsome opponents.

Adventures: Black wizards adventure for many reasons, some to prove their magical prowess, while others to find rare and elusive ingredients for their arcane arts. Others seek out rare treasures or unique spells, others to gain power or knowledge.

Characteristics: Black wizards have tremendous abilities fuelled by darkness. No longer weak, they can rise to become powerful, their spells fuelled by necromancy. The Void inevitably twists black wizards into chaos and the darkest evil. Many are megalomaniacs that seek only ever-greater power, dominance over lesser beings, or both.

Religion: While most black wizards do not bother with religion (considering it a lesser form of magic), many do hold some stock in Vangual, or other neutral or evil gods of magic or death.

Background: Black wizards group into guilds, the greatest being the Black Cabal, the elite group of vampire mages that gather in Avystervan. Even moderate level wizards are valuable to vampire society. Powers to transport and open Blood Gates makes a spellcaster a prized asset. A wizard can earn a fortune transporting wealthy vampires across the world and bringing them back again. Some vampire wizards are given the often unenviable task of training prospective wizards in the mortal realms, or protecting those vampires who have need of their services.

GAME RULE INFORMATION

A black wizard's class skills (and the key ability for each skill) are the same as a standard wizard in the PHB. They retain the same Base Attack Bonus and spellcasting abilities, as well as identical Fortitude, Reflex and Will saves.

THE BLACK WIZARD

Level	Special Ability
1	Summon Vampiric Familiar, Vitae Enhancement
5	Bonus Feat
10	Bonus Feat
15	Bonus Feat
20	Bonus Feat

CLASS FEATURES

All of the following are class features of the black wizard.

Summon Vampiric Familiar: A black wizard can obtain a familiar as detailed below.

Vitae Enhancement: A vampire can utilise his metamagic feats with the power of his blood. He can choose to expend Blood to power his spells rather than learning them at a higher level. He can use Vitae Enhancement at the time of casting, but can only enhance one metamagic feat per round. The cost in Blood is equal to the enhanced level of the spell. A wizard can use a metamagic feat on a spell and then choose to use Vitae Enhancement on it (at the time of casting), but this raises the level of the spell (and therefore the cost in Blood to further enhance it). A wizard can only enhance a spell with Vitae Enhancement once, although he can do this at the time of preparing a spell. Spells enhanced with this power are always enhanced last.

Example: A wizard maximises the spell fireball. It costs 6 Blood to do this, as the spell would normally be learned three levels higher than the 3rd level that it normally is.

Example 2: A wizard has previously learned and maximised the spell fireball (taking up a 6th level spell slot). If he wishes to Empower the spell (normally learned 2 levels higher), it would cost him 8 Blood points.

Bonus Feat: As a standard wizard.

VAMPIRIC FAMILIAR

When a spellcaster dies, the link between the original familiar and spellcaster is severed. The black spellcaster must summon a new familiar in a ritual that lasts for one full night and costs 8 Blood. The vampire must feed his familiar at least one point of Blood per week. A vampiric familiar can be summoned from the following forms:

Undead Familiar	Powers
Blood Ooze	Store Blood (HD)
Bloodling	Immune to bladed weapons, Store Blood (HD). *Note:* Bloodlings must be given one point of blood per day or dissolve.
Dire Wolf	-
Minor Undead	-
Stirge	Store Blood (4)
Dire Vampire Bat	-

Note: The vampiric familiar has half the hit points of the master, and has all the standard powers as listed in the PHB, except where noted below:

Touch: If the master is 3rd level or higher, the familiar can deliver the caster's touch spells. This also includes level draining powers although the familiar can only drain one level per successful attack.

Store Blood: The familiar can store blood for its master. The number in parentheses is the maximum amount of Blood the familiar can store (or its HD). The master can remove or replenish this Blood at any time, draining one Blood point per round as a standard action.

Powers: A vampire familiar can share its master's Dark Gifts when they are within 100 yards of each other. It can use attuned Blood to power any Gifts that require them, but can only store Blood as noted above. The familiar cannot share *age* 1 or older Dark Gifts.

Minor Undead: All undead gain all the powers and abilities associated with being undead. Undead must be physical and can be chosen from Zombie, Skeleton or Ghoul (the master must be at least 5th level).

Note: A Shadow Vampire may choose a shadow as his familiar.

THE DARK TRINITY

When the First fled into the darkness that became Avystervan, they divided their number into three orders. These guilds formed the basis of their existence, each having province over a certain area of vampire society.

The Devoted Incarnate were the first - the order of spirit - a sect holding authority over the spiritual wellbeing of the vampire community. The next was the order of flesh - the Blood Knights - the guardians of the Children of Vangual. Finally came the order of sagacity - the Black Cabal - wizards and blood mages that thrive on knowledge and mystical secrets.

RECRUITMENT

To become a member of one of the ancient orders, a vampire must petition an elder for entrance into their desired guild. It is typically only the elite who gain access to these orders. If successful, the guild elder transforms the supplicant in a gruelling ritual. The decision is permanent and should **not** be made lightly. Potential recruits are hand picked by the head of their order. If the ancient vampire is unsatisfied with the selection, they will likely destroy the prospective candidates without question.

Entrance to one of the ancient orders grants a vampire additional powers and may considerably shift their vampiric abilities. They will be given new responsibilities and may even be sent to form a new brood in a new city. Those in the Dark Trinity have an elevated status within Avystervan.

COMPETITION

There are so many vampires in existence that not every one of the Children of Vangual can enter the Dark Trinity. Competition is fierce for the limited number of places that open up. As a result the Trinity make it difficult and dangerous for a potential vampire to enter their order. Over the last five hundred years, the recruitment process has become ever more dangerous. Hundreds of vampires have been slain trying to pass the tests set out for them by the elders of the three orders. These tests change yearly and grow ever-more demanding.

Even if a vampire has the required attributes and abilities, only those who perform exceptionally well or achieve something of note are brought into the fold. The Dark Trinity recognises talent and does not allow it to go to waste.

DMs NOTE

These Prestige Classes are very powerful. They are purely for the most evil and wicked persons alive. You should be cautious about allowing them in your game. They make far better NPCs than they do Player Characters.

If you do allow PCs access to these Prestige Classes, ensure that the challenges needed to gain admission are taxing in the extreme. If a PC is somehow successful in gaining entry into the Dark Trinity, keep the orders mysterious, their abilities vague and powerful. These guilds are literally thousands of years old, their secrets are unfathomable, as are their elders.

Never give away all of the secrets of the Dark Trinity; no one vampire can know them all.

HALL

THE BLACK CABAL

The Black Cabal are vampire wizards, sorcerers and devils. Evil to the core, they use their magic to further their black desires. The ties that bind these vampires are greater even than the powers of necromancy. A vampire that joins the Black Cabal can never leave. It is a road to absolute damnation.

Having fully attuned their bodies to the black arts, the Black Cabal are powerful beyond measure. They do not fear the *Powers of Light*. They can be found wandering the streets at night, carrying out their sinister schemes with attitudes of dark invulnerability.

The Black Cabal are steeped in ancient and bloody history. They have rituals and traditions dating back over two thousand years. They have worked closely with their religious brethren to unravel the mysteries of the Avystyx Prophecies, and work hard to prove their magical and intellectual superiority.

The Black Cabal live in the Obsidian Towers in Avystervan. There, the great towers house over a hundred vampire wizards in ranks based on *age* and spellcasting ability.

MISSIONS

The Black Cabal are responsible for the magical defences of Avystervan as well as advising the First on matters both arcane and mundane. In addition, it is the Cabal's duty to bring fresh slaves to the city. Using their portals to the mortal realms, the Cabal journey at night with a contingent of Blood Guard, spiriting mortals back to Avystervan. These hunting parties (called the Black Hunt) have been declared a terrible blight by the *Powers of Light*.

The Black Cabal place at least one of their number in every city across the Realm. These lone vampires watch the mortal world, reporting their findings back to their elders in Avystervan.

Lastly, the Black Cabal have created a network of permanent magical portals (Blood Gates) across Avystervan leading to many of the major cities across the realm. The Black Cabal grants access to whoever requires use of them (for a small fee). Although these portals are typically one way, the Cabal can send a representative with any travelling party to transport them back to the *City of Graves*, should they require it (although this can be prohibitively expensive).

ORDERS

While not every vampire wizard can join the Black Cabal, many that meet the entrance requirements do. These spellcasters gain tremendous benefits, such as access to Blood Magic, and one of the greatest and most comprehensive magical reference libraries in the known world. Those wizards who do not join the Black Cabal often ally themselves with other vampire wizards in Avystervan. These younger orders allow a wizard greater freedom but do not have the raw power of the Black Cabal.

INITIATION

The rite of initiation into the Black Cabal is called the 'Blood Moon' ritual. The initiate is taken to one of the mortal cities and has a single night to find a chosen victim as selected by the elders of their order. To make the task that much harder, some initiates are drained of almost every drop of blood whilst others are given grey Va'Vash to disable their vampiric abilities. The vampire must return to their masters with the heart of their target, intact. Only then can they feast upon their prize. Particular nasty initiations have previously involved a supplicant retrieving the hearts of their mortal parents, or their own children.

Those in the Black Cabal are expected to spend several years in various positions. All who follow the craft must donate time to the creation of a certain number of magical items per year. Others must work on Blood Gate duty, some act as guards and seers. Lastly those of a higher level become hired mages, or specialists in their various fields of magic.

MORTAL AUTHORITY

Many power hungry mortals learn of the Black Cabal. The order scrys for potential subjects and sends them visions while they sleep. After making contact, the order offers magical training in return for an eternity of loyalty. Of course, the candidate becomes a vampire after an agreed period has elapsed (they gain a short period to enjoy the remainder of their mortal lives before submitting to the Black Cabal).

There are many mortal wizards under the tutelage of the Black Cabal across the realm, most of them *vampire touched* and slavishly loyal to their vampiric masters.

THE BLACK CABAL

Class Level	Base Attack Bonus	Fort Save	Ref Save	Will Save	Special	Spells per Day
1	+0	+0	+0	+2	Consume the Arcane, Recall the Arcanum	+1 level of existing class
2	+1	+0	+0	+3		+1 level of existing class
3	+1	+1	+1	+3	Blood Magic	+1 level of existing class
4	+2	+1	+1	+4		+1 level of existing class
5	+2	+1	+1	+4		+1 level of existing class
6	+3	+2	+2	+5	Will of Blood	+1 level of existing class
7	+3	+2	+2	+5		+1 level of existing class
8	+4	+2	+2	+6	Greater Consume the Arcane	+1 level of existing class
9	+4	+3	+3	+6		+1 level of existing class
10	+5	+3	+3	+7	Vitae Dispelling	+1 level of existing class

DARK EXPERIMENTS

It is said the Black Cabal make new vampires for the single purpose of experimentation, and that there are countless mutated undead creatures living beneath their halls. The Black Cabal have created their own vampire race – the *consanguineous vampire*. Barely a vampire at all, these creatures are ravenous monsters, held together by blood and necromantic energies. Tortured by the darkest sorcery, this is a punishment for their most hated enemies.

ROLE-PLAYING THE BLACK CABAL

Powerful, protected, slavishly faithful. You are part of the elite of wizards. You know or have access to many secrets of the universe. Nothing is beyond your touch. You can steal spells from the minds of others and add them to your spell-books. Magic is a part of your blood, mortal wizards are like charlatans before you. Where you fail, your order will succeed. You are indomitable.

REQUIREMENTS

To qualify to become a member of the Black Cabal, a character must fulfil the following criteria:
Spellcasting: Must be able to cast 3rd level arcane spells
Race: Must be a vampire
Prerequisites: Advanced Energy Drain, any three magical feats
Intelligence: Must be 18+
Skills: Spellcraft 10+ ranks

CLASS SKILLS

The Black Cabal's class skills (and the key ability for each skill) are the same as a wizard.

Skill points at each additional level: 2+ Int modifier

CLASS FEATURES

All of the following are class features of the Black Cabal:

Consume the Arcane: When conferring a negative level, the Black Cabal can drain any spell lost by the spellcaster and add it to the spells they have prepared. This must be an arcane spell of a level that the Black Cabal could normally cast (even if they do not know it). They can absorb one arcane spell for every negative level they drain. Stolen spells last until dawn when they dissipate from the vampire's mind. Spells requiring material components must be located or they cannot be cast (even into a spellbook). A vampire with the Still Spell feat can still use Blood Magic to cast these spells.

Example: A member of the Black Cabal attacks a 12th level wizard. He successfully strikes his target and inflicts 2 negative levels. The wizard immediately loses his two highest level known spells. The Black Cabal vampire can choose to absorb one or both of the lost spells. If he could not cast the level of spell lost by the wizard, he could not 'consume' any spells.

Recall the Arcanum: Allows the Black Cabal to retain a stolen spell before inscribing it to their spellbook. The vampire can choose to expend half a spell's level in Blood to retain the spell for future copying to his spellbook. If he does not have sufficient attuned Blood, he cannot save the spell. A retained spell cannot be used for any purpose other than scribing into his spellbook, and a vampire can only retain as many spell levels at any one time as twice his Black Cabal levels. He does not recover Blood used to retain a spell until he voluntarily releases it.

Blood Magic: The Black Cabal can store spell energy in their blood. They can store a total number of spell levels equal to their Black Cabal levels, storing them as magical effects and not actual spells. To store a spell costs Blood equal to the level of the spell. The spell is then transformed into magical energy that is locked into the caster's blood until expended. The vampire has his Blood score reduced by the amount of Blood spent on the spell until he either casts or discharges any stored spells (*storing a 2nd level spell costs 2 Blood*). Activating a spell effect is a free action (but only one Blood Magic spell can be expended per round). The action requires no material or somatic components beyond those expended at the time of the original casting. Additional spells stored after the first cost a cumulative total of 1 additional Blood per spell, ie. it costs 1 additional Blood to store a second spell and 2 Blood to store a third spell. Blood spent on the spell level or additional spell storage cannot be recovered until the spell energy has been expended (the vampire can voluntarily discharge a spell at any time).

Example: A vampire with three 1st level spells stored in his blood would be temporarily down 6 points of Blood. It would have cost a total of 6 Blood to store all three level 1 spells: 3 for the three 1st level spells - 1 to store the second and 2 to store the third. His Blood score would be reduced by 6 points until he cast or discharged any of the stored spells. If he wanted to store one 6th level spell and one 7th level spell, the 6th level spell would cost 6 Blood and the 7th level spell would cost 8 Blood for a total of 14 Blood. The vampire's Blood score would decrease by 14 points until either one or both of the spells were discharged.

Will of Blood: The vampire can grant himself temporary Spell Resistance by focusing his blood with powerful energies. Will of Blood requires a standard action to bring into effect. The vampire gains Spell Resistance equal to 10 (+1 per *age* category per point of Blood expended) and lasts for 1 round plus the vampire's *age* in rounds (plus one round for every point of Blood expended on increasing the duration).

Example: An age 3 vampire expends 3 points of Blood (on Spell Resistance alone). For 4 rounds, his Spell Resistance is 19 (10 + (3 x 3)). If he expended 5 points of Blood (all on Spell Resistance), his Spell Resistance would be 25 and last for the same 4 rounds. An age 5 vampire expending 3 points of Blood (on Spell Resistance) would have a Spell Resistance of 25 which would last for 6 rounds. If he spent 5 points of Blood (3 on Spell Resistance and 2 on duration), his Spell Resistance would be 25 for 8 rounds.

Greater Consume the Arcane: At this level, the Black Cabal's power is so great that they may select **any** arcane spell that the target knows. The vampire may still absorb only one spell per level drained.

Vitae Dispelling: The Black Cabal member can counter or negate any magical effect he can see simply by expending blood. He must make a spellcraft check to determine the nature of the spell, and expend blood to negate it at a cost of twice the spell's level. He can do this as a standard action.

Example: A wizard casts a fireball on a Black Cabal member. Seeing the fireball hurtling toward him, the Black Cabal member makes a spellcraft check. Succeeding, he knows the spell is indeed a fireball and expends six points of Blood. The spell is negated, the magical energies dissipating harmlessly around him. While a Black Cabal member could relatively easily negate a magic missile or fireball, he might not be so willing to negate a 9th level spell.

Spell List: As black wizard - plus access to Black Cabal personal spells. These spells are jealously hoarded by the Black Cabal and kept in the obsidian towers in Avystervan. Any vampire revealing these secrets to another outside the order is viciously slain and those who somehow gain access to the spells are sought out and destroyed.

BLOOD MAGE

Blood Mages are the alchemists and researchers of the Black Cabal. They have chosen to specialise in the powers of the blood rather than in the traditional magics of the Black Cabal. A powerful order in their own right, they have the full backing of the Black Cabal and are considered very much a part of it.

MISSIONS

Blood Mages control much of the blood that flows into Avystervan and are responsible for obtaining and keeping a sample of blood from every important mortal across the realm. Their ability to attune standard blood makes them invaluable and many Blood Mages accompany vampires on missions across the land, utilising their powers to enhance the might of an already formidable vampire hunting party. Lower level Blood Mages spend their time learning the arts of their craft, spending time cataloguing and collecting blood for the order. Medium level mages perform experiments and are responsible for creating new monsters, creatures and magical items. High level Blood Mages journey with vampire hunting parties, providing powerful magical backup and conjuring creatures when they are required. Blood Mages have one great purpose, to create a vampire that can withstand the day. Rumours are that their experiments are close to fruition. Only time will tell.

ORDERS

Blood Mages have their own tower in the Black Cabal's obsidian towers. There, they practise their dark experiments, creating abominations by splicing together creatures of multiple types and races. They wear crimson robes adorned with blood pearls and various magical devices. They are divided into three separate ranks: Alchemical, Anatomical and Collectors.

* **Alchemical** Blood Mages are responsible for the creation of many of the magical items that are a part of vampire society - blood pearls, vampiric shadow armor and more.

* **Anatomical** Blood Mages are responsible for the creation of new creatures as well as researching new forms of undead.

* **Collectors** are the keepers of blood, arcane researchers and collectors. They spend a great deal of time away from Avystervan, searching out new sources of blood and the finest mortal 'vintages' from across the realms.

DARK EXPERIMENTS

Blood Mages are responsible for many of the twisted creations that lurk in the sewers of Avystervan. It is said they created many of the differing types of monster vampire that currently exist, from the vampire mind flayer to the undead troll. They take great pleasure in exploring mortality in an attempt to unlock the secrets of life and in so doing, adding to their own powers.

MORTAL AUTHORITY

The few mortals that are selected to become Blood Mages are those with exceptional alchemical or magical abilities. The Blood Mages have a great network of *thrice touched* mortals, doctors and clerics and other evil persons who insinuate themselves into mortal society in order to claim samples of blood for their order.

APPEARANCE

Blood Mages can frequently be found accompanied by bloodlings. They are fond of blood ooze familiars and can be found in their laboratories surrounded by alchemical equipment and entire libraries of blood stored in *phials of the stable pabulum*. They have many ties to the First vampire Kynosh *'the blood stained'* druid who spends much of his time creating wicked experiments in the dark corners of the mortal realms. Most Blood Mages spend at least one year with the First druid before returning to Avystervan to complete their training.

ROLE-PLAYING A BLOOD MAGE

You have both the greatest and the least respect for mortal life. You are fascinated by the forces that control both life and unlife, and you are prepared to do all you can to understand them. Cold and clinical, you study death, anatomy, and creatures alive, dead and undead, focusing all of your efforts on giving greater power to the vampire races.

REQUIREMENTS

To qualify to become a Blood Mage, a character must fulfil the following criteria:

Spellcasting: Must be able to cast 3rd level arcane spells
Race: Must be a vampire of the Black Cabal
Intelligence: Must be 18+
Skills: Spellcraft 10+ ranks

THE BLOOD MAGE

Class Level	Base Attack Bonus	Fort Save	Ref Save	Will Save	Special	Spells per Day
1	+0	+0	+0	+2	Blood Magic, Touch of Blood	+1 level of existing class
2	+1	+0	+0	+3	Turn to Blood	+1 level of existing class
3	+1	+1	+1	+3	Blood Healing	+1 level of existing class
4	+2	+1	+1	+4	Drain Blood x 1/day	+1 level of existing class
5	+2	+1	+1	+4	Attune the Blood, Blood Step	+1 level of existing class
6	+3	+2	+2	+5	Drain Blood x 2/day	+1 level of existing class
7	+3	+2	+2	+5	Blood Door	+1 level of existing class
8	+4	+2	+2	+6	Drain Blood x 3/day, Rekindle the Blood	+1 level of existing class
9	+4	+3	+3	+6	Indomitable Grip	+1 level of existing class
10	+5	+3	+3	+7	Drain Blood x 4/day, Greater Rekindle the Blood	+1 level of existing class

CLASS SKILLS

The Blood Mage's class skills (and the key ability for each skill) are the same as a wizard.

Skill points at each additional level: 2+ Int modifier

CLASS FEATURES

Blood Magic: As the Black Cabal's Blood Magic power.

Touch of Blood: The Blood Mage need but touch a target to steal a single drop of their blood as per the spell *hand of blood* (see p. 70 for more details).

Turn to Blood: The Blood Mage can transform into a blood ooze at a cost of 1 Blood point. The Blood Mage retains his own hit points and AC but has all the qualities of a blood ooze. This ability is otherwise identical to the Dark Gift, Beastform.

Blood Healing: A Blood Mage gains power from the damage he inflicts. He gains 1 hit point for every 2 hit points he physically inflicts, this includes his slam attack and any harming spells he casts. It does not include attacks from melee weapons.

Drain Blood: The Blood Mage can drain blood by touch. He need but touch his target to drain 1d3 points of Constitution or Blood. This blood seeps out through the skin and into the Blood Mage's fingertips. This spell otherwise works identically to the spell *drain blood*.

Blood Step: As the Dark Gift, Vampire (Blood) Step. A Blood Mage can also 'step' from any of his summoned blood creatures, or even from a wound on an individual (so long as it equals no fewer than twice his *age* in hit points damage).

Attune the Blood: The most prized and valuable power of a Blood Mage: the power to attune his own blood. A Blood Mage can attune blood equal to his Blood Mage level plus his *age* category once per night by concentrating on his blood. It takes 1 minute to attune one point of blood.

Blood Door: As the Dark Gift, Vampire (Blood) Door. A Blood Mage can also 'step' from any of his summoned blood creatures, or even from a wound on an individual (so long as it equals no fewer than twice his *age* in hit points damage).

Rekindle the Blood: As Attune the Blood but the Blood Mage can attune the blood of other vampires. He can attune blood equal to his Blood Mage level plus his *age*. He can divide the blood attuned amongst any number of vampires up to his attunement limit. It takes 1 minute to attune one point of blood.

Indomitable Grip: Once per day a Blood Mage can cast any spell providing he has a sample of the target's blood - adding his blood mage level to the DC of the spell. The use of this power costs three points of Blood.

Greater Rekindle the Blood: This power functions as Rekindle the Blood except the Blood Mage can attune up to his age +1 blood per night on any vampire he touches. This power can only be used on the same vampire once in every twenty four hour period.

Example: An age 3, 10th level Blood Mage can rekindle up to 10 points of blood on 4 separate vampires every night.

> *"Undeath? Why this fuss about undeath?*
> *Use your imagination, try to visualize a world without death! . . .*
> *Undeath is the essential condition of life, not an evil."*
> Charlotte Perkins Gilman - Black Cabal

Vampirica Anatomica
(excerpt from Black Cabal lecture)

Of great interest to spellcasters are the mystical properties attached to the physiology of a vampire.

Some parts of a recently destroyed vampire (preferably taken from younger vampires as they do not decompose as quickly) are exceedingly useful in magical spells and enchantments. I will go into specifics later but some of the most unusual items and their properties are:

Canines: The sharp pointed teeth of a vampire. Now you all have these. Please take a moment to feel your own, and do be careful, they are sharp. The teeth are very resilient and are typically the last thing to deteriorate on a slain vampire. They can withstand a substantial period of sunlight before finally succumbing to the destructive forces of the day.

Fangs have many properties. When ground down, they grant an increased potency to certain necromantic potions and elixirs. When used as a material component in any spell that causes bleeding, they allow the caster to cast those spells at +1 caster level. Now before you go around trying to steal each other's fangs, I wouldn't advise it. They take quite a few days to grow back and feeding can be unpleasant without them.

Vampire Heart: The heart of a vampire is literally their link to the Void. Shatter the heart, slay the vampire. It's as simple as that. A vampire heart allows a spellcaster to cast the *energy drain* and *enervation* spells at +4 caster levels. It has other, more complex uses, but that is for another class - when you are all paying *more* attention!

Ichor: The blood of a vampire as we all know can be used to power our Dark Gifts, but what is little known is that vampire ichor can be used as a material component to cast the *animate dead* spell at +2 caster levels.

Vampire Skull: When ground down into a fine powder, the skull makes a rather potent sleeping draught. Additionally, it grants the +2 caster levels when casting the *slay living* and *circle of death* spells.

Bones: When ground down into a fine power (you'll notice how brittle they are now their original owner no longer needs them), they augment the caster's ability to cast the *finger of death* spell by +4 levels.

Eyeballs: Vampire eyeballs are actually quite potent. When mushed into a paste they allow the caster to temporarily increase the potency of their energy drain attacks.

Of course not just any old vampire parts will do. It seems that a vampire must have been in existence for over a year before any magical properties can be gained from their bodies. The older the vampire, the more powerful their material components.

There are certainly countless other uses for vampire organs which we have not yet discovered. Our research is ongoing, both in Avystervan, and in the mortal realms.

BLOOD KNIGHTS

The Blood Knights are an organisation of utterly corrupted black paladins in the service of Vangual and the Devoted Incarnate. Malchosius Rembaré is their leader, a powerful and diabolical figure who has brought their order to greatness over the two millennia since its creation. He is wise and powerful and bloodthirsty and has great plans for the future of his Blood Knights.

The Blood Knights are opposite to the holy paladins of the *Powers of Light* in every way. Although they are few in number, they are powerful indeed. Known as anti paladins, they have a reputation for taking what they will and doing what they like. They are unquestionably the single most powerful faction of vampires in existence. When in mortal company, they cause the living to bleed uncontrollably and strike terror into even the most hardened of hearts. They are at the very top of the unholy hierarchy and are given considerable latitude by the rest of vampire society.

There are very few Blood Knights in the world, perhaps twenty. Vangual cannot support any more than that at any one time. Given strength from the night, they are favoured amongst the Black Council and spend much time in the defence of the *City of Graves*. Fearless in battle, there are few that can claim to be their equal.

They live in the Cathedral in Avystervan where they work closely with the Devoted Incarnate. They are the warriors and defenders on the most important of missions. Few Devoted are ever seen in numbers beyond Avystervan without Blood Knight protection. Blood Knights wear their gleaming vampiric shadow armor and wield powerful magical weapons.

RECRUITMENT

Only the most skilled are chosen to become Blood Knights. Taken from the best performing black paladins, those selected are transformed personally by Vangual, who removes their hearts and keeps them safe in his Fortress of Shadow. The selection process is dangerous. Those chosen are tested against the *Powers of Light*. They must find and slay a high-ranking paladin of the orders of good, as personally selected by Malchosius himself.

Success indicates invitation into their ranks, failure and they do not return.

MISSIONS

Blood Knights are only ever given the most important missions. They neither have the strength nor the numbers to do everything the Black Council desires of them. They are only ever called upon when their particular strengths are required. Where lesser warriors are required, the Black Council turn to the Blood Guard.

ROLE-PLAYING A BLOOD KNIGHT

You are powerful and despicable. Mortals are like cattle before you. You take what you want from both mortal and undead alike. All fear you. You have no equal, even amongst the *Powers of Light*. Although you are sorely tested by Vangual, your black faith and strength of will shall always prevail.

REQUIREMENTS

To qualify to become a Blood Knight, a character must fulfil the following criteria:
Race: Must be a vampire
Religion: Vangual
Base attack bonus: +10
Special: Must have previously been a black paladin (or black fighter) in good standing with the *Powers of Darkness*.
Special: Must have Wisdom 18+
Special: Must have Strength 24+

CLASS SKILLS

The Blood Knight's class skills (and the key ability for each skill) are the same as a black paladin.

Skill points at each additional level: 2 + Int modifier.

> *"I can do you blood and love without the rhetoric,*
> *and I can do you blood and rhetoric without the love,*
> *and I can do you all three concurrent or consecutive but I can't do*
> *you love and rhetoric without the blood.*
> *Blood is compulsory - they're all blood you see."*
> Tom Stoppard, Blood Mage

BLOOD KNIGHTS

Class Level	Base Attack Bonus	Fort Save	Ref Save	Will Save	Special	Spells per Day
1	+1	+2	+0	+0	Cause Fear, Heartless	+1 level of existing class
2	+2	+3	+0	+0		+1 level of existing class
3	+3	+3	+1	+1	Lesser Aura of Wounding	+1 level of existing class
4	+4	+4	+1	+1		+1 level of existing class
5	+5	+4	+1	+1	Blood Fire	+1 level of existing class
6	+6	+5	+2	+2		+1 level of existing class
7	+7	+5	+2	+2	Aura of Wounding	+1 level of existing class
8	+8	+6	+2	+2	Unquenchable Fear	+1 level of existing class
9	+9	+6	+3	+3		+1 level of existing class
10	+10	+7	+3	+3	Greater Aura of Wounding	+1 level of existing class

Class Features

Cause Fear: As the black paladin's cause fear ability but more potent. Against greater level characters your cause fear has the same effect, but against lower level opponents, your victims suffer a penalty to their Will save equal to the difference in your levels.

Example: A 7th level Blood Knight uses his cause fear power on a 3rd level character. The character suffers -4 to his Will save.

Heartless: Blood Knights gain the Dark Gift, Heartless (and they must also move one step towards evil - see p. 60).

Lesser Aura of Wounding: As Aura of Wounding (below), but characters bleed at 1 hit point per round in a 20 ft. radius.

Blood Fire: This terrible power causes agony to all those upon whom the Blood Knight has previously inflicted damage (within the last 24 hours). The effect lasts for 1 round + 1 round per *age* category and costs 1 Blood and a standard action to evoke. All wounds caused by the Blood Knight within a 40 ft. radius instantly flare up with white-hot agony.

Every character so afflicted must make a Fortitude save (DC 10 + Blood Knight's Level + Charisma modifier) or be stricken with paralysing spasms for the remainder of the round. Characters in this state lose any Dexterity bonus to their AC and can only take partial actions (suffering -2 to any actions they do take). Additionally, attacking foes gain +2 to hit.

Aura of Wounding: The greatest and most feared of the Blood Knight powers, the aura of wounding makes the living bleed uncontrollably.

A haze of bloody necromancy surrounds the Blood Knight. Everyone in a 30 ft. radius of the vampire bleeds at a rate of 2 hit points per round. There is no save for this - the mystical powers of the Blood Knight directly clash with the energies of the living.

This power does not affect vampires or other undead. A Blood Knight can choose to voluntarily lower this effect at any time as a standard action.

Unquenchable Fear: Once per night, the Blood Knight can use their cause fear power with a rush of black energy. The target receives no save against against their fear attack.

The power inflicts *Panic* in the target and is otherwise identical to the black paladin power, cause fear.

Greater Aura of Wounding: As Aura of Wounding (above), but characters bleed at 3 hit points per round and the radius of effect is 40 ft.

Pictured below: the sacred crypt of the elders, the Mausoleum, Avystervan

"What we commonly call undeath does not destroy the body, it only causes a separation of spirit and body."
Brigham Young, Devoted Incarnate

THE DEVOTED INCARNATE

The Devoted Incarnate is the oldest and largest of the vampire orders. They are dark clerics of the most despicable alignment. Even amongst vampires, they are considered monsters. Their leader Ishtyx is the eldest of the First and is perhaps the most wicked of all the children of Vangual.

The Devoted live in the *Noctarius*. The stepped pyramid lies just beyond Avystervan's walls in a smaller cavern, home to more than two hundred vampires, mortal slaves and guards. There are ten levels to the ziggurat, with the Devoted allowed access to a tier dependant on their standing within their order. The lowest ranking clerics have access to the bottom three levels (tiers eight, nine and ten), which are for those clerics who can cast only 1st through 3rd level divine spells. Access to an upper floor is by special invitation only or on those rare moments of promotion. As a black cleric rises in spellcasting ability, so are they promoted up the ladder.

The *Noctarius* has the best-stocked library of divine materials across the realm as well as a library on the 2nd tier filled with artifacts and powerful items stolen from the *Powers of Light*. The legendary *Staff of Solaris*, the holy stave of the sun god is held there. Surrounded by protective darkness it is a perpetual reminder of the indomitable power of the Devoted Incarnate and of their mission: the utter subjugation of the mortal realms.

The Devoted have many tasks; they tend to the spiritual needs of Avystervan; they collect blood for their masters; they tend to the Mausoleum. A great many travel the world spreading suffering and death and corrupting that which they cannot destroy. They work well with the Black Cabal and concentrate their efforts on protecting Avystervan from discovery and creating new and ever more powerful weapons, spells and items of destruction for use against the *Powers of Light*.

There are many stories about the Devoted Incarnate; that they have feeding habits so refined that they may only drink from the warm blood of new-born babies. They spread death wherever they go, and cavort with both the dead and the living at every opportunity. They are formidable necromancers and hardy warriors. Blood rituals and sacrifice accompany their passing, along with crazed slaughter and screaming destruction.

The darkest enemy of the *Powers of Light*, they travel the mortal realms with growing bravery, their robes literally dripping with the blood of the innocent. They think nothing of flaunting their powers in public; openly staging attacks against lesser temples when they come across them. Along with the Black Cabal, they create elaborate raids under the guise of known enemies in order to sow seeds of doubt and fear. They loom out of the darkness, summoning undead and causing wounds that cannot easily be healed.

The Devoted Incarnate slavishly follow the Avystyx Prophecies, a book of revelations written in blood by Avystyx, a vampire bard long since turned to dust. It is said the prophecies detail the transformation of the mortal realms into a vampiric Eden, but the prophecies have proved impossible to decipher, and the Devoted Incarnate have only managed to unravel the vaguest outline of the book's meaning after two thousand years. It is whispered that the Devoted Incarnate hold the ashes of Avystyx, but that all attempts to restore him to unlife have proved unsuccessful.

ORDER

The Devoted Incarnate are divided into groups, based on ability. Lesser clerics are given missions beyond Avystervan in order to increase their power. Those of greater status are given command of groups of lesser clerics. All lower ranking clerics must spend at least a year working in the Mausoleum, while moderate level clerics spend their time creating new magical items and spells. All would be clerics of the Devoted Incarnate must spend one full year as supplicant to the order, performing the least of duties in order to prove their devotion.

MORTAL AUTHORITY

There are many black clergies to Vangual across the realms. Some are so twisted in secrecy that even their own disciples do not know the true name of the deity they revere. These churches are typically led by the Devoted, who form covens across the realms, gaining recruits and selecting the most promising for bringing into darkness. *Thrice touched* mortals can be found lurking in shadow, tending to the needs of the vampire community during the day and sewing seeds of darkness in the mortal realms whenever they can. These people have betrayed their own kind, abandoning the light in exchange for greater power in darkness.

THE DEVOTED INCARNATE

Class Level	Base Attack Bonus	Fort Save	Ref Save	Will Save	Special	Spells per Day
1	+0	+2	+0	+2	Black Harm, Consume the Divine	+1 level of existing class
2	+1	+3	+0	+3	Bleeding 1/day	+1 level of existing class
3	+2	+3	+1	+3		+1 level of existing class
4	+3	+4	+1	+4	Bleeding 2/day	+1 level of existing class
5	+3	+4	+1	+4	Turn Living	+1 level of existing class
6	+4	+5	+2	+5	Bleeding 3/day	+1 level of existing class
7	+5	+5	+2	+5	Greater Consume the Divine	+1 level of existing class
8	+6/+1	+6	+2	+6	Bleeding 4/day	+1 level of existing class
9	+6/+1	+6	+3	+6		+1 level of existing class
10	+7/+2	+7	+3	+7	Bleeding 5/day	+1 level of existing class

ROLE-PLAYING THE DIVINE INCARNATE

You belong to an order that is both ancient and powerful. Its plan are far reaching indeed. A darkness is coming and you fully intend to be a part of it. Your heart is as black as midnight and your soul utterly devoted to Vangual.

REQUIREMENTS

To qualify to become a member of the Devoted Incarnate, a character must fulfil the following criteria:

Spellcasting: Must be able to cast 3rd level divine spells
Race: Must be a vampire
Religion: Must be a cleric of Vangual in good standing or better
Base Attack Bonus: +5
Other: Must be *age* 1or older
Prerequisites: Advanced Energy Drain
Special: Must have Wisdom of 18+
Spellcraft: 10+

CLASS SKILLS:

The Devoted Incarnate's class skills (and the key ability for each skill) are the same as a black cleric.

Skill points at each Additional Level: 2 + Int Modifier

CLASS FEATURES

Black Harm: Physical damage done by the Devoted Incarnate cannot be healed magically. This also applies to any magical spells they cast from the domain of Harm or use of their special powers.

Consume the Divine: When conferring a negative level, the Devoted Incarnate can drain any spell lost by the spellcaster and add it to the spells they have prepared. This must be a divine spell of a level that the Devoted could normally cast. They can absorb one divine spell for every negative level they drain. Stolen spells last until dawn when they dissipate from the vampire's mind. Spells requiring material components must be sourced or they cannot be cast.

Example: A member of the Devoted Incarnate attacks a 12th level cleric. He successfully strikes his target and inflicts 2 negative levels. The cleric immediately loses his two highest level prepared spells. The Devoted Incarnate vampire can choose to absorb one or both of the lost spells. If he could not cast the level of spell lost by the cleric, he could not 'consume' any spells.

Bleeding: You can make a bleeding attempt (similar to a turning attempt) either selecting your targets before making your *bleeding* attempt or affecting everyone in a 30 ft. radius. Everyone affected by this power begins to bleed at a rate of your *age* in hit points per round. Undead are unaffected. Bleeding lasts while you maintain the *bleeding*, or for your *age* in rounds thereafter (magical healing is not effective). You can stop your *bleeding* at any time. The effects of this power are cumulative with other bleeding/dark harm spells.

Turn Living: At 5th level, the Devoted Incarnate can attempt to turn any living being as per the turning rules. Mortals that would be slain are instead put into a deep slumber and will awaken 1d4 hours later. They cannot be woken during this period except for the use of powerful restorative magic. They can purchase the Extra Turning feat.

Greater Consume the Divine: As above, but the Devoted Incarnate can use any divine spell lost from his victim, even one he could not normally cast.

New Domains: The Devoted Incarnate gain three new clerical domains: Blood, Harm and Faithful Undead.

> *"When one man dies, one chapter is not torn out of the book, but translated into a better language."*
> John Donne - Devoted Incarnate

CHAPTER FIVE: VAMPIRE DARK GIFTS

Dark Gift	Prerequisites	Dark Gift	Prerequisites
Advanced Energy Drain	Energy Drain	Fire Scrying	-
Alternate Form	-	Flight	-
Attunement	Age 2	Fresh Corpse	-
Aura of Fear	-	Gaseous Form	-
Beastform	Alternate Form	Heartless	Age 2
Black Mantle	Age 1	Invisibility	-
Black Touch	Advanced Energy Drain, Age 1, Energy Drain	Long Shadow	Shadow Step
		Mask of Mortality	Age 1,
Black Will	Age 1		Cloak of the Outsider
Blinding Speed	Blood Agility, Improved Initiative	Mass Charm	Dire Charm, Domination, Far Charm, Mesmerize
Blood Agility	-	Mesmerize	Domination, Far Charm
Blood Armor	-	Multiple Coffins	-
Blood Binding	-	Noxious Breath	Ravenous Vampire
Blood Speed	Blinding Speed, Blood Agility, Improved Initiative, Lightning Reflexes, Mobility	Resistance to Turning	Age 3 , Turn Resistance
		Reverse Turning	Age 4, Resistance to Turning
		Sap the Agility	Energy Drain
		Sap the Ego	Energy Drain
Blood Spittle	-	Sap the Grace	Energy Drain
Blood Stamina	-	Sap the Potence	Energy Drain
Blood Strength	-	Sap the Vigor	Energy Drain
Blood Vault	-	Sap the Will	Energy Drain
Body of Flame	-	Sense	-
Bonds of the Earth	Alternate Form	Shadow Dancing	Long Shadow, Shadow Step
Brew Va'Vash	Alchemy 15+, Brew Potion	Shadow Form	Shadow Step
Children of the Night	-	Slumbering Dreams	Age 2, Black Mantle
Claws	-	Spider Climb	-
Cloak of the Outsider	-	Stifle the Chill	Age 1
Cloudkill	Age 3, Gaseous Form, Ravenous Vampire	Telekinesis	-
		Transformation	Alternate Form
Conjure Darkness	-	Turn Resistance	-
Control Weather	-	Umbral Mist	Shadow Vampire
Dark Avatar	Age 4, Beastform, Transformation	Unquenchable Aura	Age 1
		Unturnable	Turn Resistance
Dark Mantle	Age 3, Black Mantle, Slumbering Dreams	Vampiric Door	Vampiric Step
		Vampiric Healing	-
Dire Charm	Age 1, Domination	Vampiric Senses	-
Domination	-	Vampiric Step	-
Energy Drain	-	Vampiric Touch	Advanced Energy Drain, Age 2, Energy Drain
Eyes of the Night	-		
Far Charm	Dire Charm, Domination, Mesmerize	Will of Blood	-

Advanced Energy Drain

You can draw power from the levels you drain.

Prerequisites: Energy Drain.

Benefits: Whenever you drain a negative level, you can absorb certain additional benefits (as described under your vampiric race).

Note: Abilities drained by this power can only be restored through powerful curative magic (*heal* spell or better) by a cleric of 15th level or greater.

Alternate Form

You can assume different forms.

Benefits: You can assume the form of a bat, a dire bat, a wolf, or a dire wolf as a standard action. This ability is similar to a *polymorph self* spell cast by a 12th level sorcerer, except that you can only assume one of the forms listed here. You can remain in your new form until you assume another or until sunrise.

Attunement

You can attune your blood at the cost of Blood.

Prerequisites: Age 2.

Benefits: You can attune up to your *age* +1 in Blood per night at a cumulative cost of 1 point of blood per Blood point attuned. It takes a full minute to attune a single point of Blood.

Aura of Fear

You radiate a powerful aura that strikes fear into mortals.

Benefits: You radiate an aura of fear that functions as the spell *cause fear*, except it has a radius of 30 ft. and affects creatures of your HD or lower. The Aura of Fear will continue to affect those within range until they save against it. A character who has successfully saved is not affected by your Aura of Fear until you have slept (or twenty four hours have passed - whichever is sooner). You can voluntarily choose to lower your Aura of Fear at any time as a standard action.

Beastform

You can transform into a dire creature.

Prerequisites: Alternate Form.

Benefits: You can transform into any **one** Tiny, Small, Medium or Large animal or dire animal as a standard action. You retain your own combat skills, Armor Class and Hit Points, but you cannot spellcast or use your energy drain ability while transformed. Using Beastform costs 1 Blood point and can be done at will, once per round. Each form you assume lasts until you choose another or until sunrise. You can choose a new form in which to shapechange for every *age* you advance **after** you gain this Dark Gift, or you can choose this Gift multiple times in order to gain additional forms.

Black Mantle

You can rouse yourself during the day at the expense of Blood.

Prerequisites: Age 1.

Benefits: You can rouse yourself more easily from sleep while the sun is in the sky. The DC for your Waking checks is 15. If you are woken or are already awake you can stave off sleep for 10 minutes plus an additional 5 minutes per point of Blood you spend. Use of this power for more than 10 minutes times your *age* category per day results in you gaining no benefit from sleeping that day (see p. 32).

Black Touch

Your energy drain powers are advanced beyond those of a typical vampire.

Prerequisites: Advanced Energy Drain, Age 1, Energy Drain.

Benefits: You can focus your negative energies so that your energy drain powers work on physical contact, rather than through your slam attack. You must consciously choose to do this, requiring a standard action to activate this power.

To drain an unwilling subject you must make a successful touch attack (although anyone actively touching you will be energy drained). You will continue to drain energy in this way until you choose otherwise or until sunrise. This power cannot be combined with the Dark Gift, Stifle the Chill.

Note: When this power is in effect, you will feel colder and seem more inhuman. The air around you will be chilled with necromancy.

Black Will

You can walk upon holy ground.

Prerequisites: Age 1.

Benefits: You can focus your will and walk on holy ground, although to do so harms you. This power costs three Blood points and requires a full round action to activate. Thereafter you can walk upon holy ground although you take 1 hit point damage per round and suffer additional penalties as detailed in Holy Ground on p. 31.

Blinding Speed

You move at amazing speeds.

Prerequisites: Blood Agility, Improved Initiative.

Benefits: You can move blindingly fast, travelling astonishing distances in the blink of an eye. You move at a base rate of your speed x 5, +1 for every *age* you possess (so you would move at a base of x 8 at *age* 3). While using Blinding Speed, you gain an additional partial action (at the end of your normal actions), and can dodge and defend yourself, gaining a +8 bonus (+1 per *age* category) to your Armor Class while so doing. Every use of this power costs 1 point of Blood. If you attack or otherwise enter melee, you must reactivate this power after your attack. Otherwise, this power lasts until sunrise or you resume normal speed.

Example: An age 3 vampire with a standard run of 40 ft. uses Blinding Speed to follow his prey. He takes a full round action moving at x4 his normal speed (160 ft. per round). Using Blinding Speed, his run would be multiplied by 8 (x5 plus x3 for his age). He would run at 1280 ft. per round, or about 145 miles per hour. Very fast indeed. The vampire is completely at ease moving at these speeds; the dark powers allow him to speed up and slow down magically. He can move from standing to full speed in an instant. However he cannot move and attack in the same round, although he can make two move-equivalent actions in the same round, moving from place to place in the blink of an eye.

Blood Agility

You can increase your Dexterity at the cost of your Blood.

Benefits: For every point of Blood you expend, as a standard action you can increase your Dexterity by +1 (to a maximum bonus at any one time of twice your *age* +1). This Dexterity bonus is temporary and lasts for 1 minute + 1 minute for every *age* you possess. At the end of this period, your Dexterity falls by 1 per round until it returns to normal. You must wait a full round before using this power again.

Blood Armor

You can increase your Armor Class at the cost of your Blood.

Benefits: For every point of Blood you expend up to your *age* +1, you can increase your Armor Class by +2. A crimson aura surrounds you while this power is in effect. This AC bonus is temporary and lasts for 1 minute, plus 1 minute for every *age* you possess. At the end of this period, your AC falls by 1 per round until it returns to normal. Use of Blood Armor requires a standard action.

Blood Binding

You can increase the difficulty of your spells with Blood.

Benefits: You can expend 1 plus your *age* category in Blood to increase the difficulty of any spell you cast by that amount. Thereafter, you can further increase the difficulty by expending 6 minus your *age* category in Blood to increase the difficulty by +1 (maximum bonus of twice your *age* category).

Blood Speed

You gain an additional attack at the cost of Blood.

Prerequisites: Blinding Speed, Blood Agility, Improved Initiative, Lightning Reflexes, Mobility.

Benefits: You gain an additional attack at a cost of 1 Blood. This attack is made at the start of your attack, at your full attack bonus.

Blood Spittle

You can spit blood at your enemies.

Benefits: You can make an attack and spit Blood at your opponents. This can count as one of your attacks (in place of any multiple attacks you may have). You can spit up to 1 plus your *age* points of Blood per attack, doing damage dependent on your *age* (see below). As you age, your blood has more potent effects, although you can choose to use a younger *age* effect as you see fit. Unless otherwise stated, all effects last for the amount of Blood you expend in rounds +1.

Example: An age 3 vampire can spit 4 points of Blood per attack doing 1d8 damage with each point. He can choose to use the Adhesive, Acid or Blinding effects (only one per attack), and each effect lasts for 4 rounds.

Blood Spittle Damage Chart

Age	Damage	Effect	Description
0	1d4	None	
1	1d6	Blinding	Burns for same damage minus one damage die per round.
2	1d6	Acid	Your target is *Blinded*.
3	1d8	Adhesive	Your blood is thick, like glue. You can prevent your target from speaking or breathing. You can prevent a target from dropping an item or even stick their feet to the floor (requiring a Strength check DC 15 + *age* category) to escape.
4	1d8	Entangled	Your blood is viscous, *Entangling* your target.
5	1d10	Nausea	You can spit thick, black blood. Your target must make a Fortitude save (DC 15 + your *age* category) or be *Nauseated*.

Blood Stamina

You can increase your hit point total at the cost of your blood.

Benefits: For every point of Blood you expend (to a maximum equal to 1 plus your *age* category), you can increase your hit point total by d12. These additional hit points are temporary and last for 1 minute, plus 1 minute for every *age* you possess. Thereafter, if you have not lost these temporary hit points, they fall at a rate of 5 per round until your hit point total reverts to normal. Any damage sustained during this period is removed from any temporary hit points you have remaining before being subtracted from your normal hit point total. Effects of this power do not stack. You must wait a full round before all of your bonus hit points have expired before you can use this power again.

Note: You can only use this power while you have a positive hit point total. Use of Blood Stamina requires a standard action.

Blood Strength

You can increase your strength at the cost of your blood.

Benefits: For every point of Blood you expend, you can increase your Strength by +1 (to a maximum amount of Blood equal to 1 plus twice your *age* category). This Strength is only temporary and lasts for 1 minute, plus 1 minute for every *age* you possess. At the end of this period, your Strength falls by 1 each round until it reverts to its normal score. You must wait a full round before using this power again. Use of Blood Strength requires a standard action.

Blood Vault

You can increase your Blood score.

Benefits: This Gift increases your Blood score by 3 points. You can only take this Dark Gift once for every *age* you possess.

Body of Flame

You can cover yourself in flames.

Benefits: You can set yourself afire, burning with flames of varying colours, crimson, purple and blue. While these flames do not harm you, they are harmful to living beings. You attack your victims for an additional 1d4 (+1 per *age* category) points of fire damage. Additionally, unless protected, those in melee with you suffer -2 to their actions from the intense heat. Lastly, all within 5 ft. of you must make a Reflex save (DC 15 +1 per *age* category) or catch fire (as per the DMG).

Bonds of the Earth

You can turn yourself to stone.

Prerequisites: Alternate Form.

Benefits: When you sleep you can turn yourself to stone, becoming statue-like for the duration of the day. This has both benefits and disadvantages. First, you can withstand the rays of the sun, but you are dormant and unaware of your surroundings until you waken. Secondly, you cannot restore your wounds while sleeping and will awaken in the condition you were in when you turned to stone. You cannot rouse yourself from sleep during the day and are powerless to protect yourself should your enemies find you. Your statue is Hardness 10 (+1 per *age* category) and has the same hit points as your current hit point total. A statue that does not have its heart ground to dust assumes its death form at nightfall and restores itself as normal.

BREW VA VASH

You can create the various forms of Va'Vash.

Prerequisites: Alchemy 15+, Brew Potion.

Benefits: This functions exactly like the Brew Potion feat, except it is needed to create Va'Vash in its three forms. Va'Vash is detailed on p. 79. The difficulty rating is the chance of successfully creating Va'Vash of that color. Anything under that check results in a failed potion that has no magical qualities whatsoever.

CHILDREN OF THE NIGHT

You can summon the creatures of the night.

Benefits: You can command the lesser creatures of the world and once per day can call forth a pack of 4d8 dire rats, a swarm of 10d10 bats or a pack of 3d6 wolves as a standard action. These creatures arrive in 2d6 rounds and will serve you for up to 1 hour.

CLAWS

You can grow vicious claws or fangs.

Benefits: You can grow razor-sharp claws or fangs as a standard action. You can automatically use these in place of your normal attacks, delivering your standard damage plus damage dependent on your age. If you have energy draining powers, these claws may only inflict one negative level per successful attack. Growing either claws or fangs costs 1 Blood point and they remain until you choose to retract them or until sunrise.

ADDITIONAL DAMAGE CHART

Age	Additional Damage
0	+0
1	+1d4
2	+1d6
3	+1d8
4	+1d10
5	+2d6

CLOAK OF THE OUTSIDER

You can hide your vampiric nature.

Benefits: You can conceal your true nature to others for a short period of time per night. By expending 2 points of Blood you can 'cloak' yourself for 10 minutes plus 10 minutes per age category. Each additional 10 minute period thereafter costs a cumulative 1 Blood point. While you may appear mortal, you do not necessarily look as you did when you were alive. There will always be something vaguely inhuman about you. You may have strangely colored hair, eyes or flesh, or just feel 'odd' or 'different' to mortals.

Note: Using any of your Dark Gifts immediately negates this power and the cloak does not negate the *Chill* or the *Stench of the Grave*.

CLOUDKILL

You can assume a cloud of noxious mist.

Prerequisites: Age 3, Gaseous Form, Ravenous Vampire.

Benefits: You can transform into a cloud of noxious mist that acts like the spell *cloudkill*. You have a movement rate of 20 ft. and can assume this form for 1 round plus 1 round per age category for every Blood point you spend. While in this form you have the trait *incorporeal*.

CONJURE DARKNESS

You can summon darkness.

Benefits: You can create darkness as per the spell *darkness* thrice per night as a standard action plus an additional time for every age you possess. Additional uses thereafter cost 1 Blood point.

CONTROL WEATHER

You can control the weather.

Benefits: You can control the weather at will as a full round action. The power acts as the spell *control weather* - however you are restricted to conjuring: Clouds, Fog, Lightning, Thunder, Torrential Rain and Storms. Alternatively you can elect to use the spell *fog cloud* once per round (to a maximum number of uses per day equal to 1 plus your age) or the spell *solid fog* (at the cost of 1 Blood point per use).

DARK AVATAR

You have a monstrous form.

Prerequisites: Age 4, Beastform, Transformation

Benefits: You can transform into a monstrous creature when you are reduced to 0 hit points or lower. You recover your age +1 x d12 hit points, plus an additional 1d12 hit points for every Blood point you are willing to expend during your transformation. You gain additional powers as detailed in your choice of Avatar, below.

Upon your return to normal form you immediately lose 10 minus your age category points of Blood. If this reduces you to 0 Blood, you must sleep for 10 minus your age in days at which point you awaken, ravenously hungry and must feed immediately. If you were reduced to –1 Blood or lower, you immediately fall into the *eternal quiescence* for 10 minus your age category months at sunrise.

Demon Form: You assume the form of a massive muscular demon with barbed horns and gnarled shadow draped skin. Your exact shape is hidden behind the waves of shadow that pour from you. You gain +8 modifier to your Strength, Dexterity and AC. Your fast healing ability increases by +8 and you gain an additional Damage Reduction bonus of +10/+1. In addition you drain 3 negative levels upon successfully inflicting a slam attack.

Dragon Form: You can transform into a huge-size skeletal dragon. You gain all the standard powers of a Black Dragon (Adult at age 4 and Old at age 5) with the following benefits: You gain a +6 modifier to your Strength, Dexterity and AC. Your fast healing ability increases by +6 and you gain an additional Damage Reduction bonus of +5/+1. In addition you can use many of your dragon abilities as listed in the MM. Your breath weapon takes the form of a concentrated cone of negative energy that flays the flesh from the living and drains 1d4 levels per successful attack. This attack is negativity based and is not subject to standard elemental resistances. Reflex save still applies for half damage and half-level drain (to a minimum of 1 level).

Giant Form: You assume the towering form of a huge and skeletal giant. Standing just over 20 ft. tall you gain a +10 modifier to your Strength, Dexterity and AC. Your fast healing ability increases by +10 and you gain an additional Damage Reduction bonus of +15/+1. You can attack with your massive hands at 4d6 + strength bonus draining 2 levels per successful slam attack.

Notes: In addition to the powers listed above, you confer 1 negative level upon any you touch or who voluntarily touch you. You can use any of your other powers and Gifts while in your Dark Avatar form. This power lasts until you assume another form or sunrise.

Dark Mantle

You no longer need to sleep during the day.

Prerequisites: Age 3, Black Mantle, Slumbering Dreams.

Benefits: You are powerful and do not need to sleep during the day, although you can do so if you choose (to heal your wounds).

Even when you sleep, you only need to do so for 6 - *age* category hours. You suffer a reduced -2 penalty to acting during the day (although you suffer the full penalty when acting in bright sunlight).

Additionally while in any kind of sunlight, you can expend one point of Blood per round (cumulative until you stop expending Blood for 1 round) to give yourself a normal action for that round, ie. you can take full actions as opposed to only being allowed to take a partial action.

Dire Charm

You can give a single mental command to anyone who meets your gaze.

Prerequisites: Age 1, Domination.

Benefits: You can implant a command in your target's mind. Your victim makes a Will save. Failure means the dire charm lies dormant until activated. The target may not know they have been affected at all and may continue for weeks or even months with this charm lying waiting to be activated. A vampire can only dire charm as many persons as he has levels plus his *age* category.

Examples of dire charms are 'Defend Me!' causing your target to suddenly leap to your defense, or 'sleep!' in which case your target will fall into a deep slumber until awoken. The dire charm dissipates after a year and a day.

Domination

You can control a mortal's will.

Benefits: You can crush an opponent's will by looking into his or her eyes. This is similar to a gaze attack, except that you must take a standard action, and those merely looking at you are not affected. Anyone you target must succeed at a Will save or fall instantly under your influence as though affected by a *dominate person* spell.

Note: If you have previously bitten your target, you can further bend them to your will. For more information on biting your victims, see p. 29.

Energy Drain

Your slam attacks drain levels.

Benefits: Living creatures hit by your slam attacks suffer 1 negative level. If you can already drain 1 level, this Gift allows you to drain 2 levels with your slam attack.

Saves against your energy drain attack have a DC of $10 + 1/2$ vampire's HD + *age* + Charisma modifier.

Eyes of the Night

You can see far off locations through the shadows.

Benefits: You may cast your consciousness out into darkness, seeing through the shadows into any location with which you are familiar.

This Gift acts exactly as the spell *clairvoyance* (although your sight can penetrate any darkness you may encounter). You can spy through cracks in walls, or from patches of darkness while you concentrate.

Far Charm

You can charm your victims from a great distance.

Prerequisites: Dire Charm, Domination, Mesmerize.

Benefits: You can affect your victims over great distances. After *once touching* your target, you can influence them with greater control, using any other mind powers with enhanced effect. You can issue several commands:

Command: You can compel your victim to do as you please. They will be reluctant to carry out dangerous instructions but will endeavour to carry out your orders to the best of their ability. Any task your target would be unwilling to perform grants them a Will save (DC $10 + 1/2$ HD + *age* + Charisma modifier). Failure means they reluctantly carry out your instructions, success means they overwhelm your compulsion and pass into unconsciousness. You cannot attempt to Command them again until twenty four hours have passed.

Summon: You can compel your victim to seek you out by any means possible (DC $10 + 1/2$ HD + *age* + Charisma modifier). You can choose to send them dreams of your location (if they do not know it).

Sleep: Your target falls instantly into a deep and dreamless sleep for your *age* +1 rounds (DC $10 + 1/2$ HD + *age* + Charisma modifier). They cannot be woken by any means during this time, although you can wake them at any time.

Talk: You can overwhelm your victim's senses and speak through their mouth (DC $10 + 1/2$ HD + *age* + Charisma modifier).

You maintain a telepathic link to your victim, even seeing/sharing their senses. You can watch your victim through their eyes, learning their secrets and following their footsteps. A Far Charmed target gets a chance to resist your compulsion when you first bring it to bear and once per day thereafter. Success indicates you cannot use your Far Charm powers upon them again until you have slept or twenty four hours have passed (whichever is sooner).

Note: Being able to share your target's thoughts can be both a good and a bad thing, as not only will you know their exact location, but they *may* in turn know your mind. Strong willed victims might even be able to see your thoughts probing very thoughts and feelings. They can make one Will check per day (DC $10 + 1/2$ HD + *age* + Charisma modifier) to be able to know your thoughts.

Fire Scrying

You can see through any fire or flame.

Benefits: You may cast your consciousness out into the world, seeing through fire in any location with which you are familiar. This Gift acts exactly as the spell *clairvoyance* and lasts while you concentrate. You can scry through any fire or flame, from a candle to a bonfire.

Flight

You can fly at will.

Benefits: You can fly, levitate or float at will. This power works as the fly spell, with a maneuverability of good.

> *"Death is a very dull, dreary affair, and my advice to you is to have nothing whatsoever to do with it."*
> W. Somerset Maugham, Black Cabal

FRESH CORPSE

You do not smell of death.

Benefits: Your corpse is remarkably well preserved. The *Stench of the Grave* is far less noticeable in you than in other vampires. Rather than reeking of death, you instead smell fusty and strange. When others get close to you, the smell is unpleasant. You can mask your scent by bathing or with perfumes, although you must do so every few hours, or the smell rises again. Your odor can still be sensed by other vampires and sensitive goodly aligned characters.

GASEOUS FORM

You can turn gaseous at will.

Benefits: You can assume *gaseous form* at will, as per the spell *gaseous form*. You can remain gaseous indefinitely (or until sunrise) and have a fly speed of 20 ft. with perfect maneuverability.

HEARTLESS

You do not need your mortal heart to exist.

Prerequisites: Age 2.

Benefits: Your mortal heart has turned to dust. You are immune to staking, but you are *heartless* and must immediately move one rank towards evil when selecting this Dark Gift.

INVISIBILITY

You can turn invisible at will.

Benefits: You can turn invisible as a move-equivalent action. This Gift functions as the spell *invisibility,* except you can remain invisible indefinitely, or until sunrise. Use of this power costs 1 Blood point.

LONG SHADOW

You can send forth your shadow to scout for you.

Prerequisites: Shadow Step.

Benefits: You can cast forth your shadow, which can journey out from you. Silent and almost invisible, it can fly at a rate of 40 ft. (good). You maintain a sensory link to your shadow at all times, and can see through its eyes no matter where it is.

Your shadow cannot be destroyed, although light based spells aimed directly at it have a 10% chance per spell level of shattering it (leaving you without a shadow for 2d4 nights). You can recall your shadow to you at any time as a standard action.

MASK OF MORTALITY

You appear wholly mortal for a time.

Prerequisites: Age 1, Cloak of the Outsider.

Benefits: You can look as you did when you were mortal, or like anyone else you choose. This Gift costs 1 Blood per 10 minutes of use and allows you to take any form you like. You *must* combine this power with the Dark Gift, Stifle the Chill if you are to appear wholly mortal. Each use of Mask of Mortality costs 1 Blood point

MASS CHARM

Your charm powers work in a large area.

Prerequisites: Dire Charm, Domination, Far Charm, Mesmerize.

Benefits: As Domination, but you can affect a total number of creatures within a 30 ft. radius of no more than twice your character level + *age*.

Example: a 10th level, age 3 vampire could mass charm 26 HD worth of people. Creatures affected do not have to be looking into your eyes, nor do you have to target a single individual. You can affect a crowd, or a single victim. You must be able to see your targets for this power to work on them. Hidden or invisible targets are unaffected by this power (although those that become invisible after they have been affected are still influenced by the mass charm).

MESMERIZE

You can project your thoughts into someone's mind.

Prerequisites: Dominate, Far Charm

Benefits: You can stare into your victim's eyes and make them see whatever you want them to see. You can influence their emotions, or implant an entire scene, making everything appear contrary to how it actually is. The target is granted a Will save to resist the effects, but once failed, you can influence them in any way you desire. You can amend memories, adding or removing thoughts and feelings. You can instil powerful desires, or remove urges.

Memories lost are typically gone forever, although a *restoration* spell has a 50 % chance of restoring altered memories. You could make a character forget how to use their spellcasting abilities, but deep ingrained memories have a chance of returning (although this is unpredictable and has no certainty of working). Careful vampires only alter insignificant memories, or those not deeply seated in their target's mind.

MULTIPLE COFFINS

You can have more than one coffin.

Benefits: Using soil from your home grave, you can attune additional coffins to yourself. You can have a total number of coffins equal to 1 (+1 additional coffin for every *age* that you have).

NOXIOUS BREATH

You can breathe a cloud of poisons.

Prerequisites: Ravenous Vampire.

Benefits: You can breathe a cloud of toxins in a 10 ft. long and 5 ft. wide cone. These toxins are not harmful to the dead, but deal 1d6 points of damage for every *age* you possess to all living beings in the area of effect. This power causes dizziness and *nausea* as per the spell *stinking cloud* (Fortitude save DC 15 + *age* or be *nauseated* for 1d4 rounds). If you so choose, you can forego any damage inflicted to raise the Nausea DC to 20 + *age*. Characters with fewer than a quarter of your levels will be overwhelmed by the stench and pass into unconsciousness for 1d4 rounds.

You can only use your noxious breath attack once every 6 (- *age*) rounds.

RESISTANCE TO TURNING

You are resistant to turning or commanding attempts.

Prerequisites: Age 3, Turn Resistance

Benefits: You are more difficult to turn than a standard vampire of your *age*.

When you would normally be turned, you can choose to expend Blood on a point per point basis to increase your effective HD (to negate the turning attempt). This happens at the time of turning; you are not turned until you either resist or choose to allow the turning attempt.

Reverse Turning

You can reverse turning attempts made against you.

Prerequisites: Age 4, Resistance to Turning.

Benefits: You are old and powerful; the energies within you are too potent to be turned by any mundane cleric, no matter how powerful they may be. Any cleric attempting to turn you will sense your power even as they raise their holy symbol. You must first resist their turning attempt (as Resistance to Turning). If you are successful, you can then make an Opposed Will Check against the turning cleric (this can be further modified by +1 for every Blood point you expend). Success indicates the turning is reversed, causing the cleric's holy symbol to blacken and the cleric to suffer 1d8 points of damage per your *age* +1 (Will save for half). If you roll a natural 20, the Void will shatters the cleric's holy symbol, causing him to suffer 8d8 points of damage and stunning him for 2d4 rounds. He also loses 2d4 of his remaining turning attempts for the day.

Sap the Agility

Prerequisites: Energy Drain.

Benefits: For every negative level that you would normally inflict, you can choose instead to drain 1 point of Dexterity from your victim. They suffer a penalty of -2 to their Reflex saves for 2d4 minutes.

After twenty four hours, they must make the standard check; success indicates the lost Dexterity returns.

Sap the Ego

Prerequisites: Energy Drain.

Benefits: For every negative level that you would normally inflict, you can choose instead to drain 1 point of Intelligence from your victim. They become *confused* as per the spell for 1d4 rounds.

After twenty four hours, they must make the standard check; success indicates the lost Intelligence returns.

Sap the Grace

Prerequisites: Energy Drain.

Benefits: For every negative level that you would normally inflict, you can choose instead to drain 1 point of Charisma from your victim. They suffer a penalty of -1 to their actions for 1d4 rounds.

After twenty four hours, they must make the standard check; success indicates the lost Charisma returns.

Sap the Potence

Prerequisites: Energy Drain.

Benefits: For every negative level that you would normally inflict, you instead drain 1 point of Strength from your victim. They suffer -2 to their attack rolls for 2d4 rounds.

After twenty four hours, they must make the standard check; success indicates the lost Strength returns.

Sap the Vigor

Prerequisites: Energy Drain.

Benefits: For every negative level that you would normally inflict, you can choose instead to drain 1 point of Constitution from your victim. They suffer -2 to their Fortitude saves for 2d4 minutes.

After twenty four hours, they must make the standard check; success indicates the lost Constitution returns.

Sap the Will

Prerequisites: Energy Drain.

Benefits: For every negative level you would normally inflict, you can choose instead to drain 1 point of Wisdom from your victim. They suffer a penalty of -2 to their Willpower saves for 2d4 minutes.

After 24 hours, they must make the standard check; success indicates the lost Wisdom returns.

Sense

You have the ability to sense both positive and negative energy.

Benefits: The older you get, the more powerful your ability to discern the presence of other vampires, clerics and magical beings. You can make a Sense Motive check when something is magically concealed, or a vampire, cleric or magical creature is nearby. You can also sense when you are being scryed upon or when enchantments are being used against you.

Sense	DC
Vampires	DC 15 +/- difference in *age* (if any)
Invisible Creatures	DC 15
Good Clerics	DC 10
Magical Creatures	DC 25
Enchantments	DC 20
Scrying	DC 20

Modifiers to Sense Motive Check: Target within 1000 yards: +1, Target within 100 yards: +2, Target within 10 yards: +3.

Note: Older vampires have a better chance to sense younger vampires. They gain a bonus in the difference between ages, while younger vampires suffer a penalty to their checks.

Example: An age 3 vampire is invisibly watching an age 1 vampire conduct a transaction. The age 1 vampire has the Dark Gift, Sense. He gets to make a Sense Motive check to sense the older vampire spying on him. The DC is 16 (15 minus the difference in ages of the vampires - 2). The age 1 vampire gains +3 to his roll as the older vampire is within 10 yards of his location.

Shadow Dancing

Your shadow engages in melee.

Prerequisites: Long Shadow, Shadow Step.

Benefits: You can set loose your shadow that can attack for you. It springs forth, attacking as a character of your level (including any combat feats you may have) with its freezing claws.

Your shadow remains in existence for 1 round plus 1 round per *age* category and deals 1d6 points of damage per attack plus additional damage and bonuses to hit dependent on your *age* (see below). It has half your hit points and if destroyed, reforms in 2d4 nights. This power costs three Blood points to bring into effect and your shadow dances for a number of round equal to your Character Level.

Note: Your shadow is *incorporeal* and can only be struck by weapons that would normally be able to strike you. It otherwise has all the powers, characteristics and vulnerabilities of a standard shadow.

Additional Shadow Damage Chart

Age:	0	1	2	3	4	5
Damage:	+0	+1d6	+1d8	+2d6	+2d8	+3d6
To Hit:	+0	+1	+2	+3	+4	+5

Shadow Form

You can transform your body to living shadow.

Prerequisites: Shadow Step.

Benefits: You can transform yourself into living shadow as a standard action. You gain the trait *Incorporeal* and can pass through solid objects at will. Your physical attacks pass through armor. You may only deliver a standard negative energy drain attack in this form, although you derive no benefits from so doing. Creatures slain while in this form rise up as Vampire Scion 1d4 nights later with Shadow Form as one of their Dark Gifts.

Note: While in this form you are considered to be a shadow. Although you still turn at your vampiric level, spells that affect shadows will also affect you.

Slumbering Dreams

You can rouse yourself mentally during the day.

Prerequisites: Age 2, Black Mantle.

Benefits: Although your body must sleep during the day, you can rouse yourself mentally from slumber. You can cast forth your mind into the mortal realms. You can roam the halls of your home or even journey forth into the world in the form of a ghostly apparition. You can send a compulsion to those you have *touched* or use your powers to summon creatures to do your bidding. You can even conjure darkness or manipulate the weather.

Manifesting to those around you is difficult. They will see a hazy apparition (that a cleric can easily dispel with a simple turning attempt). The use of your vampiric powers costs double the normal amount of Blood (or 1 Blood if there is normally no cost) and the DC lowers by 5 to resist the effects of your abilities. Should your sleep be disturbed, you suffer no penalty to your Waking check.

Spider Climb

You can walk on walls, ceilings and even smooth surfaces.

Benefits: You can cling to walls, surfaces and even ceilings at will. This Gift works as the spell *spider climb*.

Stifle the Chill

You can still the Vampiric forces within you.

Prerequisites: Age 1.

Benefits: You can still the forces of necromancy in your body for a short time allowing you to come into contact with mortals. Your flesh is cold and you still appear dead, but the *Chill* has subsided and you are no longer cloaked in a freezing aura of icy darkness.

Use of this power requires a full round action to bring into effect and costs 3 points of Blood. It can be negated at any time as a standard action. You can still the flows of necromancy for 10 minutes plus 10 minutes per *age* category. Every additional 10 minutes thereafter costs 1 Blood point.

Note: While you have stifled the chill, you lose the use of your energy drain and fast healing powers.

Telekinesis

You can use the power of your mind to move objects.

Benefits: The forces of necromancy swirl within you. You can use telekinesis as per the spell *telekinesis* cast by a 12th level sorcerer once per night, with additional uses costing 1 Blood.

Transformation

You can change your form.

Prerequisites: Alternate Form.

Benefits: You can transform yourself into one of the following *additional* forms, plus one form for every *age* you gain *after* buying this Dark Gift. The transformation requires a move-equivalent action and costs 1 Blood point. Reforming requires a standard action. While transformed, you assume a number of creatures equal to your current hit point total. So long as at least one creature remains, you can reform yourself (at that hit point total).

Standard Creatures of the Night (Choose One):
Bats - Rats - Moths - Birds

Blood: You can turn yourself into a pool of blood that can move and climb at a rate of 10 ft. round. You are immune to physical melee attacks and so long as the smallest portion of you remains, you can reform yourself.

Leech: You can transform into leeches, worms or any form of burrowing grub, one for each of your hit points. You can drain blood in this way, one point for each leech you create. It takes 5 rounds for one leech to drink 1 point of blood from a target.

Mosquito: You can transform into a mosquito that can suck blood. You can drain 1 point of blood from a victim in 10 rounds.

Note: If you have the Dark Gift, Dark Avatar, you can transform yourself into a flock of stirges, dire rats or dire bats as above.

Turn Resistance

You have increased resistance to clerical turning.

Benefits: You add your *age* to your effective HD for the purposes of turning. See Master *Age* Table on p. 127 for more details.

Umbral Mist

You can transform into a freezing mist.

Prerequisites: Shadow Vampire.

Benefits: By expending 3 Blood and a move-equivalent action you can transform into a hazy mist of freezing razor-sharp particles of an area no greater than 5 ft. x 5 ft. x 5ft. for every *age* that you have. You can move at 30 ft. (good). Anyone entering the mist takes 1d6 points of slashing damage per round and mortal characters suffer an additional 1d4 (+1 per *age*) points of cold damage (no save). The freezing chill is so intense that all mortal characters must make a Fortitude save (DC 15 + *age* + Charisma modifier). Those that successfully resist are dazed until the end of the round. Those that fail are dazed and lose 1 point of Strength and Dexterity (regained at 1 per full turn of rest). Umbral Mist lasts for 5 + your *age* rounds.

Unquenchable Aura

Your essence can not easily be destroyed.

Prerequisites: Age 1.

Benefits: You are powerful, the necromantic energies surrounding you cannot easily be dissipated. If you would be destroyed in a turning attempt you instead lose one point of Blood for every two of the cleric's turning levels and are immediately reduced to your death state. You are unable to reform for a number of days equal to the turning cleric's level and awaken on 1 hit point with 0 Blood. You must feed immediately or fall into the *eternal quiescence*. If your Blood score falls to 0 as a result of any turning attempt, you do not awaken for 1 week multiplied by the turning level of the cleric.

Unturnable

Once a cleric has failed to turn you he can never turn you again.

Prerequisites: Turn Resistance.

Benefits: Whenever a cleric fails to turn you (or you manage to resist his turning attempts), he can never again turn you. You know his soul and have have learned to forever resist his abilities (but not his spells or any other divine powers he may have).

Vampiric Door

You can travel using shadow, flame or fire as a gateway.

Prerequisites: Vampiric Step.

Benefits: There are three forms of this power: Blood Door, Fire Door and Shadow Door. You must choose one when gaining this Gift.

* **Blood Door:** You can 'teleport' into any source of blood, so long as you can see your point of origin. This is a move-equivalent action and costs a single Blood point. You can only teleport into blood that has at least twice your *age* in hit points damage, one point of Blood or a single point of mortal Constitution.

* **Fire Door:** You can 'teleport' into any flame or fire, so long as you can see your point of origin. This is a move-equivalent action and costs a single point of Blood.

* **Shadow Door:** You can 'step' into any shadow, so long as you can see your point of origin. This is a move-equivalent action and costs a single point of Blood.

Note: You do not have to be able to physically 'see' your destination to use this power. You could scry for it, or be looking through the eyes of your simulacrum, undead minion or even a *vampire touched* victim.

Vampiric Healing

You can use blood to heal your wounds.

Benefits: You can expend blood to heal yourself far more quickly than a typical vampire. Each point of Blood you expend heals you of 1d12 hit points. You can expend up to 1 Blood plus your *age* category per round as a standard action. You can also expend up to your *age* +1 Blood in every twenty four hour period to heal 1d4 points of sunlight/holy damage per Blood point spent.

Vampiric Senses

Your five senses are greatly enhanced.

Benefits: Your sense of smell, touch, taste, hearing and sight are all far beyond those you experienced when you were alive. You gain a bonus of +4 to your Listen, Spot and Search checks.

You gain the *scent* ability and suffer no penalty to fighting when you could not otherwise see your opponent.

You can concentrate to hear a conversation in a crowded room (although exceptional noise will deafen you momentarily) and read texts, or even lips from a hundred yards away in almost total darkness.

> *"I am death. I am shadow. I am night.*
> *I am the killer of ages...*
> *I have murdered the old, the young, the strong and the weak.*
> *And now I shall kill you, perhaps..."*
> Illian Mort Drellian, Shadow Vampire

Vampiric Step

You can travel using shadow, flames or fire.

Benefits: There are three forms of this power: Blood Step, Fire Step and Shadow Step. You must choose one when gaining this Gift.

* **Blood Step:** You can step into one source of blood and out of another as a move-equivalent action. You can only step into or out of blood that has at least twice your *age* in hit points damage, one point of blood or a single point of mortal Constitution.

* **Fire Step:** You can step into one flame and out of another as a move-equivalent action. There must be fire at both your point of entrance and your destination and both must be within line of sight.

* **Shadow Step:** You can step into one shadow and out of another as a move-equivalent action. There must be shadow at both your point of entrance and your destination and both must be within line of sight.

Vampiric Touch

You have increased energy drain powers.

Prerequisites: Advanced Energy Drain, Age 2, Energy Drain.

Benefits: Your energy draining powers are advanced beyond those of a typical vampire. It has two forms:

* **Dark Drain:** You can focus all of the Void's energies within you into a single burst of necromantic energy. You may drain a single **permanent** level from your target at a cost of 3 Blood points. To do so greatly weakens you; you lose all vampiric Strength and Dexterity bonuses and cannot drain levels for 2d4 rounds.

* **Enhanced Energy Drain:** Your energy drain ability is increased by +1. Use of this power costs a single point of Blood for every round in effect (regardless of whether you use it or not).

Note: It takes a standard action to activate either of these powers. Only one can be active at any one time.

Will of Blood

You can focus your domination powers by expending your Blood.

Benefits: When engaging in any charm attempt, you can force your victim to reroll a successful Will save by expending Blood to match their roll (if you can). The victim must then make a further Will save. If they again succeed, you can continue to force them to reroll by expending Blood, until they either fail their roll or you are unwilling to expend further Blood. No matter how much Blood you have, you can only force a total number of rerolls equal to your *age* +1. Every use of Will of Blood costs 1 Blood point.

Note: In addition you can choose to expend up to your *age* +1 Blood before any domination attempt to increase the difficulty by +1 for each point of Blood expended.

Example: A 12th level, age 2 vampire (with a Charisma modifier of +3) attempts to use his domination power on a cleric. The Will save is 21 (10 (base) +6 (half HD) +2 (age) +3 (Charisma)). The cleric rolls a 24. A save. The vampire must expend 4 points of Blood to force the cleric to make a reroll (3 to match his roll and +1 for the attempt). He chooses to do this, and concentrates, focusing all his dark energies on the task at hand. The cleric makes his Will save again, this time rolling a 22. The vampire again chooses to expend 2 points of Blood, forcing the cleric to reroll a third time. This time he rolls an 11, and fails, falling victim to the vampire's dark charms.

CHAPTER SIX: MAGICAL SPELLS

ZERO LEVEL SPELLS

Blood Light. Creates light from your blood for 1hr/level.

Corpus Enhancement. Increase the power of your spells with blood.

FIRST LEVEL SPELLS

Blood Dart. Does 1d4+1 points of damage per 2 levels, +1 per point of Blood spent (max *age* category).

Cause Light Wound. Deals 1d8 (+1 per round) damage.

Hand of Blood. Steals one point of blood from your target.

Summon Undead I. Summons undead to fight for you.

SECOND LEVEL SPELLS

Attune the Blood. Attunes a single point of blood.

Aura of Repulsions. Creates a protective skin that repels liquids.

Blood Bolt. 1d6 points of damage per 2 levels, +1d6 per Blood spent (max *age* category).

Cause Moderate Wound. Deals 2d8 (+2 per round) damage.

Dark Aura. An inky blackness surrounds the caster.

Open Blood Gate. Unlocks a Blood Gate.

Purge the Void. Purge Void on the destruction of an evil vampire.

Silent Charm. Alerts the vampire to intrusion of his crypt.

Summon Undead II. Summons undead to fight for you.

THIRD LEVEL SPELLS

Blood Geyser. Does 1d6 damage per level to all within the spell's effect.

Cause Serious Wound. Deals 3d8 (+3 per round) damage.

Conjure Bloodling. Summons bloodlings to fight for you.

Drain Blood. Steals blood on touch.

Eyes of the Damned. See through the eyes of your minions.

Increase the Bloody Receptacle. Increases your Blood score.

Scry the Blood. Know the power level of the blood.

Summon Undead III. Summons undead to fight for you.

Touch the Mortal. Up to *twice touch* a mortal.

Wall of Blood. Conjures a wall of blood.

FOURTH LEVEL SPELLS

Agoravaal's Boon. Protects you against being staked.

Cause Critical Wound. Deals 4d8 (+4 per round) damage.

Circle of Blood. A circle of blood to springs up around you. Anyone stepping through the blood takes your level in damage.

Conjure Blood Hound. Summons a Blood Hound for 1 hr/lvl.

Summon Blood Leech. Conjure 1 or more Blood Leeches.

Summon the Necrotic Ally. Calls a friend to the Arch.

Summon Undead IV. Summons undead to fight for you.

FIFTH LEVEL SPELLS

Blood Bite. Do damage at the cost of Blood.

Cloak of Blood. Protective cloak of blood, +4 to AC and can attack at your level.

Circle of Lesser Harm. 1d8 (+1 per round) damage to in circle.

Conjure Katharein. You endure a Katharein when you next sleep.

Conceal the Nosferatu. Makes a vampire appear human

Create Consanguineous Vampire. Transforms a mortal into a consanguineous vampire.

Inducing the Willing Quiescence. Voluntarily fall into *eternal quiescence* for a stated period.

Journey to the Arch. Transport yourself to the Necrotic Arch.

Summon Blood Gate. Conjures magical Blood Gate

Summon Undead V. Summons undead to fight for you.

SIXTH LEVEL SPELLS

Bind Vampiric Simulacrum. You can create your own Vampire Simulacrum.

Blood Curse. A creature cannot heal for 1 day per level.

Call Necrotic Allies. Summons your level in allies to the Necrotic Arch.

Circle of Harming. Deals 2d8 (+2 per round) damage to all within the circle.

Focus the Chill. Increases your energy drain abilities by +1 for 1 rd/level.

Neutral Countenance. Protects one target against divination attempts.

Steal Blood. Drains 1d6 (+1 per *age* category) Blood from a vampire or 1d8 (+1 per *age* category) Constitution from a mortal.

Summon Undead VI. Summons undead to fight for you.

SEVENTH LEVEL SPELLS

Blood Fire. Sets a target's blood on fire causing agony and inability to act.

Circle of Greater Harm. Deals 3d8 (+3 per round) damage to all within the circle.

Consanguineous Curse. You can transform a vampire into a consanguineous vampire.

Inducing the Black Sleep. Save or a vampire falls into *eternal quiescence* for a time.

Stifle the Chill. Prevents a vampire from using their energy drain powers.

Summon Undead VII. Summons undead to fight for you.

EIGHTH LEVEL SPELLS

Boil Blood. Deals your level in Constitution damage to one target.

Circle of Pain. Cause all hurt by you to suffer agonising pain.

Curse of the Transient Nosferatu. Temporarily transmutes a mortal into a vampire.

Bleeding. Target bleeds at your level in hit points per round (-1 hit point per round).

Restore the Favored. Fully restores a vampire if you have their heart.

Summon Undead VIII. Summons undead to fight for you.

NINTH LEVEL SPELLS

Aura of Tranquility. Masks the necromantic aura of a vampire or undead creature.

Circle of Maleficence. Deals 4d8 (+4 per round) damage to all within the circle.

Curse of Vampirism. Slays a mortal and transforms them into a free-willed fledgling vampire.

Exsanguinate. Drains your caster level in Blood from your target.

Necromancy's Dark Transfiguration. Drain a single level from all you can touch in 1 minute.

Summon Undead IX. Summons undead to fight for you.

Veil of Ash. Affects an area around you with *disintegration*.

Will of the Ages. Temporarily increases your *age* category to a maximum of *age* category 5.

> "I want to go on living even
> after my death."
> Anne Frank, Black Sorcerer

Agoravaal's Boon

Abjuration
Level: Sor/Wiz 4
Components: V, S, F
Casting Time: 1 action
Range: Personal
Target: You
Duration: 1 day/level or until discharged
Saving Throw: None
Spell Resistance: No

This spell protects you against being staked. Any stake or sharp wooden implement pressed against your chest immediately shatters. Any attack of this nature while sleeping grants you +8 to your Waking check.

Arcane Focus: A tiny sliver of silver that must be kept on the caster's person throughout the duration of the spell.

Attune the Blood

Necromancy [BC]
Level: Sor/Wiz 2
Components: V, S, M
Casting Time: 1 minute
Range: Touch
Target: Blood touched
Duration: Instantaneous
Saving Throw: None
Spell Resistance: No

This spell attunes a single drop of mortal blood. You must put a point of blood into a specially created silver chalice. Upon completion of the spell, the point of blood becomes attuned. However the attuned Blood has an *age* category of 0 and cannot be used to power Dark Gifts that require higher *age* category Blood.

Material Components: A point of blood.

Aura of Repulsions

Abjuration
Level: Sor/Wiz 2
Components: V, S
Casting Time: 1 action
Range: Touch
Target: Vampire touched
Duration: 1 round/level
Saving Throw: None
Spell Resistance: No

This spell creates a glistening aura that protects you against liquids. The spell is not powerful enough to protect against submersion in water, but will cause water, and other liquids to splash harmlessly off you. If you are fully submerged under water, the spell confers but one additional round of protection before expiring.

Note: While this spell is in effect you cannot benefit from imbibing potions or from any salve or ointment that could be applied to your skin.

Aura of Tranquility

Necromancy
Level: Clr 9, Sor/Wiz 9
Components: V, S, M, F
Casting Time: 1 hour
Range: Special
Target: Special
Duration: 1 day/level
Saving Throw: None
Spell Resistance: No

This spell is identical to *neutral countenance* except that you may cast it upon one vampire for each of your caster levels. You can increase the spell's duration by expending one point of Blood for every additional day you require the spell to remain in effect.

Material Components: A pint of warm mortal blood

Arcane Focus: A perfectly smooth sphere of obsidian.

Bind Vampiric Simulacrum

Necromancy
Level: Sor/Wiz 6
Components: V, S, M
Casting Time: One full month
Duration: Permanent
Saving Throw: None
Spell Resistance: No

You can transform a mortal into a vampiric simulacrum. Only you can use this spell, Bind Vampiric Simulacrum cannot create or bind a simulacrum to another vampire. The spell requires a suitable mortal and a full month to cast. You must spend at least 8 hours per night on the process. If you are interrupted for more than one night during the casting the spell fails and the mortal is destroyed. More information on vampire simulacra is available on p. 103.

Material Components: 30 points of attuned Blood and 5,000gp multiplied by the HD of the mortal to be transformed. It also requires at least one rare organ from a magical creature. This is typically fresh unicorn horn although other spells have different ingredients.

Bleeding

Necromancy [Harm]
Level: Clr 8, Sor/Wiz 8
Components: V, S
Casting Time: 1 action

Range: Touch
Target: Person touched
Duration: Instantaneous
Saving Throw: Will negates
Spell Resistance: Yes

You can cause your target to bleed. They lose your caster level in hit points at the end of every round, with a reduction of 1 per round. They can make a Will save at the end of each round to negate the bleeding effects for that round only. Any magical healing will prevent any bleeding for that round.

Example: A 16th level vampire wizard casts bleeding on a paladin. The paladin loses 16 hit points in the first round, then 15 on the next, and so on, until on the 16th round, he loses 1 hit point and the bleeding stops altogether. At the end of every round, the paladin may make a Will save against the caster's level to negate the spell and prevent any bleeding for that round.

Blood Bite

Necromancy [Blood]
Level: Sor/Wiz 5
Components: V, S, M
Casting Time: 1 action
Range: Short (25 ft. + 5 ft./level)
Area: Cone
Duration: Instantaneous
Saving Throw: Reflex half
Spell Resistance: Yes

A swirling torrent of blood surges out from your fingertips doing 1d6 points of burning acidic damage per caster level (to a maximum of 10d6) to all those within the spell's area of effect. In addition, you can expend up to 1 plus your *age* category points of Blood to bolster the spell's power. For every point of Blood you spend, the spell's damage is increased by 1d6 (to a maximum of 6d6). This additional damage is not subject to a Reflex save; targets automatically suffer this damage even if they save against the spell's standard damage.

Material Components: Your own blood.

Blood Bolt

Necromancy [Blood]
Level: Sor/Wiz 2
Components: S, V, M
Casting Time: 1 action
Range: 10 ft.
Target: One creature
Duration: Instantaneous
Saving Throw: None
Spell Resistance: No

You can conjure a bolt of blood that unerringly strikes a living target doing 1d6 points of damage per two of your caster levels (to a maximum of 5d6). In addition, you can expend Blood up to your *age* category to enhance the spell's damage by 1d6 to a maximum of 10d6.

Material Components: A point of your blood.

BLOOD CURSE

Necromancy [Blood]
Level: Clr 6, Sor/Wiz 6
Components: V, S, M, DF
Casting Time: 1 action
Range: Touch
Target: Person touched
Duration: 1 day/level
Saving Throw: Will negates
Spell Resistance: Yes

You prevent a mortal from healing naturally. For the duration of the spell they do not recover health or hit points while resting. Additionally, all curing spells only heal half normal. When cast upon a vampire, the target cannot attune blood and they derive no nourishment from any blood they drink.

Material Components: A drop of poison.

BLOOD DART

Necromancy [Blood]
Level: Clr/Drd 1, Sor/Wiz 1
Components: V, S, M
Casting Time: 1 action
Range: Close (25 ft. +5 ft./2 levels)
Target: Up to 5 creatures, no two of which can be more than 15 ft. apart
Duration: Instantaneous
Saving Throw: None
Spell Resistance: Yes

You can conjure a glistening dart that deals 1d4+1 points of damage to any opponent you choose. The darts will always strike your intended targets unless there is an obstacle in the way, in which case they will strike that instead. You gain an additional blood dart for every 2 levels to a maximum of 5 missiles at 9th level. A single missile can only strike one target and the spell only effects living creatures.

In addition, you can expend up to your *age* category in Blood to deliver that amount of additional damage to every opponent you strike with the spell. An *age* 5 vampire could deliver 1d4+1 points of damage to 5 targets and expend 5 points of Blood to inflict a further 5 points of damage to each of them. This damage is only applied once to each target struck by the spell and is not subject to the target's spell resistance.

Material Components: A point of your blood.

BLOOD FIRE

Necromancy [Blood]
Level: Clr 7, Sor/Wiz 7
Components: V, S, F
Casting Time: 1 action
Range: Close (25 ft. +5 ft./2 levels)
Target: One living creature
Duration: 1 round +1 round per 2 levels
Saving Throw: Will negates
Spell Resistance: Yes

You can cause agony to any target whom you have previously wounded (within the last 24 hours). The target is stricken with a paralysing agony, their wounds burning with terrible fire. Characters in this state lose all dexterity bonuses to their AC, can only take partial actions and suffer -2 to any actions they do take.

Arcane Focus: A perfectly smooth agate of no less than 1000gp value.

BLOOD GEYSER

Necromancy [Blood]
Level: Sor/Wiz 3
Components: V, S, M
Casting Time: 1 action
Range: Medium (100 ft. + 10 ft./level)
Area: Cylinder (10 ft. radius, 20 ft. high)
Duration: Instantaneous
Saving Throw: None
Spell Resistance: No

You can call forth a column of blood that explodes at the designated point, causing all living beings to suffer 1d6 points of damage per level of the caster to a maximum of 15d6.

Material Components: A point of your blood.

BLOOD LIGHT

Necromancy
Level: Sor/Wiz 0
Components: V, S, M
Casting Time: 1 action
Range: Personal
Effect: Up to your *age* category +1 in blood red lights, all within 10 ft of you.
Duration: 1 hour/level
Saving Throw: None
Spell Resistance: No

You can cause a single globe of bloodlight to appear for every *age* you possess (or 1 if you are mortal). Globes can be positioned at a distance of up to 10 ft. from you. The crimson light provides barely enough for a mortal to see more than a few feet, but does not impede a vampire's *darkvision* in any way.

Material Components: One point of Blood or Constitution.

BOIL BLOOD

Necromancy [BC]
Level: Clr 8, Sor/Wiz 8
Components: V, S, F
Casting Time: 1 action
Range: Touch
Target: Person Touched
Duration: Instantaneous
Saving Throw: Will half
Spell Resistance: Yes

You deal your caster level in Constitution damage to a mortal, or in Blood damage to a vampire.

A mortal reduced to 0 Constitution rises as a bloodling on the Negative Energy Plane 1d4 days later.

Arcane Focus: A drop of mercury.

CALL NECROTIC ALLIES

Conjuration (Calling)
Level: Sor/Wiz 6
Components: V, S
Casting Time: 1 action
Range: Personal
Effect: 1 creature per level
Duration: Instantaneous
Saving Throw: None
Spell Resistance: No

While at the Necrotic Arch, you can summon up to your caster level in allies. You need but whisper their names and the spell will call them. Additionally, you may attach a message to the call of no more words than your character level. Characters willing to aid you will appear at the Arch in 1d4 rounds.

If the summoned characters are not asleep, a character may accept the call, falling into a deep slumber in a single round and passing to the Arch. For more information on the Katharein, see p. 114.

CAUSE CRITICAL WOUND

Necromancy [Harm]
Level: Clr 4, Sor/Wiz 4
Components: V, S
Casting Time: 1 action
Range: Touch
Target: Creature touched
Duration: Instantaneous
Saving Throw: Will negates
Spell Resistance: Yes

You cause a grievous wound upon your target. It does 4d8 points of damage and causes the wound to bleed at 4 hit points per round for a number of rounds equal to your level (max 10). Any amount of healing will immediately stop the bleeding.

CAUSE LIGHT WOUND

Necromancy [Harm]
Level: Clr 1, Sor/Wiz 1
Components: V, S
Casting Time: 1 action
Range: Touch
Target: Creature touched
Duration: Instantaneous
Saving Throw: Will negates
Spell Resistance: Yes

You cause a tiny wound upon your target. It does 1d8 points of damage and causes the wound to bleed at 1 hit point per round for a number of rounds equal to the level of the caster (max 5). While this spell is hardly fatal, it does look gruesome. Any amount of healing will immediately stop the bleeding.

CAUSE MODERATE WOUND

Necromancy [Harm]
Level: Clr 2, Sor/Wiz 2
Components: V, S
Casting Time: 1 action
Range: Touch
Target: Creature touched
Duration: Instantaneous
Saving Throw: Will negates
Spell Resistance: Yes

You cause a moderate wound upon your target. It does 2d8 points of damage and causes the wound to bleed at 2 hit points per round for a number of rounds equal to the level of the caster (max 5). Any amount of healing will immediately stop the bleeding.

CAUSE SERIOUS WOUND

Necromancy [Harm]
Level: Clr 3, Sor/Wiz 3
Components: V, S
Casting Time: 1 action
Range: Touch
Target: Creature touched
Duration: Instantaneous
Saving Throw: Will negates
Spell Resistance: Yes

You cause a major wound upon your target. It does 3d8 points of damage and causes the wound to bleed at 3 hit points per round for a number of rounds equal to the level of the caster (max 10). Any amount of healing will immediately stop the bleeding.

CLOAK OF BLOOD

Necromancy [BC]
Level: Sor/Wiz 5
Components: V, S
Casting Time: 1 action

Range: Personal
Target: Self
Duration: 1 round per level
Saving Throw: None
Spell Resistance: No

You conjure a cloak of blood into being around you. The cloak has a reach of 10 ft. and can attack anyone who comes within its threat range as if it were a character of your caster level (this includes attacks of opportunity if applicable).

The cloak confers an AC bonus of +4 and lashes out with its barbed folds, dealing 1d6 points of damage +1 per three of your caster levels.

In addition, if you are a vampire, base damage dealt by the cloak can be absorbed up to a total of your *age* category in hit points per round. You cannot exceed more than your maximum hit point total in this way.

CIRCLE OF BLOOD

Conjuration (Creation) [BC]
Level: Sor/Wiz 4
Components: V, S, M
Casting Time: 1 action
Range: Close (25 ft. + 5 ft./level)
Effect: 20 ft. radius circle of blood, centered no more than 40ft. from the caster
Duration: 1 round/level
Saving Throw: None
Spell Resistance: No

You can cause a circle of blood to spring up at your desired location. The circle is 10 ft. (+1 ft. per level) high and undulates with bloody menace. Anyone stepping through the circle suffers 1 hit point of damage for each of your caster levels plus your *age* category. You can expend one additional Blood to increase the radius of the circle by 10 ft. You can also create a dome of blood with similar dimensions (at a cost of four Blood points). Upon expiration of the spell, any unused blood splashes messily to the ground.

Material Component: Two points of your own Blood.

CIRCLE OF HARMING

Necromancy [Harm]
Level Clr 6, Sor/Wiz 6
Components: V, S
Casting Time: 1 action
Range: 20 ft.
Area: All living creatures within a 20 ft. burst centered on you
Duration: Instantaneous
Saving Throw: Will negates
Spell Resistance: Yes

You cause all within the spell's area of effect to suffer a *cause moderate wound* spell. It does 2d8 points of damage + bleeding at 2 hit points per round for a total number of rounds equal to your caster level (max 5). Any amount of healing will stop the bleeding.

CIRCLE OF GREATER HARM

Necromancy [Harm]
Level: Clr 7, Sor/Wiz 7
Components: V, S
Casting Time: 1 action
Range: 20 ft.
Area: All living creatures within a 30 ft. burst centered on you
Duration: Instantaneous
Saving Throw: Will negates
Spell Resistance: Yes

You cause all within the area of effect to suffer a *cause serious wound* spell. Any amount of healing will immediately stop the bleeding.

CIRCLE OF LESSER HARM

Necromancy [Harm]
Level: Clr 5, Sor/Wiz 5
Components: V, S
Casting Time: 1 action
Range: 20 ft.
Area: All living creatures within a 20 ft. burst centered on you
Duration: Instantaneous
Saving Throw: Will negates
Spell Resistance: Yes

You cause all within the area of effect to suffer a *cause light wound* spell. It does 1d8 points of damage and causes the wound to bleed at 1 hit point per round for a number of rounds equal to your caster level (max 5). Any amount of healing will immediately stop the bleeding.

CIRCLE OF MALEFICENCE

Necromancy [Harm]
Level: Clr 9, Sor/Wiz 9
Components: V, S
Casting Time: 1 action
Range: 20 ft.
Area: All living creatures within a 30 ft. burst centered on you
Duration: Instantaneous
Saving Throw: Will negates
Spell Resistance: Yes

You affect those within the area of effect with a *cause critical wound* spell. It does 4d8 damage + bleeding at 4 hit points per round for a total number of rounds equal to your caster level (max 10). Any amount of healing will stop the bleeding.

CIRCLE OF PAIN

Necromancy [Blood]
Level: Clr 8, Sor/Wiz 8
Components: V, S, F
Casting Time: 1 action
Range: 20 ft.
Area: All wounded creatures (by you) within a 20 ft. burst centered on you
Duration: Special
Saving Throw: Will negates
Spell Resistance: Yes

You cause all within the spell's area of effect to be afflicted with the *blood fire* spell.

Arcane Focus: A blood ruby of no lower than 1000gp in value.

CONCEAL THE NOSFERATU

Illusion
Level: Sor/Wiz 5
Components: V, S, M
Casting Time: 1 minute
Range: Touch
Target: Person touched
Duration: 1 hour/level
Saving Throw: None or Will negates
Spell Resistance: No or Yes

You can make a vampire seem fully human for a short time. Lasting until dawn, your target will appear to be mortal, even under close scrutiny. They will have warm flesh and even appear to breathe. Although the vampire is concealed behind an illusion, they are still affected by all their traditional weaknesses. Holy auras may startle them and they cannot enter private buildings uninvited or walk upon holy ground. They still have full use of their vampiric powers. Powerful characters may have a chance to sense the presence of the vampire behind the magic. To sense the unnatural presence, the character must succeed at a caster level check (1d20 + character level) against a DC of 15 + the caster level of the spellcaster who cast *conceal the nosferatu* + their *age* category.

Material Components: A drop of warm mortal blood and a phoenix feather.

CONJURE BLOOD HOUND

Conjuration (summoning) [BC]
Level: Drd 4, Rgr 4, Sor/Wiz 5
Components: V, S, M
Casting Time: 1 action
Range: Close (25 ft. + 5ft./level)
Effect: One summoned creature
Duration: 1 hour/level (D)
Saving Throw: None
Spell Resistance: No

You can conjure a Blood Hound. Providing you have a sample of blood, a Blood Hound will locate the source if it is able. For more information on Blood Hounds, see p. 98.

Material Components: Three points of your own attuned Blood.

CONJURE BLOODLING

Necromancy (conjuration) [BC]
Level: Sor/Wiz 3
Components: V, S, M
Casting Time: 1 action
Range: Close (25 ft. + 5ft./level)
Effect: One or more summoned creatures, none of which can be more than 40ft. apart.
Duration: 1 hour/level (D)
Saving Throw: None
Spell Resistance: No

You can conjure one or more bloodlings, the faithful of Vangual. You can summon a bloodling for every level you have. You must expend at least 8 hit points of blood or 1 attuned Blood point (equal to 12 hit points + age category), from which a bloodling will rise up and act immediately. You can create a total number of bloodlings equal to 1 plus your *age* category for every point of Blood expended.

Example: An age 3 vampire can conjure 4 bloodlings per point of Blood. If he were 12th level, he would need to expend 3 points of Blood to create 12 bloodlings. See p. 98 for more information on bloodlings.

Material Components: Enough blood to conjure at least one bloodling.

CONJURE KATHAREIN

Necromancy
Level: Sor/Wiz 5
Components: V, S
Casting Time: 1 action
Range: Touch
Target: Vampire touched
Duration: Instantaneous
Saving Throw: Will negates
Spell Resistance: Yes

You can voluntarily undergo a Katharein. The spell must be cast at the moments before dawn, timing its completion at the exact moment you fall into slumber. You will awaken at the Necrotic Crypt, and must pass through the Arch before you can waken (see Katharein p. 114).

CONSANGUINEOUS CURSE

Necromancy [BC]
Level: Sor/Wiz 7
Components: V, S, M, F

Casting Time: 1 full night
Range: Touch
Effect: One vampire touched.
Duration: Permanent
Saving Throw: Special
Spell Resistance: Yes

You can curse a vampire, transforming them into a consanguineous vampire (see p. 103 for more information on consanguineous vampires). The spell takes a full night to cast and requires at least six points of attuned Blood to seal the transformation.

A vampire is allowed a Will save to resist the effects of the spell, DC 15 plus the Intelligence modifier of the caster. Success indicates the spell fails and the vampire remains unharmed. You can increase the difficulty of the spell by adding three points of your attuned Blood to the casting for each +1 difficulty added.

Note: You can only control as many consanguineous vampires as you have levels. Once you reach your level limit, you cannot create further consanguineous vampires until some of your existing creatures are destroyed.

Material Components: Powdered amber of no less than 1000gp mixed with vampire blood.

Arcane Focus: A silver scalpel and a pinch of Grey Va'Vash.

CORPUS ENHANCEMENT

Necromancy [BC]
Level: Sor/Wiz 0
Components: V, S, M
Casting Time: 1 action
Range: Personal
Target: Self
Duration: 1 round/level
Saving Throw: None
Spell Resistance: No

If you have at least a point of the target's blood you may cast this spell to increase the DC of all your spells against that target by +4. The blood must be no more than 24 hours old but it can be stored magically for later use. The Black Cabal have entire libraries of stored blood from famous and powerful persons across the mortal realms.

Material Component: A drop of your target's blood.

CREATE CONSANGUINEOUS VAMPIRE

Necromancy [BC]
Level: Sor/Wiz 5
Components: V, S, M, F
Casting Time: 1 full night

Range: Touch
Duration: Permanent
Saving Throw: None
Spell Resistance: Yes

You can transform a mortal into a consanguineous vampire, the least of vampires. The spell takes a full night to cast and requires at least three points of attuned Blood to seal the transformation. Upon completion of the spell, the mortal's life essence will be destroyed and his corpse will rise up as a consanguineous vampire the following night. See p. 100 for more information on consanguineous vampires.

Note: You can only control as many consanguineous vampires as you have levels. Once you reach your level limit, you cannot create further consanguineous vampires until some of your existing creatures are destroyed.

Material Components: Powdered amber of no less than 500gp.
Arcane Focus: A silver scalpel.

Curse of the Transient Nosferatu

Necromancy
Level: Clr 8, Sor/Wiz 8
Components: V, S, M
Casting Time: Special
Range: Touch
Target: Person touched
Duration: Special
Saving Throw: Will negates
Spell Resistance: Yes

You can temporarily infuse a mortal with powerful necromantic energies. Their bodily functions will be halted, and they will be transformed into a newly created fledgling Black Blood until sunrise. The target must drink a concoction of vampire blood and wine for the spell to take effect. The transformation is agonising for a few moments, then the target falls into unconsciousness, waking as a vampire on the following turn. At dawn, they will pass into a black sleep, awaking 1d4 hours later, taking their first gulping breath as a mortal once again.

Note: Frequent use of this spell can corrupt the target with necromantic energies, and can transform the target permanently into a vampire. For every use of this spell in each 28 day period, the target must make a Will Save DC 15 (+1 for each additional casting) or be irreversibly transformed into a Vampire Scion.

Curse of Vampirism

Necromancy
Level: Clr 9, Sor/Wiz 9
Components: V, S, M
Casting Time: 1 hour
Range: Touch
Target: Person touched
Duration: Permanent
Saving Throw: Will negates
Spell Resistance: Yes

You can transform a mortal into a vampire. Upon the spell's completion, your target will be slain and will rise up as a Vampire Scion under your control or a fledgling vampire (your choice) 1d4 nights later.

Material Components: A mortal heart marinated in red wine with a pint of attuned vampire Blood and a pinch of vampire dust that the mortal must (be forced to) drink.

> This spell is traditionally used by the Devoted Incarnate upon their enemies. Captured and forced to drink the dreaded elixir of undeath these enemies become permanent slaves of the vampire race.

Dark Aura

Evocation
Level: Sor/Wiz 2
Components: V, S
Casting Time: 1 action
Range: Personal
Target: You
Duration: 1 turn/level
Saving Throw: None
Spell Resistance: No

An inky aura surrounds you, utterly obscuring you from view. If you cannot see through darkness, you cannot see though the dark aura. This spell confers some protection against sunlight and grants half damage against any one light/sunlight based spell. The *dark aura* is immediately cancelled upon absorbing one round of direct sunlight or damage from any light based spell.

Drain Blood

Necromancy [BC]
Level: Sor/Wiz 3
Components: V, S, M
Casting Time: 1 Action
Range: Touch
Target: One person
Duration: Instantaneous
Saving Throw: Will negates
Spell Resistance: Yes

You can absorb 1d4 (+1 per *age category*) points of blood from a vampire or 1d4 (+1

per *age* category) points of temporary Constitution from a mortal.

Note: If blood is drained from a vampire who has stores of both attuned and unattuned blood, blood will be drained from their supply of unattuned blood first.

Material Components: A silver needle wrapped in crimson velvet.

Exsanguinate

Necromancy [Blood]
Level: Clr 9, Sor/Wiz 9
Components: V, S
Casting Time: 1 action
Range: Touch
Target: Person touched
Duration: Special
Saving Throw: None
Spell Resistance: Yes

You can drain the blood from a victim. This spell drains 1 point of Blood from a vampire or 1 point of Constitution from a mortal for each of your caster levels. If you are a vampire, you can choose to absorb this blood as part of your daily requirement.

Eyes of the Damned

Divination
Level: Clr/Drd 3, Sor/Wiz 3
Components: V, S
Casting Time: 1 full round
Range: Unlimited
Target: One person or creature
Duration: 1 turn/level
Saving Throw: None
Spell Resistance: No

You can see through the eyes of your simulacrum, *vampire touched* or your progeny. Distance is not an object but you cannot see through magically warded or extra-planar locations. In addition, you must rely on the vision of your target. If they cannot see in darkness (or are asleep or blinded), you will see nothing.

Focus the Chill

Necromancy
Level: Sor/Wiz 6
Components: V, S, M
Casting Time: 1 action
Range: Personal
Target: Self
Duration: 1 round/level
Saving Throw: None
Spell Resistance: No

You can focus your powers of necromancy, increasing your energy draining abilities by

+1. The frigid aura around you will be intense and it will be difficult - if not impossible - to hide amongst mortals. Characters suffer a penalty -1 to any fear saves they must make in your proximity while this spell is in effect.

Material Components: A drop of mortal cleric blood mixed with vampire dust wrapped in the skin of a black dragon.

HAND OF BLOOD

Necromancy [BC]
Level: Sor/Wiz 1
Components: S
Casting Time: 1 action
Range: Touch
Target: Person touched
Duration: Permanent.
Saving Throw: Will negates
Spell Resistance: Yes

You can steal a single point of blood from your target. Mortals will lose 1 point of Constitution, while a vampire will lose 1 point of Blood. A mortal may not notice the theft (other than experiencing a momentary weakness).

Note: Powerful characters have a chance to realise that they have been affected by magic (Sense Motive check DC 30). They will not necessarily realise they have been the victim of an attack, but may associate the momentary chills and weakness to some form of magic. A vampire will always know they have lost a portion of their blood.

INCREASE THE BLOODY RECEPTACLE

Necromancy [BC]
Level: Sor/Wiz 3
Components: V, S, M, F
Casting Time: 8 hours
Range: Touch
Target: Creature touched
Duration: See below
Saving Throw: Will negates
Spell Resistance: Yes

You can temporarily increase a vampire's Blood score by 1 plus your *age* category for a total number of days equal to 1 plus your *age* category. These variables can be further increased if you expend Blood to increase either Blood score or spell duration.

Example: The spell grants an age 3 vampire +4 to his Blood score for 4 days. However, a vampire wishes to greatly increase this. He expends 10 further points of Blood, 5 to increase his Blood score and 5 to increase the spell's duration. When he wakens, his Blood score will have risen by 9 for a total of 9 days.

The spell will come into effect when target next wakes from slumber. At the spell's expiration, all excess blood dissipates. The spell cannot be stacked, and multiple castings result in all spells being cancelled. Lastly, the spell cannot be recast for a total number of days equal to the duration of the last increase. In the example above, the vampire could not recast this spell for a total of 9 days.

Arcane Focus: A pinch of vampire dust and a ruby worth at least 100gp.

Material Components: A fragment of mirror and bundle of wax wrapped in a silken cloth.

INDUCING THE BLACK SLEEP

Necromancy [BC]
Level: Sor/Wiz 7
Components: V, S, M
Casting Time: 1 action
Range: Touch
Target: One vampire touched
Duration: Special
Saving Throw: Will negates
Spell Resistance: Yes

The target must make a Will save or fall into the *eternal quiescence* for 1 year for each of your caster levels. If you have any of the target's blood, the DC to resist this spell is increased by +4.

Material Components: Ruby dust mixed with a pinch of raw Va'Vash.

INDUCING THE WILLING QUIESCENCE

Necromancy [BC]
Level: Sor/Wiz 5
Components: V, S, M
Casting Time: 1 action
Range: Personal
Target: Self
Duration: Special
Saving Throw: Will negates
Spell Resistance: Yes

You can voluntarily enter the *eternal quiescence*. You can state any one condition that will awaken you (example: *anyone entering my crypt*), but other than that, you will not awaken until the specified time period (as stated in the casting) has elapsed.

While sleeping, you do not lose any blood and can remain in the *black sleep* for as long as you wish. Many ensure they are sufficiently protected, and slumber for a single year, ten, or a thousand, awaking for brief periods every so often to see what is happening with the world. A successful *dispel magic* (against your caster level) will break the *black sleep* and cause you to awaken.

Material Components: A flawless jewel of no less than 5,000gp in value.

JOURNEY TO THE ARCH

Necromancy
Level: Sor/Wiz 5
Components: V, S, M
Casting Time: 1 action
Range: Personal
Target: Self
Duration: Instantaneous
Saving Throw: None
Spell Resistance: No

You can journey to the Arch. You must begin your casting at the moments before dawn, timing the spell's completion to the exact moment you fall into slumber. You will appear in the Necrotic Crypt from which you can enter a Katharein at any time by passing through the Arch (see Katharein p. 114).

Material Components: A precious stone of no less than 100gp in value wrapped in newly woven silk.

NECROMANCY'S DARK TRANSFIGURATION

Necromancy (conjuration)
Level: Sor/Wiz 9
Components: V, S
Casting Time: 1 action
Range: Touch
Target: All living creatures touched
Duration: 1 minute
Saving Throw: None
Spell Resistance: No

You can confer a single negative level upon all you can touch in one minute. You need but touch your victims to confer one (and only one) negative level upon them. To strike an unwilling target you must make a successful touch attack.

If you have the Dark Gift, Black Touch, you can drain as many levels as you could in a single attack, but you cannot drain more than a single attack's worth of levels on any one target in the spell's duration.

NEUTRAL COUNTENANCE

Necromancy
Level: Clr 6, Sor/Wiz 6
Components: V, S, M
Casting Time: 1 action
Range: Touch
Target: Creature touched
Duration: 1 hour/level
Saving Throw: None
Spell Resistance: No

You can occlude the necromantic energies surrounding a vampire. While in effect, a vampire gains a powerful resistance to being magically detected by others. Although he visibly remains a vampire, the magical energies around him seem to be those of a 0 level mortal.

If a divination is attempted against the warded creature the caster of the divination must succeed at a caster level check (1d20 + caster level) against a DC of 15 + the caster level of the spellcaster who cast the *neutral countenance* + their *age* category. To any failed scrying attempt, the vampire appears normal. Their magical energies are dull and grey, but they do not have any evidence of vampirism about them.

Material Components: A pint of warm mortal blood and a perfectly smooth sphere of obsidian.

Open Blood Gate

Conjuration
Level: Sor/Wiz 2
Components: V, S, M
Casting Time: 1 action
Range: Touch
Effect: 1 Blood Gate
Duration: Instantaneous
Saving Throw: None
Spell Resistance: No
You can unlock any Blood Gate you can touch. Most lead to the Plaza in Avystervan, although other exit points exist.

Material Components: A single point of attuned Blood.

Purge the Void

Necromancy
Level: Clr 2, Sor/Wiz 2
Components: V, S, F
Casting Time: 1 action
Range: Touch
Target: Vampire touched
Duration: 1 round/level
Saving Throw: None
Spell Resistance: No
When cast within 10 rounds of the death of an evil vampire, you can purge yourself of 1 plus the slain vampire's *age* category in Void points. You must have been personally involved in the destruction of the vampire to benefit from this spell. This spell is typically taught by the Arcane to fledgling vampires in exchange for favors.

Arcane Focus: A wand fashioned from the preserved bone of a lich.

Restore the Favored

Necromancy
Level: Clr 8, Sor/Wiz 9
Components: V, S, M, XP
Casting Time: 1 action
Range: Touch
Target: Vampire touched
Duration: Instantaneous
Saving Throw: None
Spell Resistance: No
You can restore a vampire to unlife if his heart remains. He will reform in 1d4 hours with his heart once again in his body. This spell is favored by the Devoted Incarnate.

Material Components: An exquisite ruby of no less than 1000gp in value dipped in gold dragon blood.

XP Cost: 500

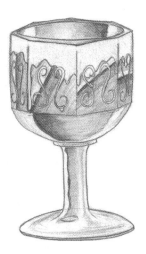

Scry the Blood

Divination [BC]
Level: Sor/Wiz 3
Components: V, S, M
Casting Time: 1 Action
Range: Touch
Target: 1 drop of blood touched
Duration: Instantaneous
Saving Throw: None
Spell Resistance: No
You can understand the nature of blood. Holding a drop of blood in your palm, you can ascertain the target's level(s), classes, hit points, any feats and Dark Gifts they may have. If the target is an arcane spellcaster, you can also ascertain the general types of spells they have learned, evocation, necromantic, etc.

Material Components: A drop of the target's blood.

Silent Charm

Abjuration
Level: Sor/Wiz 2
Components: V, S, M
Casting Time: special
Area: Lines of no greater than the caster's level in ft.
Duration: Permanent or until discharged
Saving Throw: None
Spell Resistance: No
This spell involves tracing a ward across any threshold in a vampire's lair. When anyone other than the designated creatures (as stated in the spell's casting) crosses the ward, the spell triggers, alerting the vampire to the intrusion. The silent charm attempts to rouse the vampire from sleep, granting a +8 bonus to their Waking check. If the spell fails to wake the vampire, he suffers only a -2 penalty to waking from sleep for the next 10 turns.

Note: You can tie this spell into a *contingency* spell (for example: it could *teleport* you from your current resting-place to another if your *place of rest* is disturbed).

Example: 'When the silent charm is triggered, teleport me to my safe haven.'

Material Components: A pinch of powdered silver mixed with mortal blood. This is traced across the threshold(s) the vampire wishes to ward with the *silent charm*.

Steal Blood

Necromancy [BC]
Level: Sor/Wiz 6
Components: V, S, M
Casting Time: 1 action
Range: Medium (100 ft. + 10ft./level)
Target: One mortal or vampire
Duration: Instantaneous
Saving Throw: Will negates
Spell Resistance: Yes
You can drain 1d6 (+1 per *age* category) points of Blood from a vampire, or 1d8 (+1 per *age* category) points of Constitution from a mortal.

Note: If the blood is stolen from a vampire who has both attuned and unattuned blood within them, blood stolen will be first drained from their supply of unattuned blood.

Material Components: A silver needle wrapped in crimson velvet.

Stifle the Chill

Necromancy
Level: Sor/Wiz 7
Components: V, S, M
Casting Time: 1 action
Range: Touch

Target: Person touched
Duration: 1 hour/level or until sunrise.
Saving Throw: Will negates
Spell Resistance: Yes

You can temporarily disassociate a vampire with their link to the Negative Energy Plane. This spell wholly prevents a vampire from using their energy drain powers or any necromantic based Dark Gifts. This spell fully negates the effects of the *Chill* and makes a vampire seem almost human. Although a vampire is barred from using their negative energy powers, they are still free to use their shapechanging or other vampiric abilities.

Note: The caster cannot cancel the spell until dawn when the spell naturally expires.

Material Component: A pint of fresh mortal blood.

Summon Blood Gate

Conjuration (Creation)
Level: Sor/Wiz 5
Components: V, S, M
Casting Time: 1 minute
Range: Close (25ft. +5 ft. /2 levels)
Effect: 1 portal of 5 ft. radius
Duration: 1 round/level
Saving Throw: None
Spell Resistance: No

You need but drip two points of your own Blood onto a smooth surface to conjure a Blood Gate. The Blood Gate manifests as a swirling portal of your own gore that remains in existence until the expiration of the spell. You must specify the exit Blood Gate during the casting of the spell. You can link to one Blood Gate for each of your caster levels but you must first journey to that location and expend three points of Blood to attune your magic to that Blood Gate (see Blood Gates p. 88). There are over a hundred such portals across the mortal realms, each with its own name. You can voluntarily lose a link to one Blood Gate to attune your magic to another.

Material Components: Two points of your own attuned Blood.

Summon Blood Leech

Conjuration (Summoning) [BC]
Level: Drd 4, Sor/Wiz 4
Components: V, S, F
Casting Time: 1 action
Range: Close (25 ft. + 5ft./level)
Effect: One or more summoned creatures
Duration: 5 rounds +2 rounds/level (D)
Saving Throw: None
Spell Resistance: No

You can summon your caster level in blood leeches. The blood leeches appear where you designate and act immediately. See blood leeches on p. 104.

Arcane Focus: A pearl for every blood leech conjured.

Summon the Necrotic Ally

Conjuration (Calling)
Level: Sor/Wiz 4
Components: V, S
Casting Time: 1 action
Range: Touch
Target: 1 ally summoned
Duration: Instantaneous
Saving Throw: None
Spell Resistance: No

This spell is identical to *call the necrotic allies*, but you may only call one ally to the Arch with each casting of the spell.

Summon Undead I

Conjuration (Summoning) [Faithful Undead]
Level: Clr/Drd 1, Sor/Wiz 1
Components: V, S, M, F
Casting Time: 1 action
Range: Close (25 ft. + 5ft./level)
Effect: One summoned creature
Duration: 1 round/level (D)
Saving Throw: None
Spell Resistance: No

This spell works as per all the spell *summon monster*, but summons undead from Vangual's domain (the *Black*) on the Negative Energy Plane. This spell is otherwise identical to *summon monster I*.

Arcane Focus: The heart of a mortal that has been dead for no longer than seven days.

Material Components: One drop of mortal blood for every creature summoned.

Summon Undead II

Conjuration (Summoning) [Faithful Undead]
Level: Clr/Drd 2, Sor/Wiz 2
Components: V, S, M, F
Casting Time: 1 action
Range: Close (25 ft. + 5ft./level)
Effect: One or more summoned creatures, no two of which can be more than 30 ft. apart.
Duration: 1 round/level (D)
Saving Throw: None
Spell Resistance: No

As *summon undead I*, except you can summon one undead from the 2nd level list, or 1d3 undead from the 1st level list.

Summon Undead III

Conjuration (Summoning) [Faithful Undead]
Level: Clr/Drd 3, Sor/Wiz 3
Components: V, S, M, F
Casting Time: 1 action
Range: Close (25 ft. + 5ft./level)
Effect: One or more summoned creatures, no two of which can be more than 30 ft. apart.
Duration: 1 round/level (D)
Saving Throw: None
Spell Resistance: No

As *summon undead I*, except you can summon one undead from the 3rd level list, or 1d3 undead of the same type from the 2nd level list or 1d4+1 creatures of the same type from the 1st level list.

Summon Undead IV

Conjuration (Summoning) [Faithful Undead]
Level: Clr/Drd 4, Sor/Wis 4
Components: V, S, M, F
Casting Time: 1 action
Range: Close (25 ft. + 5ft./level)
Effect: One or more summoned creatures, no two of which can be more than 30 ft. apart.
Duration: 1 round/level (D)
Saving Throw: None
Spell Resistance: No

As *summon undead I*, except you can summon one undead from the 4th level list, or 1d3 undead of the same type from the 3rd level list or 1d4+1 creatures of the same type from a lower level list.

Summon Undead V

Conjuration (Summoning) [Faithful Undead]
Level: Clr/Drd 5, Sor/Wiz 5
Components: V, S, M, F
Casting Time: 1 action
Range: Close (25 ft. + 5ft./level)
Effect: One or more summoned creatures, no two of which can be more than 30 ft. apart.
Duration: 1 round/level (D)
Saving Throw: None
Spell Resistance: No

As *summon undead I*, except you can summon one undead from the 5th level list, or 1d3 undead of the same type from the 4th level list or 1d4+1 creatures of the same type from a lower level list.

Arcane Focus: The heart of a mortal that has been dead for no longer than twenty four hours.

Summon Undead VI

Conjuration (Summoning) [Faithful Undead]
Level: Clr/Drd 6, Sor/Wiz 6
Components: V, S, M, F
Casting Time: 1 action
Range: Close (25 ft. + 5ft./level)
Effect: One or more summoned creatures, no two of which can be more than 30 ft. apart.
Duration: 1 round/level (D)
Saving Throw: None
Spell Resistance: No

As *summon undead I*, except you can summon one undead from the 6th level list, or 1d3 undead of the same type from the 5th level list or 1d4+1 creatures of the same type from a lower level list.

Arcane Focus: The heart of a mortal that has been dead for no longer than twenty four hours.

Summon Undead VII

Conjuration (Summoning) [Faithful Undead]
Level: Clr/Drd 7, Sor/Wiz 7
Components: V, S, M, F
Casting Time: 1 action
Range: Close (25 ft. + 5ft./level)
Effect: One or more summoned creatures, no two of which can be more than 30 ft. apart.
Duration: 1 round/level (D)
Saving Throw: None
Spell Resistance: No

As *summon undead I*, except you can summon one undead from the 7th level list, or 1d3 undead of the same type from the 6th level list or 1d4+1 creatures of the same type from a lower level list.

Arcane Focus: As *summon undead VI*.

Summon Undead VIII

Conjuration (Summoning) [Faithful Undead]
Level: Clr/Drd 8, Sor/Wiz 8
Components: V, S, M, F
Casting Time: 1 action
Range: Close (25 ft. + 5ft./level)
Effect: One or more summoned creatures, no two of which can be more than 30 ft. apart.
Duration: 1 round/level (D)
Saving Throw: None
Spell Resistance: No

As *summon undead I*, except you can summon one undead from the 8th level list, or 1d3 undead of the same type from the 7th level list or 1d4+1 creatures of the same type from a lower level list.

Arcane Focus: As *summon undead VI*.

Summon Undead IX

Conjuration (Summoning) [Faithful Undead]
Level: Clr/Drd 9, Sor/Wiz 9
Components: V, S, M
Casting Time: 1 action
Range: Close (25 ft. + 5ft./level)
Effect: One or more summoned creatures, no two of which can be more than 30 ft. apart.
Duration: 1 round/level (D)
Saving Throw: None
Spell Resistance: No

As *summon undead I*, except you can summon one undead from the 9th level list, or 1d3 undead of the same type from the 8th level list or 1d4+1 creatures of the same type from a lower level list.

Arcane Focus: As Summon Undead VI.

Touch the Mortal

Necromancy
Level: Sor/Wiz 3
Components: V, S, F
Casting Time: 1 action
Range: Touch
Target: Mortal touched
Duration: 1 round/level
Saving Throw: Yes
Spell Resistance: Yes

You can up to *twice touch* a mortal without having to physically bite them. The mortal must make Will save DC 15 + your *age* + Intelligence modifier. Failure results in nausea and disorientation for a round. This spell can only be cast once on the same mortal in every twenty four hour period. These bites do not count towards the *Black Kiss*. A vampire must perform a *visitation* on three separate occasions if he wants to create a true vampire.

Arcane Focus: A shard of silver and a blood pearl containing a point of *age* 2 or older vampire Blood.

Veil of Ash

Necromancy
Level: Sor/Wiz 9
Components: V, S, M
Casting Time: 1 action
Range: Personal
Effect: 10 ft. radius sphere of annihilation around the caster
Duration: 1 round/level
Saving Throw: Fortitude partial
Spell Resistance: No

This spell affects everything in a 10 ft. radius around you with an aura of destruction similar to the spell *disintegration*.

Arrows, missiles, even certain magical effects are utterly annihilated by this spell. Veil of Ash affects everything, from inanimate objects to living beings. It turns the ground around you to dust and slays 1 HD or fewer creatures instantly. Creatures in the spell's area of effect suffer the effects of the spell every round. This spell is otherwise identical to *disintegration* in every other way.

Material Component: A black diamond taken from the Ash Plane of no less than 1000gp value.

Wall of Blood

Conjuration (Creation) [BC]
Level: Clr 3, Sor/Wiz 3
Components: V, S, M
Casting Time: 1 action
Range: Close (25 ft. + 5ft./level)
Effect: Anchored plane of blood, up to 10 ft. x 1 ft. per level
Duration: 1 round/level (D)
Saving Throw: None
Spell Resistance: No

You expend a point of Blood to cause a wall of blood to spring up before you. The wall is viscous and immobile. Anyone stepping through it suffers 1 point of damage for each of your caster levels (no save).

Material Component: One Blood point.

Will of the Ages

Necromancy [BC]
Level: Sor/Wiz 9
Components: V, S, M, XP
Casting Time: 1 turn
Range: Touch
Target: Person touched
Duration: 1 hour per level
Saving Throw: None
Spell Resistance: Yes

You can increase the *age* of any vampire you touch. Powerful necromantic energies broil within your target, distilling their link to the dark powers and temporarily increasing their *age* category. You can only increase an *age* category by 1 per casting. The spell expires at dawn and cannot be cast again for 10 minus your *age* category in days. The effects of the spell stack but you cannot increase any vampire's *age* category above 5 with the use of this spell.

Arcane Material Components: A black diamond of no fewer than 5,000gp value that is destroyed in the casting.

Xp Cost: 200 XP.

SPELLS AND DOMAINS

BLACK PALLIUM DOMAIN

Granted Power: Once per day for 1 round/level, the caster can assume partial undead form. The caster gains the trait *undead* and has all the powers and abilities associated therein. They can be affected by holy items and magic in the same way as any of the undead.

Note: If a turning attempt would normally destroy the character, the character is returned to normal and is suffers -4 to all actions for 1d4+1 rounds.

1. Spider Climb
2. Darkvision
3. Gaseous Form
4. Polymorph Self
5. Dominate Person
6. Eyebite
7. Control Undead
8. Mass Charm
9. Energy Drain

BLOOD DOMAIN

Granted Power: You cast Blood spells at +1 caster level.

1. Blood Dart
2. Blood Bolt
3. Blood Geyser
4. Wall of Blood
5. Blood Bite
6. Blood Curse
7. Blood Fire
8. Circle of Pain
9. Exsanguinate

FAITHFUL UNDEAD DOMAIN

Granted Power: You may cast any one Faithful Undead spell with twice the normal duration, once per day.

1. Summon Undead I
2. Summon Undead II
3. Summon Undead III
4. Summon Undead IV
5. Summon Undead V
6. Summon Undead VI
7. Summon Undead VII
8. Summon Undead VIII
9. Summon Undead IX

HARM DOMAIN

Granted Power: You cast Harm spells at +1 caster level.

1. Cause Light Wound
2. Cause Moderate Wound
3. Cause Serious Wound
4. Cause Critical Wound
5. Circle of Lesser Harm
6. Circle of Harming
7. Circle of Greater Harm
8. Bleeding
9. Circle of Maleficence

BLACK CABAL SPELLS

0. Corpus Enhancement
1. Hand of Blood
2. Attune the Blood
3. Blood Hound, Conjure Bloodling, Drain Blood, Increase the Bloody Receptacle, Scry the Blood, Wall of Blood
4. Circle of Blood, Summon Blood Leech
5. Cloak of Blood, Create Consanguineous Vampire, Inducing the Willing Quiescence
6. Steal Blood
7. Consanguineous Curse, Inducing the Black Sleep
8. Boil Blood
9. Will of the Ages

FAITHFUL UNDEAD SUMMONING LIST

1st Level: Medium Skeleton, Small Zombie
2nd Level: Large Skeleton, Ghoul, Medium Zombie
3rd Level: Allip, Blood Elemental, Small, Shadow
4th Level: Blood Ooze, Huge Skeleton, Ghast, Wight, Large Zombie
5th: Level: Blood Elemental, Medium-size, Ghost, Vampire Ghoul, Wraith
6th: Level: Blood Elemental, Large, Mummy
7th Level: Blood Elemental, Huge, Spectre, Feral Vampire
8th Level: Blood Elemental Greater, Huge, Huge Zombie
9th Level: Blood Elemental, Elder, Huge, Bodak

Chapter Seven: Magical Items

d%	Item	Market Price (gp)
01-10	Blood Pearl	500
11-12	Blood Talisman	5,000
13-14	Consanguine Chalice	120,000
15	Elixir of the Radiant Mortality	5,000
16-17	Elixir of the Void	5,000
18-25	Glowering Cloak	12,000+
26	Heart of Blood	-
27-30	Incarnadine Vestibule	2,000
31-35	Manual of the Simulacrum	60,000
36-45	Phial of the Stable Pabulum	1,000
46	Philtre of the Forbidden Transmutation	50,000
47-50	Potion of the Nosferatu	-
51-55	Ring of the Necromantic Countenance	30,000
56-60	Ring of Repulsion	5,000
61	Salubrious Chalice	60,000
62-70	Shadow Clothing	1,000
71-75	Shroud of Darkness	5,000
76-85	Talisman of Corpus	2,000
86-89	Vampire Dust	-
90-91	Vampiric Coffins	10,000
92	Vampiric Shadow Armor	-
93	Vampiric Weapons	Varies
94	Va'Vash	Varies
95-00	Volkath	85

Blood Pearl

The Blood Pearl is a magical item that can store normal or attuned blood for a vampire. Created by alchemists and wizards, it can be used as a source of blood when a vampire is far from civilisation. They appear as milky white pearls, yet when filled with a point of blood, become glistening rubies. A vampire need to place the pearl to his lips to absorb the blood, or to imbue a pearl with some of his own. Some wealthy vampires have bags of these pearls, enough attuned Blood to last for weeks.

Caster Level: 8, **Prerequisites:** Craft Wondrous Item, *cause light wound*, **Market Price:** 500gp, **Weight:** -.

Blood Talisman

These ornate pendants allow a vampire to store Dark Gifts in the form of attuned Blood within the crimson jewel at their centre. A vampire can imbue a Blood Talisman with any Dark Gifts he knows up to the Talisman's Blood Value. The Blood Value is the maximum amount of Blood a talisman can store at any one time (typically between 5 and 20 points).

Imbuing: To imbue a Blood Talisman with a Dark Gift costs five times the *age* category of the Dark Gift in Blood (or 3 Blood for age 0 Dark Gifts). If a Dark Gift does not have a duration, the duration is 10 minutes multiplied by the *age* of the imbuing vampire.

Example: Imbuing a Blood Talisman with the Dark Gift, Spider Climb would cost the vampire 3 points of Blood per Spider Climb added. To imbue Resistance to Turning (age 3) would cost 15 Blood. All powers work as if the imbuing vampire were actively using the power.

Use: Anyone can use a Blood Talisman. To activate the device requires a free action on the part of the bearer and costs either one Blood or 1 point or temporary point of Constitution.

Caster Level: 9, **Prerequisites:** Craft Wondrous Item, *imbue with spell ability*, **Market Price:** 5,000gp; **Weight:** -.

Consanguine Chalice

Providing at least half of their ashes can be recovered, this chalice will completely restore a vampire from their *Second Death*. The remains are placed in the chalice and mixed with fresh virgin blood. The vampire will rise again, within 1d8 hours. If the sun rises before the resurrection is complete, the process fails and the vampire is forever destroyed. There is no limit to the time vampire dust can remain dormant before being restored in a *Consanguine Chalice*.

Caster Level: 12, **Prerequisites:** Craft Wondrous Item, Raise Dead, **Market Price:** 120,00gp, **Weight:** 2lbs.

Elixir of the Radiant Mortality

This very rare potion allows the vampire to seem wholly mortal until sunrise. Although they maintain their vampiric strength and speed, they cannot use their energy drain powers, nor any necromantic based abilities. They can still use any power that requires blood to use.

If a divination is attempted against the concealed vampire the caster of the divination must succeed at a caster level check (1d20+caster level) against a DC of 30. Powerful characters may make a Sense Motive check at DC 40. DC 30 for powerful holy characters. Even characters who sense something is amiss with the character may not know exactly what, only that there is something strange and that a 'darkness' surrounds them.

Caster Level: 15, **Prerequisites:** Brew Potion, *veil*, **Market Price:** 5,000gp, **Weight:** -.

Elixir of the Void

This glimmering potion allows the drinker to remove 2d4 points of Void. The necromantic energies in these potions are powerful. Use of two or more potions in a single month result in all effects being negated and the drinker gaining 1d4 points of Void. Both rare and expensive, these potions are crafted by liches in Kethak.

Caster Level: 15, **Prerequisites:** Brew Potion, *restoration*, **Market Price:** 5,000gp, **Weight:** -.

Glowering Cloak

This ragged black cloak stinks of death and decay. When worn by a vampire, it allows certain protection against sunlight and holy spells. Made by the Black Cabal, they are rare indeed.

* Against holy spells, it grants the vampire +2 to all saves and the wearer takes half damage from all holy/goodly aligned spells.
* It has more power against sunlight. It will allow a vampire to remain awake in sunlight for up to 2 hours per month. Vampires only suffer -2 to actions during the day while wearing the cloak (but can still only take partial actions). Additionally, it will reduce the effects of sunlight. A vampire can stand an additional 2 rounds in the sun before being destroyed. However, once a glowering cloak has absorbed 10 full rounds of sunlight, it dissolves entirely and can never be used again.

A mortal wearing one of these cloaks (not advised due to the foul smell) must make a Fortitude Save (DC 20) or be immediately slain. **Caster Level (Greater):** 12, **Prerequisites:** Craft Wondrous Item, *dark aura, deeper darkness,* **Market Price:** 30,000gp, **Weight:** 5lb.

Glowering Cloak - Lesser

Lesser cloaks are made by the vampire guilds that have not yet mastered the art of creating greater Glowering Cloaks.

* Against holy spells, it grants the vampire +1 to all saves and the wearer takes normal damage from holy/goodly aligned spells
* A vampire can remain awake in sunlight for up to 1 hour per month. Additionally, it will reduce the effects of sunlight, a vampire can stand an additional 1 round in sunlight before being destroyed. However, once it has absorbed 5 full rounds of sunlight, it dissolves entirely and can never be used again.

Mortals wearing these cloaks suffer the same effect as above (DC 15). Whether they save or not, they take 8d8 points of necromantic damage and the cloak is destroyed.

Caster Level (Lesser): 9, **Prerequisites:** Craft Wondrous Item, *dark aura, darkness,* **Market Price:** 12,000gp, **Weight:** 5lb.

Heart of Blood

These powerful artefacts are unique, created for a vampire by the master Agoravaal for special services rendered to the Black Cabal. The Heart looks like a metallic bloody sphere, and replaces a vampire's own decayed heart. It has the following powers:

* Increases a vampire's *age* category by +1 (maximum of *age* 5). This costs a permanent reduction in the vampire's Blood score by the *age* category to which they have advanced.
* Allows a vampire to survive for twice the number of rounds in sunlight. The Heart of Blood allows a vampire to endure sunlight for his *age* category in rounds before he starts to take any damage.
* Gives a vampire a +6 blood store in which he can store any blood he desires.
* A vampire can only be destroyed if his Heart of Blood is shattered. Each Heart is different; magical spells or weapons will not break them. Their destruction should be tied in to a quest of some considerable difficulty.

Creation Notes: These items cannot be bought, and only Agoravaal knows the secret of their creation. **Weight:** 2lb.

Incarnadine Vestibule

This device is made from a lurid crimson metal. It is designed to store a vampire's heart. The vampire must first have their hearts removed (typically by a willing member of the Devoted Incarnate who have perfected the ritual). A jewel of no less than 1000gp value is placed where the vampire's heart was, and the remains of the heart are placed in the vestibule.

Without a heart, a vampire cannot be staked. A vampire will be destroyed should their heart be destroyed. The Divine Incarnate have a vault filled with vampire hearts, all stored in Incarnadine Vestibules. Perhaps it is a way of controlling their faithful. Many vampires outside the Devoted Incarnate that have removed their hearts place the vestibule in a very safe place indeed.

Caster Level: 12, **Prerequisites:** Craft Wondrous Item, *create undead;* **Market Price:** 2,000gp; **Weight:** 2lbs.

Manual of the Simulacrum

These tomes allow a vampire to create a Blood Simulacrum, a powerful altered mortal for use as bodyguard and servant. The tome can only be used by a character of 12 HD or greater and requires a full month to comprehend. The process requires a suitable mortal and a full month to complete the transformation. It requires a total of 30 points of attuned Blood and at least one thousand gold pieces times the HD of the victim to be transformed into the simulacrum. It also requires several organs of rare and magical creatures (as determined randomly by the Manual). Vampire simulacra are detailed on p. 103.

Caster Level: 15, **Prerequisites:** Craft Wondrous Item, *animate dead,* **Market Price:** 60,000gp, **Weight:** 2lbs.

Phial of the Stable Pabulum

This clear glass or earthenware container is about the size of a holy water vial. It can store any liquid, although only fresh blood triggers its magic. Any blood poured into a phial will stay fresh and warm for hundreds, if not thousands of years. The storage capacity of a phial depends on the container from which it was created. A standard phial can typically store two blood, although greater phials have been created that can store up to ten.

Phials of the stable pabulum radiate powerful necromantic magic and can only be crafted by the Black Cabal, who invented them for the purpose of vampiric trade. It is said there is a vault deep within the Black Cabal's obsidian tower that is filled with thousands upon thousands of phials of varying types of blood.

Caster Level: 9, **Prerequisites:** Craft Wondrous Item, *permanency,* **Market Price:** 1000gp, **Weight:** -.

Philtre of the Forbidden Transmutation

Using vampire dust and high quantities of blood, these elixirs instantly slay the drinker who rises up as a vampire 1d4 nights later. Contact with the black and viscous liquid confers two negative levels upon a mortal. Even smelling it bestows a single negative level (DC 14 to resist). *Philtres of the Forbidden Transmutation* are very rare and their secret is known only to a handful of vampires and liches. Many have been confiscated by the clerics of the sun god, who keep them safe in temples across the mortal realms.

Caster Level: 15, **Prerequisites:** Craft Wondrous Item, *finger of death,* **Market Price:** 50,000gp, **Weight:** -.

Potion of the Nosferatu

This rare potion allows a PC to become a vampire for a short time. The effect wears off shortly before dawn, but grants the drinker **all** the powers and weaknesses of a fledgling vampire. However, they are not true vampires and will be destroyed should their hit point total be reduced to zero. Being partially mortal, they gain +4 to turning attempts against them, and where a cleric would otherwise destroy them, the magic is instantly dispelled, with the mortal making a Fortitude save DC 20 or falling into a deep unconsciousness for 1d8 hours.

Note: An old or powerful vampire may be aware that there is something amiss about the fledgling vampire. They will certainly radiate considerable necromantic and illusory magic.

Caster Level: 15, **Prerequisites:** Brew Potion, *finger of death, restoration,* **Market Price:** N/A, **Weight:** -.

Ring of the Necromantic Countenance

This ring, bound by necromancy makes the wearer look exactly like a vampire. Powerful illusion magic makes the wearer look dead, while necromantic magics surrounds the wearer with a vampiric aura. The character will seem cold and dead, and radiating the *Chill of the Grave*. Under normal circumstances, this will be enough to fool most unsuspecting vampires.

A Sense Motive check (DC 25) will reveal the character to be something out of the ordinary. Exceptional vampires (especially those with the Dark Gift, Sense) might be able to perceive the illusion.
Caster Level: 15, **Prerequisites:** Craft Ring, *conceal the nosferatu*, **Market Price:** 30,000gp, **Weight:** -.

Ring of Repulsions

This ring repels water, of any kind. While worn, each single attack by water is repelled as if by the spell *aura of repulsions*. These rings typically have 20 charges.
Caster Level: 7, **Prerequisites:** Craft Ring, *protection from elements*, **Market Price:** 5,000gp, **Weight:** -.

Salubrious Chalice

This dark magical item allows a vampire to brew blood to create a powerful restorative. Once per month when filled with blood it has the following properties:

❊ **Unholy Restoration:** Will restore a vampire to health - healing all wounds and disabilities.

❊ **Black Strength:** The elixir will also imbue a vampire with strength, granting them +4 to their saves against holy magic and adding +4 to their turning resistance. This lasts until the vampire next sleeps.

❊ **Black Mantle:** Allows a vampire to remain alert during the day (but they still suffer all the standard daytime penalties). This elixir must be prepared in advance, and a vampire can only spend one full day per month awake. Further attempts to remain awake will result in the brew failing and the chalice not working for 1d4 months.

❊ **Blood Store:** Finally the chalice can store up to six points of blood within it that will remain fresh for a year and a day. To do this means that the chalice cannot be used for anything else other than storage. The blood can be drunk or used to brew an elixir, but when removed from the chalice, immediately clots and is useless (unless drunk immediately by the vampire).

Notes: It costs six points of Blood to fill the chalice and each power can work but once in every monthly cycle. Each potion takes a full hour to distil within the chalice.
Caster Level: 15, **Prerequisites:** Craft Wondrous Item, *darkness*, *harm*, **Market Price:** 60,000gp, **Weight:** 1lb.

Shadow Clothing

Vampire drow hold the secret to crafting shadow clothing: magical garments fashioned from cloth woven on the Shadow Plane. These clothes appear to be sewn from midnight. When used by a vampire, neither their clothes nor the undead will make so much as a footfall. A full set of these clothes grants the wearer +8 to their Move Silently checks. A shadow cloak grants the wearer +8 to their Hide in darkness checks, and +4 to standard Hide checks.
Caster Level: 5, **Prerequisites:** Craft Wondrous Item, *silence*, **Market Price:** 1,000gp, **Weight:** 2lbs.

Shroud of Darkness

Allows limited protection against sunlight. Vampires wearing these rare cloaks are surrounded by an aura of sheer pitch. Even vampiric vision is hazy through the darkness. They can, however, move freely under the protection of the cloak for 1 turn per point of Blood expended. Vampires still suffer the same penalties to their actions while the sun is in the sky. When the cloak has absorbed 1 full hour of sunlight it is forever destroyed.
Caster Level: 15, **Prerequisites:** Craft Wondrous Item, *darkness*, **Market Price:** 10,000gp, **Weight:** 1lb.

Talisman of Corpus

This amulet prevents a vampire from being staked. It shatters anything pressed against the vampire's chest and typically has 20 charges.
Caster Level: 9, **Prerequisites:** Craft Wondrous Item, *shatter*, **Market Price:** 2,000gp, **Weight:** -.

Vampire Dust

The remains of a vampire, used in magical research by wizards the world over. If enough of the dust remains, a vampire can be fully restored by use of certain spells or magical items.

Vampiric Coffins

Lockable from the inside, these coffins are magically protected. Dispel magic or opening spells have no effect; they are designed to be impenetrable. They take a tremendous amount of damage to break open and only magical weapons of +2 or greater will have any effect. A sleeping vampire will always be roused by a forcible entry into their coffin. They can then choose how they will react to this. Vampiric coffins are very expensive and only the most affluent can afford them. Hardness: **40**   Hit Points: **100**
Caster Level: 12, **Prerequisites:** Craft Wondrous Item, *ironwood*, **Market Price:** 10,000gp, **Weight:** 200lbs.

Vampire Shadow Armor

The vampire artificers of Avystervan jealously guard the secret of this armor's creation. It has the appearance of black metal with a bloody sheen, and wisps of darkness pour from it.

Shadow Armor attaches itself to the wearer's flesh, biting into their skin with razor-sharp barbs. Donning it is a complicated process and requires 10 full minutes to do so. It cannot be hurried. Removing the armor requires a special bladed tool and around 30 minutes. Each segment must be prised from the wearer's skin causing 1d4 points of damage in the process.

When worn, the Shadow Armor drains 1 point of Blood and its AC level in hit points that cannot be recovered until twenty four hours after the armor has been removed.

As light as silk, Shadow Armour acts as any form of armor, from simple leather up to full plate. Forged from shadow, it is only half-substantial. It confers protection as traditional armor, yet has the penalties of studded leather. It must absorb 1 point of blood per day plus an additional point for each of its magical plusses. If it cannot get its full requirement, it loses 1 point of AC per day. Vampiric Shadow Armor that falls to 0 AC turns to dust.

A vampire can absorb blood from his shadow armor, gaining 1d12 hit points for every point of AC drained. He can do this as a move-equivalent action, but can only drain 1 point of AC per round.

A successful turning attempt against the vampire also drains 1 point of AC from Vampiric Shadow Armor. Holy water harms not only the vampire, but also causes 1d2 points of AC damage as does a light spell. The armor loses 1d3 points of AC for every round it spends in Bright Sunlight and 1d2 at any other time.

Vampire Shadow Armor cannot be bought, it must be made for an individual vampire, typically those of the order of Blood Knights. If the armor is worn by a mortal, it does nothing until it is fully in place, then drains 1d4 points of Constitution per round until it is removed. Dhampyre can wear Vampiric Shadow Armor.

Caster Level: 20, **Prerequisites:** Craft Magic Arms and Armor, *create undead, harm,* **Market Price:** N/A, **Weight:** As studded leather.

Vampiric Weapons

Vampiric weapons are magical items imbued with the necromantic energies of the undead. They are typically fashioned from the souls of vampires who have failed Vangual; sentenced to an eternity bound to an inanimate object. Forged on the Planes of Ash and Negativity, they have multiple powers, yet as potent as they are, they also have considerable disadvantages.

Requirements

Most vampiric weapons drain at least 1 point of Constitution from their owner and (x) hit points at nightfall. Constitution is restored after one full week of relief from the weapon. The weakest weapons drain 1d4 hit points, the most powerful 1d12 hit points per night (a lesser character could feasibly die from picking up one of these weapons). These hit points cannot be healed by any means. Only the toughest of characters can withstand the drain the most powerful vampiric weapons place upon a mortal. This damage is not caused in melee, only when a character picks up a weapon of their own volition and holds it for more than 1 round.

Shadowcrafting

Fabricated by liches who hoard the secret of their creation, they transfer the essence from captured (or willing) vampires into these weapons. The secret of this and the vampiric items is known as shadowcrafting and is known only to various liches. The older the vampire, the more powerful the weapon.

Powers

These weapons can drain negative levels, pass hit points to their owner, even grant them Strength and Constitution, drained from their victims. They can also confer some vampire powers to the wielder. These swords can normally only be used by one owner, although anyone who comes into flesh contact with the weapon will suffer the contact for touching the weapon (taking hit points damage).

The most powerful of these items have very strong wills that can devour the will of a lesser character. Additionally, these weapons may desire the wielder to perform other actions - for example: most require the flesh or blood of a mortal at least once per day.

Notes: All weapons are dependent on the bound vampire and the crafter who made it. Vampire weapons are priceless and even lesser items sell for many thousands of gold pieces.

Caster Level: 15, **Prerequisites:** Craft Magic Arms and Armor, *control undead, imprisonment, curse of vampirism,* **Market Price:** Varies (but very high), **Weight:** as weapon.

VAMPIRIC WEAPON: ANDAVAAL

HISTORY

Andavaal has had many owners, although none can claim to be its master. The sword has a powerful will of its own, and many of its previous bearers have fallen to its dark desires. In unlife, *Andavaal* was a bloodthirsty and despicable vampire. He lived only for battle - to drink upon the life essence of the purest mortals. The sword is no different: it will do all it can to accomplish this aim.

Some say that Arikostinaal himself bound the ancient vampire into the sword as punishment for devouring one of his most promising mortal students.

DESCRIPTION

Andavaal is a longsword with a black leather hilt and a blood-red jewel set into the pommel. The blade flickers with crimson when unsheathed and seems to pulse with the beating of an ancient heart when in melee. When it takes a life, *Andavaal* bursts into bloodlight and droplets of blood roll from the blade.

POWERS

At night *Andavaal* is a *keen* +4 Longsword. The bearer cannot be disarmed while using *Andavaal.* It grants a bonus of +2 to both Strength and Dexterity and +4 bonus to AC. The wielder can use the Dark Gifts, Spider Climb and Gaseous Form a total of thrice per day and can cause bloodlight as the spell, cast as a 12th level sorcerer at will. Lastly the wielder regenerates 1 hit point per round.

OTHER POWERS

Every 12 hit points damage *Andavaal* inflicts in a single attack (or on every natural 20), *Andavaal* confers a negative level upon the target and grants 5 temporary hit points to the bearer and adds +1 to their Strength and Dexterity for 2d4 rounds. These temporary hit points remain for 1 hour.

✿ During the day but underground *Andavaal* is a +1 longsword with no other powers.

✿ During the day in sunlight *Andavaal* is a -4 longsword.

✿ When *Andavaal* so chooses, any bearer cannot easily use another sword or discard *Andavaal.* To lay down the sword a character must make a Willpower save DC 25. Failure means they are unwilling to use any sword other than *Andavaal. Andavaal* can consciously choose to lower this compulsion at any time.

✿ *Andavaal* can exert a compulsion over the bearer during the hours of darkness. He can force the bearer to do his bidding as per the *domination* spell (DC 25 to resist). He can only make one such attempt per night.

REQUIREMENTS

Andavaal drains 1d10 hit points of damage per day at nightfall from its current bearer or from anyone that holds it for more than one minute. These hit points cannot be healed by any means other than naturally. It requires (reduces) 2 points of mortal Constitution or 4 points of Blood from a vampire per day.

Va'Vash

Va'Vash in its natural state is a bluish-black crystalline deposit found only on the Ash Plane. Collected by Ash Vampires and distilled by the Ravenous, Va'Vash has a powerful effect on both mortals and vampires alike. When properly brewed, it takes one of three forms, depending on its purity and the skill of the alchemist. It can appear as liquid, oil or powder and can be delivered in an attack, by contact, ingestion or inhalation.

Va'Vash

Red Va'Vash: Dulls a vampire's senses making them intoxicated. While influenced by Red Va'Vash, a vampire suffers a penalty of -4 to all of their actions.

Duration: 1d4 hours
Difficulty: 15
Cost: 500gp

Grey Va'Vash: Strips a vampire of many of their magical qualities. They lose access to their Supernatural (Su) powers, Dark Gifts, and can only use Extraordinary (Ex) abilities. They suffer -2 to all of their actions due to the disorienting qualities of Va'Vash.

Duration 2d4 hours
Difficulty 20
Cost: 1000gp

Black Va'Vash: A vampire ingesting black Va'Vash automatically collapses into the *black sleep*. He may make a Will save twenty four hours later to attempt to waken (DC 25). If he fails, he slumbers for 2d8 years per dose of Va'Vash.

Duration: * Varies
Difficulty: 25
Cost: 10,000gp

The Effects of Va'Vash

A vampire receives no save against Va'Vash that is ingested or inhaled, the effects directly attack their necromantic energies.

When using Va'Vash as a contact poison, a vampire gains a Fortitude save to avoid its effects (DC as to create Va'Vash).

It is very difficult to force a vampire to inhale. They do not breathe unless they are speaking. They get to make a Reflex save (DC10) to avoid any airborne attacks, even if the attack was successful.

Note: Va'Vash is highly addictive. Many vampires become hooked on it, and a number of guilds use Va'Vash to control their vampires.

Va'Vash and Mortals

Giving any form of Va'Vash to a mortal makes them drowsy and confers 2 negative levels instantly upon them (DC to remove as to create Va'Vash). If a vampire feeds from a Va'Vash polluted mortal, they immediately suffer the effects of the Va'Vash without any save.

The Forbidden Drug

Black Va'Vash has been used on several powerful vampires over the years and is expressly forbidden on pain of *Second Death* in Avystervan. The *Occularum* in Avystervan can sense the presence of Black Va'Vash within 100 yards.

Caster Level: N/A, **Prerequisites:** None, **Market Price:** As above, **Weight:** -.

> *"A pint of blood laced with Red Va'Vash is just about the only way I can get through the day."*
> Canton Derrin, Lost Vampire

Volkath

A volkath is a Vangaard weapon. A great scythe-like blade, the volkath has grooves running down each side of the weapon to collect blood. The Volkath requires a Strength of 18 to wield properly.

A volkath is a double weapon. You can fight with it as if fighting with two weapons, but if you do, you incur all the normal attack penalties associated with fighting with two weapons, as if you were wielding a one-handed weapon and a light weapon. A creature using a double weapon in one hand can't use it as a double weapon.

Volkath: Exotic Weapon

Cost: 80gp
Damage: 2d4/2d4
Critical: 19/20 x4
Range Increment: -
Weight: 35 lb.
Type: Slashing and Piercing

CHAPTER EIGHT: AVYSTERVAN THE CITY OF GRAVES

Avystervan (Av-Iss-Ter-Van) is a sanctuary where the oldest and most powerful vampires live in safety. A haven for the undead, the *City of Graves* is the vampiric seat of power and mortal home to the Black Council. It is a realm of screams and dark practices, forbidden gods and blood sacrifices.

Located several miles under the ruins of the still-smouldering city of Veil, Avystervan consists of just over five hundred homes, houses, taverns and shops. It lies in a vast cavern, wreathed in secret and shadow in the depths of the underworld. Cobbled streets and gothic architecture fill the darkness, remnants of beautiful dwarven construction and a civilisation long since faded to dust.

After their banishment from the mortal realms, the ancient First fled into the earth, coming upon a band of duergar working on what was then a much smaller cavern. They transformed their first captives into vampire slaves and set them to creating the city of darkness that is now Avystervan. Some of the dark dwarves are still in existence, building even now in the far-off depths of the underworld.

For two thousand years the city has slowly decayed. The buildings succumb to the persistent touch of time, losing more of their character with every passing century. A haze of ancient dust lingers in the air and everything has a solemn feel, as though the ages have passed Avystervan by. The world changes, yet the *City of Graves* remains the same.

Avystervan is a black city - the buildings are designed to appeal to an eye that cannot perceive color. Arched ceilings, intricately carved doors, wrought iron gates and stone carved by hands that lived over two thousand years ago are the norm.

Avystervan feels ancient. Claustrophobic darkness presses heavily upon the city. Crumbling gargoyles peer down through ever-present mist and age worn statues with empty eyes stand at every corner. The streets are narrow, only two can walk abreast. As space is limited, many buildings are narrow, but made up of many floors. The more affluent can afford to build in the new caverns some distance from the main city, but this is only for the very wealthy.

A great number of vampires come to Avystervan when they have lived out the lives of many mortals. With cooling blood, they grow weary of life, choosing to reside where they can live out their nights without fear of the day or being pursued by endless vampire hunters. As the sun is far from Avystervan, many vampires find they only need to sleep for a short period each day. Many even deeper under ground find they never need to sleep at all.

But not only the undead live in the *City of Graves*. For the living, it is a place of great suffering. Mortals are bred in captivity, providing a wealth of food and slaves for the community. These folk are usually sickly and weak, pale from lack of sunlight, their wills utterly crushed. Many of them have never known anything but captivity, and most do not know how to speak any language other than a smattering of vampiric. When they get too old and no longer keep their taste, they are destroyed or given to the *mocked* for their amusement.

Humans are bred in pits and branded at birth with a necromantic mark that can be seen by those with darkvision. Given ranks, from *food* or *pet* to *personal servant*, they have precious few liberties and are often kept apart even from others of their own kind. Treated like animals, they have little chance of escaping their captivity. Slaves that must move about the city are given faintly glowing rocks to light their way. Each glows with just enough *bloodlight* for them to see without blinding even the most light sensitive of vampires. Valued mortals are kept *thrice touched* so they gain a fragment of their master's powers (mainly the ability to see in the dark). Even fewer mortals are turned into vampires: they must have exceptional gifts indeed to be elevated from slavery.

PROTECTION

The city is protected against scrying and divination by powerful enchantments. Arcane sorcery, the province of liches, wards against intrusion on a variety of levels and hampers those would magically transport themselves within Avystervan's boundaries.

Avystervan's greatest protection is that it is kept secret from the *Powers of Light*. Its location is known only to a select number of mortals or by those who trade in the rarest of knowledge. To most it is a rumor, a work of fiction imagined by the most twisted bards.

HISTORY

Since their descent into darkness, the Ancients subjugated the duergar, the drow and anyone else who came too close to the foundations of their dark sanctuary. They guarded their new territory fiercely, gaining the enmity of both the drow and the Mind Flayers in the process. What they could not 'turn', they destroyed. After sustaining massive casualties in the first retaliatory strikes against the city, both the drow and the Mind Flayers gave orders for Avystervan to be left well alone. They ordered the *City of Graves* out of bounds. Within a century the Children of Vangual controlled the underworld for a hundred miles in every direction.

GETTING TO AVYSTERVAN

Finding Avystervan is difficult. Miles of tunnels in the underworld mean danger for any that do not know the way. Terrible things lurk in the darkness; creatures even the Children of Vangual fear. The safest route to the city is through a Blood Gate, although one must have a wizard that knows the correct spells to gain access to such magic. Many merchants hire vampire wizards for regular transport to and from Avystervan. The most frequently used Blood Gates lie in the largest cities, where a merchant can conduct his activities without attracting any unnecessary attention to himself. Wherever the Children of Vangual have insinuated themselves, there will be a Blood Gate lurking in the darkness, somewhere...

Gaining entry to Avystervan without invitation is not easy. There are guard posts stationed at every entrance to the city, manned by powerful undead, as well as at least one member of the Blood Guard - the powerful anti-paladins of Vangual. Magical Wards lie across many tunnels - their powers ranging from powerful defensive magic to divination - scrying for intruders and those who would mean the city harm. The Blood Guard are ever prepared for attack, whether from the outside world, or by invasion from within.

The city's greatest threat, the drow are ever watchful. While Avystervan is no longer actively bringing drow into the fold, the dark elves will never forget their huge losses suffered centuries ago, and they have very long memories indeed.

While the magical protections of the city are placed squarely in the hands of the Black Cabal, Avystervan is physically defended by the Blood Guard. These vampiric warriors in their shadow armor are formidable opponents - yet the *City of Graves* has more than just vampiric eyes looking outwards…

The Occularum

The *Occularum* are magical globes of trailing shadow that patrol the city and its tunnels. How many there are none can say, but wherever there is trouble, the *Occularum* can be found, watching almost invisibly from the shadows. They are allegedly controlled by the lich Arikostinaal, although only the Black Council knows the truth. Getting past the *Occularum* is all but impossible. They can see magically, perceive alignment, spiritual auras and necromantic forces. They make a deep humming when they get close and the air seems to vibrate as they pass. Although the *Occularum* watch the world around the city, they also take a great interest in the happenings of certain organisations and the vampires within Avystervan. Many suspect the controlling force behind the *Occularum* has its own agenda. Certainly talk of any importance ceases when the *Occularum* are about.

The *Occularum* can sense magic of any kind. Any spell cast (beyond the Obsidian Tower) will have an *Occularum* at that location within 1d4 rounds. The *Occularum* do nothing; they merely observe; yet within a matter of seconds a contingent of Blood Guard at any location within the city. In Avystervan, eyes are *always* watching...

The City of Graves

The cavern in which Avystervan stands is fashioned from smooth black rock. There are some pointed stalactites that hang down from the ceiling, but generally the cavern is smooth and dry. The main chamber spans a little over five hundred feet across with a number of satellite chambers encircling it. There are a number of magically crafted tunnels that lead into the city and on to other regions of the underworld, namely drow settlements and places deeper and much darker underground.

Towers, gothic buildings, monoliths and strange edifices stand in Avystervan, monuments to forgotten gods and ancient powers. The cityscape is a mixture of towers, pointed turrets, black stone statues and ornate spires. Occasionally the clashing of an ancient gong or chime of an age worn bell can be heard echoing through the silence.

The most noticeable building in Avystervan is the black temple to Vangual. Reaching right up to the cavern roof, the grotesque pyramid continually drips blood, a reminder of the dark sacrifices that occur within…

Equally noticeable is the gnarled tower of Arikostinaal. Reaching almost up the roof of the cavern, the tower was transported magically into Avystervan almost two thousand years ago and has stood precariously ever since, magic all that prevents it from toppling over entirely.

The Plaza lies just before the steps to the Black Temple: a wide expanse of smooth stone surrounded by the largest buildings in the city. At the centre of the Plaza, the portal to the Citadel stands, a wide arch of polished obsidian filled with roiling darkness. Stepping through the portal transports the traveler instantly to the Negative Energy Plane and the Citadel, the seat of the ancient First's power.

Around the Plaza are many taverns catering to the exotic and the depraved, the most famous being the Broken Vein. There are many shops catering for all tastes, some selling standard goods (such as mortal food) as well as mundane items and other essentials. Other establishments sell more exotic wares: slaves, magical items, works of art, or even *Red Va'Vash*. *Red Va'Vash* is not prohibited in Avystervan; if a vampire wants to lessen the pain of their existence by spending their money on a magical narcotic, the First have not yet chosen to stop them. They have, however forbidden possession of *Black Va'Vash*. Any vampire found to be carrying *Black Va'Vash* is immediately destroyed (unless on specific business of the Black Council).

Either in or close to the city itself, the First's homes stand out, almost as ancient as the elder vampires themselves. Set in their own walled grounds, each is individual to the First that built it. Many have night-blooming gardens, impressive statues and unusual works of art on display for all to see.

The caverns surrounding the main city house the residences of many important vampires. The nine guild-halls can be found in and around Avystervan on their own estates. The Black Cabal's obsidian towers lie a ten-minute walk from the city in a private and heavily guarded cavern. There, near a lake of blood, they practice their dark experiments, free from the scrutiny of other vampires. The Noctarius is home to the Devoted Incarnate; they worship in the black temple, yet live in a great stepped and angular Ziggurat a short way from the city.

The Blighted District

Down a long and winding tunnel, the Ravenous have their own town a half-hour distant from the main city. A number of houses, inns and temples, the *Blighted District* is a mirror of Avystervan. Due to a lack of control over their powers of disease, younger Ravenous are not allowed entrance into Avystervan. They have in the past, spoiled the mortal food supplies and contaminated several undead with diseases even the Devoted Incarnate find difficult to cure.

The Undercity

The caverns beneath the city belong to the *mocked*. Most vampires do not go there unless they have reason to. Nacreous green lichen casts back the darkness, and the *mocked* live off the scraps Avystervan throws them - those mortals for whom the rest of vampire society has no further use.

The Ash Plane lies only a portal away. The gateway lies in an old chapel to the north of the city. Many Ash Vampires make their home either in or around it. The portal is a swirling disk of dust and ash that instantly slays the living should they journey too close. The chapel was once dedicated to an elemental god of ash, but like so many others the god and his temple are all but forgotten.

Visitors to Avystervan

Only the wicked have any reason to seek out the *City of Graves*. Vampires come from all over the world to experience Avystervan's diabolical pleasures. Most elder vampires make the pilgrimage at least once in their unlives. Countless vampire broods, elven vampires and creatures even more unusual - vampire Mind Flayers live in the city in a strange shaped structure of metal and glass. There is talk that a small gathering of undead beholders reside somewhere within Avystervan's walls, although if this is true, only the Black Cabal are fully aware of them.

Mortals who come to Avystervan

Only the most wicked and heartless visit Avystervan. Those who come unexpected or unannounced are quickly devoured, turned into slaves, or both. Merchants, slavers and those who covet mortals for the delicate pallets of the undead are amongst those who seek out the *City of Graves*. These despicable folk trade their own kind in exchange for rich rewards. Mortals visiting Avystervan must possess the blackest hearts. Those of lesser evil are sacrificed to Vangual in the Black Temple.

By far the most common *living* visitors to Avystervan are the mortal followers of Vangual. These clerics have a special place in vampire society and are treated (almost) as equals. Some are in training to become vampires themselves, while many lead Vangual's black churches across the mortal realms. Others are summoned to Avystervan to receive special praise, or worse, punishment for failing to live up to the exacting standards of the *god of blood*.

Wizards, particularly necromancers seeking aid with their research find their way to Avystervan. Sentient undead: ghosts, liches and others seek sanctuary within its confines. Others come merely because they can, out of curiosity or to sample its unique pleasures. Thieves, assassins and worse come to the city, some because they have vital information, others work solely for individual broods, carrying secrets, messages, or even vampires across the Realm.

Many mortals belong to a specific vampire in the city. This is particularly true of the mortal clergy of Vangual. These mortals are marked with blood runes that gleam to vampire sight. These runes reveal who is owned by which vampire. Such vassals are given special dispensation to walk the streets unmolested.

Regardless, all mortals must possess nerves of steel to endure the sights Avystervan has to offer.

Vampires and Avystervan

Arrogant, vampires have no compassion and precious little humanity. They take what they want and have little respect for others. Younger vampires who are easily manipulated by the Void are constantly fighting. They have not yet learned respect for their elders and still believe they can change the world single handedly. As they age they learn control over their rage, but in many, the Blood Guard is the only force that stills the hand of violence. Fights break out in the streets some out of boredom, others, merely for entertainment. Duels are rarely fatal as vampires know they cannot kill each other. Inflict sufficient damage and an opponent dissolves to mist. The Blood Guard reward such instances of violence with imprisonment.

Punishment

Crimes typically result in a vampire being staked and left in solitude for a number of days (dependent on the crime). When released, the famished vampire is compelled to remain in the undercity for a further period, forced to eat scraps of food even the *mocked* would not touch to satisfy their desperate craving. Other punishments include burning, dismemberment or partial immersion in holy water. It is difficult to teach a vampire humility, but with enough force they can be taught to fear the rulers of the city. Vampires know fear only too well.

Society

Age is an indication of social status in Avystervan. Everything hinges on a vampire's age and the reputation of his master. If a vampire's master did well, his vassals will be favorably received. If a master performed poorly, his transgressions may be passed on to his progeny. Tracing back the long lines of heritage are very important, and many vampires take great pains to ensure their bloodline is kept pure and free from taint. A vampire who acts rashly may find the master of his master hunting him down to bring him back into line.

Because of the limited space in Avystervan, a vampire cannot easily create progeny to live with him. He must first seek permission from his master, who must in turn seek permission from the Black Council. Of course, the wizards of the Black Cabal are free to create progeny as they will. They experiment on their undead slaves, learning the secrets of vampirism and advancing their dark powers of necromancy.

Vampiric: The Language of Avystervan

Created by the Black Council two thousand years ago, Vampiric is a hissing, screeching sibilance used in Avystervan (or rarely in the mortal realms when vampires desire absolute privacy).

All vampires are taught it within their first year of unlife but mortals have trouble learning it. Good characters find it unsettling to hear as it is said to be a whisper of the Void. Few beyond the city's confines have mastered it. A person may learn the language, provided they have someone who knows it well enough. Many slaves in Avystervan know nothing but a smattering of Vampiric.

Some basic words in Vampiric

Mortal	Vampiric
Vampire	Isthee'en or Vicaruus
Death	Nak'aree
Blood	Vii'thae
Mortal	Vii'dae
Shadow	Nocturuum
Sun	Solitaarn
Night	Morithaal
Children of Vangual:	Ustarar'en orr Umathaar

Isst kath uuthulaar esto morithaal, ux ellar nust morthex orrt solitaar (though we go gravely into the night, we shall fear no *power of light*).

BLACK PRACTICES

THE LONG NIGHT

Once per year, on the night of the First's transformation, the Black Cabal host the Long Night, an evening of vampiric revelry and blood sacrifice. For a month beforehand, the Black Cabal journey out into the realms in search of suitable adventurers for their games. Chosen from all different races, classes and levels of power, these adventurers are abducted and taken back to the *City of Graves*. Much prestige is gained on how these adventurers are obtained (with emphasis on particularly cruel or cunning tactics used in their capture). Held in isolation, these adventurers are released on the evening of the Long Night to a seemingly empty city. They have one hour to do as they will, then the hunt is on. Whoever brings back the head of an adventurer wins a great reward, a philtre of ancient blood, rare jewels or a favour from one of the elders.

Note: Adventurers have been released in all kinds of ways over the centuries. One year, the vampires feigned a revolt. The adventurers were released by a mortal who pretended to help them escape. Another time, the mortals woke to a deserted city.

Despite their best efforts, no adventurer has ever reached the surface.

THE CHORUS OF SCREAMS

The *Chorus of Screams* is the ritual of bloodletting that surrounds Vangual's unholy day. Once per year, coinciding with the ascension of the god of vampires, many mortals are slain during this evil time... The screams can be heard for miles around, echoing down the tunnels across the underworld for days, even weeks after. The screams alone have been said to send a mortal man insane. Many of the living leave Avystervan during this time…

THE CARNIVAL OF FLESH

Once per month, the carnival comes. A collection of traders both mortal and vampire alike gather in the Plaza to show off their wares. Slaves from all across the realms are exchanged, sold and traded. The dirty, the rich, the powerful, the sick and the holy can be found here, trapped in tiny cages or paraded on leg chains for the citizens of Avystervan to purchase. The Black Cabal buy and trade many specimens, as do a large number of the vampire houses. The carnival is a day of much excitement. The activities commence two hours after noon in the upperworld and continue until all the mortals have been sold. What is not sold is given to the *mocked* or tossed into the Blood Pool.

CARNIVAL OF SCREAMS PRICE LIST

* A commoner - 50 to 100 Black.
* A low-level warrior - 200 Black.
* A new-born infant (less than 24 hours old) - 250 Black.
* An unspoiled child (8 to 14) - 300 Black.
* A mid-level adventurer - 400 Black.
* A low-level wizard - 500 Black.
* A high-level adventurer - 3000 Black.
* A powerful wizard - 4000 Black.
* A high-level cleric of the *Powers of Light* - 5000 Black.
* A goodly aligned Dhampyre - 10,000 Black.

CURRENCY

Aside from blood and slaves (the Children of Vangual have precious little use for actual gold), the main currency in Avystervan is the Black, the coin of Kethak. The Black is a circular coin made of a polished material similar to obsidian. Minted in Kethak, coins have the pointed skull of some strange inhuman race on one side and a black sun on the other.

The Black is worth about half its value in Avystervan and a full Black is worth around 10 gold pieces. The Black is divided up into smaller amounts. The Half Black is literally one Black cut in two. The smallest coin is the Quarter Black.

BLOOD RUNES

Blood runes are scrawling symbols that are part of the vampiric language. Using ink crafted from vampire blood and some magical elements, they take two forms:

VAMPIRIC BLOOD RUNES

Vampiric (or standard) blood runes are a standard crimson glyph drawn in blood. These runes are used to mark names, buildings and other areas of importance in Avystervan.

NECROTIC BLOOD RUNES

Necrotic blood runes glow visibly under bloodlight but are otherwise invisible to the mortal eye. They are designed to show a vampire who owns a building or which slave belongs to which vampire. A *detect magic* spell will reveal a necrotic blood rune as will the light from a fire vampire. Lastly, a vampire or any *vampire touched* creature with darkvision can see a necrotic blood rune.

Necrotic blood runes are permanent marks on people, slaves and items in Avystervan; they are also used in the mortal realms to indicate safe houses or Blood Gates (although most are carefully hidden to avoid accidental detection).

THE NECROTIC BRAND

Created by the Black Cabal, this long black rod has a circular metal plate on one end. When the correct command words are spoken (in vampiric), the rod will gleam with blazing magical energy. It can then be used to brand a mortal with the Blood Rune of a particular vampire. This process is agonising and causes 1d8 points of damage to the unfortunate mortal.

If the mark ever comes into contact with true sunlight it deals 1d4 points of damage per round to the branded mortal. There is no save for this, although a *dispel magic* cast upon the mark will negate it entirely.

The mark loses its magical properties when it has been away from Avystervan for 30 days.

> "*Now you know what we are, now you know what you are. You'll never grow old, Michael, and you'll never die. But you must feed!*"
> David, Lost Boys

Avystervan Locations

Pictured left, Dreamer's impression of how the Sanguinus Incarnum might look on The Plaza in Avystervan

The Obsidian Towers

The home of the Black Cabal, the order of vampire wizards live on their own estate in a sprawling complex fashioned entirely from obsidian. The Black Cabal appreciate their privacy and have powerful guards posted around their estate.

The towers themselves are twin edifices of black rock, with a number of lesser buildings positioned around them. Bridges and walkways criss-cross back and forth, and from above, the entire structure forms a septagram, a seven-pointed star with the great ritual hall at the very center.

The Obsidian Towers are warded with countless protective and divination magics. Anti-scrying enchantments are in place, so the Black Cabal can practice their sorcery in private. Uninvited invasion of the estate is met with instant death. There are no exceptions. The black robed members of the Cabal are deeply secretive and although they fully report to the Black Council, their order is swathed in secrecy. Few get to see the inside of the Obsidian Towers, and even fewer know their dark objectives. The inside of the towers is said to be a sprawling maze of corridors, with strange beasts and deadly dangers at every turn.

There is said to be a monstrous beast in the bloody waters of the great lake beside the towers. The Blood Pool is an underground lake whose waters turn a rich crimson the further from the shore one travels. It is said that even the Black Cabal fears what lurks beneath its placid surface. Perhaps it is one of their experiments gone horribly wrong. Occasionally, a small boat can be seen bobbing upon the bloody water, as the vampire wizards carry out their strange experiments.

The Black Temple

The largest building in Avystervan is the *Sanguinus Incarnum*, the cathedral dedicated to Vangual, god of vampires. There, the Devoted Incarnate worship their deity with bloody dedication.

The temple is a vast stepped and angular pyramid of blood red stone. Ten thousand mortals were said to have been slain in its creation. Barbs and strange markings cover its surface, and every part of the temple drips blood that gathers in the moat at its base.

Vangual himself decreed that the moat must be filled with gore at all times. What he does with the offerings is anyone's guess, but the Devoted Incarnate worship him slavishly, willing to lay down their unlives should he demand it. They wander about the pyramid, their eyes and hearts as dark as their black robes.

It is said only mortals with the blackest hearts can look upon the *Sanguinus Incarnum*. Anyone with even a hint of goodness in them will go mad at the sight of the blood-drenched pyramid.

What goes on within the many levels of the temple will not be detailed here, but needless to say, much suffering and pain is carried out in the name of the blood god, Vangual. Many vampires who have not performed well are also brought here to face the wrath of their patron deity who looks harshly upon those vampires who do not do his bidding.

> *There is something you need to understand here, Harry, and it's very important. Not all wizards are good.*
> Hagrid, Vangaard

THE BROKEN VEIN TAVERN

'Our name may be tasteless, but our blood isn't.'

The Broken Vein is famed the world over (amongst the undead). Standing on the Plaza, this fine establishment has a reputation for providing anything the traveler requires. Owned by a family of drow Black Bloods, the Broken Vein attracts vampires from all across the realm.

While not the most expensive tavern in Avystervan - with luxurious furniture and mortal virgin serving maidens - it is certainly high priced. Few fledgling vampires can afford to eat there.

The Broken Vein has a large cellar filled with a wide selection of 'vintages'. These mortals are held in appalling conditions, yet are kept healthy by a black cleric who specialises in keeping the living in perfect condition. Their screams are kept from the clientele by magical wards of silence.

Everything is for sale at the Broken Vein. Even the dancing maidens are available - for the right price. It is said the owners scour the realms for the most beautiful virgins, who are also for sale as vampire brides (for an extortionate amount of Black). Children, the fit and the sick, animals and even magical creatures are available here for the discerning tastes of the clientele.

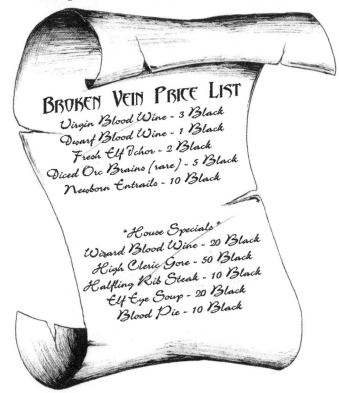

BROKEN VEIN PRICE LIST

Virgin Blood Wine - 3 Black
Dwarf Blood Wine - 1 Black
Fresh Elf Ichor - 2 Black
Diced Orc Brains (rare) - 5 Black
Newborn Entrails - 10 Black

House Specials
Wizard Blood Wine - 20 Black
High Cleric Gore - 50 Black
Halfling Rib Steak - 10 Black
Elf Eye Soup - 20 Black
Blood Pie - 10 Black

THE CORPUS ROOMS

The Corpus Rooms are a place where vampire merchants bring the most succulent mortals from around the realm - for purchase - or just a little feeding. This 'restaurant' is a place of much feasting. They hold regular auctions, bringing fresh slaves to the city from all over the realms. The remains are sent to the *Blighted District* or tossed down the gutter, food for the *mocked*.

THE CATHEDRAL

This gothic building is carved with the faces of crying children around every inch of its surface. A single storey square building, it houses the Blood Knights, the most feared vampires in the realm. What dark practices go on within, one can but imagine, as few are given invitation to enter this sacred building.

TOWER OF ARIKOSTINAAL

The second largest building in Avystervan, the lich Arikostinaal and his Death Knight bodyguards live in relative seclusion here. Although Arikostinaal spends much of his time in the city of Kethak on the Ash Plane, he can be found here from time to time, and has been careful to maintain a tangible presence on the Black Council. Arikostinaal was one of the founders of Avystervan, offering his services to the First many thousands of years ago. It is quite probable that he was the first lich in the realms, and is certainly one of the most powerful.

The lich tower rises up in the east of Avystervan, pearly white and in stark contrast to the black and grey of the rest of the city. It has a pale amethyst lambency about it which some vampires find unsettling. Ghostly lights can be seen flickering around its summit, dancing across the cavern roof on the rare occasions when Arikostinaal is at home. It has a pointed roof and many windows. At the base, surrounded by a high wall, one can spy the glowering forms of Arikostinaal's Shadow Guard, his Death Knights who watch over him at all times. Arikostinaal has never been seen without them; even when he attends Black Council meetings, he travels with his two most powerful Death Knight retainers.

THE MAUSOLEUM

This is where vampires, too weary of living go when they can no longer endure the passing ages. The years take their toll even on the undead, and some desire nothing more than to sleep away the centuries in peace and solitude. For this provision, the First created the Mausoleum; a place where vampires can lie in rest until such times as they find a reason to return to life. Most never do. These vampires allow themselves to run out of blood and will in all likelihood never awaken. Turning into desiccated husks, they are content to slumber the years away in the *eternal quiescence*. The Mausoleum is a serene place, tended by the Devoted Incarnate and other undead. There are thousands of slumbering vampires within its walls, some who have taken *Black Va'Vash*. Quite why the First do not destroy these vampires for their illegal use of Va'Vash is unknown, but they seem content to allow them to sleep away the centuries, safe from harm in the Mausoleum.

AST'ATH'KAVAAR

The strange building of glass and metal is the home to the Union, the guild of vampire Mind Flayers. There are perhaps fifty Mind Flayers in Avystervan; they can be seen wandering the city in their deep purple robes.

Ast'Ath'Kavaar means 'Place of Inculcation' in the common tongue. Their home is deathly silent as many of the Mind Flayers communicate telepathically, their mind powers greatly increased in the transformation to undeath. They do not speak, and rarely communicate with outsiders.

HOUSE AVANAAR

House *Avanaar*, the famous vampire drow house stands proudly in darkness just off the Plaza in Avystervan. The stately home with its stained glass windows and vampire drider guards is home to over three hundred drow, all of whom have severed contact with their mortal brethren and declared eternal loyalty to the First.

House *Avanaar* is shrouded in secrecy. Over the centuries, it has proved its loyalty to the vampire community time and time again, yet the drow demand their own privacy and the Black Council has given it to them. Few enter House *Avanaar* without permission, and even fewer that do, ever leave.

HOUSE SONORUUS

The 'house of screams' is the home to Avystervan's order of black bards. A tall building carved with grinning faces of children, House *Sonoruus* is a terrible place to behold. What actually goes on amidst the silken pillows and crimson drapes, many vampires do not know, but it is a place of secrets and hideous debauchery. The black bards gather regularly to discuss the affairs of the mortal realms, and to plan their information gathering strategies.

THE TOWER OF SALVATORIAN

The home of Salvatorian Vanadayne has remained dark and silent since his sudden departure some years before. A tower of smooth black stone covered with glyphs of deep sapphire, the stained glass windows are closed, the doors locked.

Although the Black Cabal laboured hard, their efforts to gain entrance to the tower have proved unsuccessful. The magic binding the ancient building is as much a mystery as the disappearance of Salvatorian himself. The lich Arikostinaal has been unable (or unwilling) to gain entrance.

The black tower continues to stand defiant and empty; a monument to the fading power of the vampire race…

THE BARRACKS

This large square building has a wide compound behind its high walls. Here the Blood Guard make their home, some two hundred vampires wearing the black-red armor of Avystervan. A moment's notice from the Plaza, the Blood Guard can be mobilised into full battle readiness in a matter of minutes.

THE GARDENS OF LIGHT

Created by the Black Cabal, this great chamber lies a short walk from the main city. Filled with sunlight, the garden is used to farm many of the foodstuffs used to feed the mortals of Avystervan.

Carefully controlled by the Black Cabal, the sunlight is captured by a crystal that lies on the roof of the great cathedral in Veil. Any vampire can utter the word 'vashaan' (darkness in vampiric) to extinguish the sunlight, but only a member of the Black Cabal can reinstate it. Many slaves are used to tend the gardens that lie in tiers around the walls and solemn trains of shackled children are brought here daily by mortal clerics to keep them healthy for feeding. Despite a momentary respite from the darkness, there is still much pain and anguish in Avystervan.

THE UPPER CITY

The ruined city of Veil lies directly above Avystervan. The First do not speak its name. Considered a terrible curse, Veil is known only as the 'upper city' to the inhabitants of Avystervan.

Veil lies deep in seclusion at the eastern most edge of a mountain range (although it can exist in any remote location). At its height it was a place of darkness and terrible evil. Centuries later, the earth is scorched, the buildings ruined, but the evil has not yet been laid to rest. Unable to find peace, the spirits of the inhabitants of Veil are in torment. Abandoned by Vangual, they continue the work they did in life amidst the destruction of the ruined city, hateful of the living, the dead, and most of all, vampires.

The city itself is small, housing perhaps ten thousand at its peak. It originally had a large stone wall encircling it, but the wall has long since collapsed. A gothic castle still stands in ruins at its eastern-most end. The stone buildings remain, burned and melted as if a flame more potent than mundane fire ravaged the streets. Only the cathedral, a black and diabolical looking building appears to have been left untouched by fire. There, the necromancers remain in spirit, vowing a terrible revenge on all who invade their misery. Some of the buildings still smoulder. Even after two thousand years, a palpable reminder of the darkness that brought the city to its knees lingers and a layer of gloomy ash hangs miserably over the city at all times.

Five thousand people were lost when the *Order Nobilis* razed the city to the ground. Their corpses lie there still, unable to rest, denied a proper burial and little chance of finding peace. When the sun falls many of them rise as undead under the command of the Necromancers, whose rage is still potent after so many endless years.

The portal to the underworld (and Avystervan) is hidden, magically concealed within the ruined temple to Vangual. When darkness falls, vampires appear amongst the burned and ruined columns, slipping into the night on their journeys across the mortal realms.

There are no maps that mark Veil's location or records that speak of it, except for a handful of texts penned by the necromancers themselves over two millennia go. The city is all but unknown to the mortal world.

Adventurers have been lured to the city by wily vampires. They have ensured a steady supply of fresh blood to Avystervan by spreading stories of great wealth and adventure to be found amongst the ruins. They are correct: much treasure can be found within the ruined buildings, but when the sun goes down and the undead rise up from their graves there is little escape…

The ruins of the city are enough of a challenge for most adventurers. The city and its walking dead should occupy their time entirely. Certainly the restless spirits of the necromancers should prove tough enough for any party, should they manage to penetrate that far into the city to encounter them.

No one has ever discovered the entrance to the secret city of the vampires. The necromancers are forbidden to mention it.

Avystervan belongs to the undead. The living have no place there…

Using Avystervan in your Game

Avystervan can be used in many ways. Typically it is not a place where mortals should ever go without a reason of the highest importance. It is secret - although the *Powers of Light* know of its existence - the Arcane have kept the sanctity of the city intact. Their sorceries are a deterrent to any that would plot against the city, and the liches have worked with Vangual to keep Avystervan safe from harm for thousands of years.

A journey to the city would almost certainly mean death for a party of even the highest level mortal characters.

For evil characters, Avystervan can be used in many ways, as a base of operations, a place of rest, or simply as a new location for vampires to visit. There are enough possibilities within the city for months of adventure. It is even a portal to the Planes of Negativity and Ash - and the city of Kethak.

The Black Council is always scheming. Even the most evil mortals are occasionally summoned to the city for quests that cannot be performed by vampires alone.

Future sourcebooks will reveal scenarios involving the *City of Graves*, but certainly, for adventures, the upper city can easily be slotted into any campaign. The burned and shattered ruins have enough ghosts, monsters and dangers inhabiting its environs to keep the attention of any group of adventurers happy (and occupied) for weeks.

How do vampires get goods to Avystervan?

Vampires have many *thrice touched* mortals that operate in the mortal realms. These evil characters procure items for the city, and work with the Black Cabal to bring goods on a regular basis to Avystervan. Many evil merchants have agreements with vampires for weekly drops, and many of the allies of Vangual use Blood Gates to move back and forth from the city to the mortal realms. Individual organisations have their own methods, but most involve magical transportation and frequent use of Blood Gates.

Blood Gates

There are over a hundred Blood Gates scattered across the mortal realms. There is at least one in every small town and many more in the largest cities. Each Blood Gate is linked to a particular location - typically Avystervan - although this isn't always the case. Many private Blood Gates exist for which only those with the correct magical passwords can gain access.

A Blood Gate's exit portal looks like a series of strange bloody runes inscribed into the ground or upon a large flat surface. They are typically hidden behind tapestries or rugs and kept away from prying eyes. A Blood Gate detects as magical and can be seen by those with *darkvision*. They gleam when viewed under bloodlight.

A Blood Gate can only be unlocked with the *open blood gate* spell. When activated, a Blood Gate becomes a swirling oval of liquid crimson. They are typically stand around six feet high, although many sizes exist. The two greatest Blood Gates lead from the Plaza to the City and are called *Tas'kaskan* (route to the docks) and *Ith'kaskarar* (entrance to the secret temple).

Magical Goods

Avystervan is a highly magical city. There are countless alchemists, sages, scholars and wizards in permenant residence crafting all manner of magical items. While the prices may be extortionate, the *City of Graves* is an excellent place to buy enchanted items of all kinds and descriptions, providing one has the purse strings to match the exorbitant rates the undead craftsmen charge for their wares. Prices are twice those listed in the DMG.

How many vampires are there in Avystervan?

There are around 2000 vampires that hold permanent residence in Avystervan at any one time. This is broken down into the following numbers:

Vampire Race	%	Total Number
Black Bloods	80%	1600
Mock Vampires	5%	100
Ravenous Vampires	4%	80
Vangaard	4%	80
Ash Vampires	3%	60
Shadow Vampires	2%	40
Fire Vampires	1%	20
The Lost	<1%	5
Dhampyre	<1%	15

In addition, there are around 25 Drider Vampires and at least 3 Blood Tyrants in Avystervan.

How many Mortals are there in Avystervan?

There are a surprising number of mortals in Avystervan. Many are slaves, and the actual number of mortals used for food changes so regularly, that number has not been included here.

Number of Mortals and other races approximately:

Mortal slaves/servants	300
Mortal students	100
Other Mortals (merchants)	50
Liches	30
Mind Flayers	50
Drow	300

In addition there are a limited number of the more exotic creatures and over one hundred mortal drow in residence in Avystervan at any one time. There are also a large number of lesser undead, ranging from one hundred zombie slaves to over three hundred ghosts, spectres and other incorporeal beings.

There are in addition always merchants moving back and forth from the Plaza on a regular basis, as well as a large number of spies, bards and information gatherers.

Crests and Symbols

The crest of the Black Council is a black disk containing the eight blood runes of the First around its outer edge.

The seal of Avystervan is a black disk with the blood-red teardrop of Vangaual in the centre, surrounded by a black inhuman skull with burning red eyes.

CHAPTER NINE: VANGUAL

Name: Vangual
Status: God of Vampires
Symbol: Crimson Blood Droplet
Worshipper's Alignment: Any Evil
Portfolio: Vampires, Blood, Undead, Self-Fulfilment

Without a patron deity, no race could flourish. Vampires are no exception. Although Vangual is so known in Avystervan, the god of vampires has many names: The Lord of Suffering, Champion of the Void, Patron of Vampires.

Vangual was once a Feral Vampire who found his way to the city of Veil. Then but a hamlet, Veil had another name and was a small but thriving community. Masquerading as a powerful sorcerer, Vangual concealed his true nature and took to aiding the people of the mountain village in an attempt to gain their trust. Over the decades, Vangual's influence grew until he was practically a god in the villagers' eyes, mysterious and near mythical in power. When he returned from a long absence, a shrine had been erected to him and he took his first steps towards apotheosis.

As his influence spread, he began to take on followers, disciples who wished to learn his secrets and pass on his wisdom. Vangual's powers grew until the city became a thriving community. The people of Veil did anything Vangual asked of them. They trusted him and all he represented. Slowly darkness crept over Veil, the people were corrupted by necromancy and many became sorcerers under the tutelage of the *Powers of Darkness*. Vangual renamed the village Veil and began construction of a great city for his people. Although many good people still lived in Veil, as the city grew and more strangers came, the city became a haven for darkness.

No one knows exactly how Vangual became a god. Neither Vangual nor the other Powers will say. What is known is that Vangual sent out his followers into the world in an attempt to spread his influence. They attracted the attention of the *Powers of Light* and the *Ordo Nobilis* proved to be the ruin of Veil. But that was a very long time ago, and the members of the noble order were merely pawns in the earliest battles between the powers of light and darkness.

Now Veil is long destroyed and Vangual rarely visits the mortal realms. He makes his home in the *Black*, the seat of the Void beyond the Negative Energy Plane. No one knows what the *Black* is or even where it lies, only that it resides somewhere beyond the Negative Energy Plane in a realm of terrible suffering. The only portal lies deep within the Citadel that opens only when a vampire is summoned.

Vangual oversees the Black Council from his Fortress of Shadow. The Fortress itself is said to be a brooding castle that lies on a plane of endless night with the Void flickering around it.

It is said Vangual resides in a great pool of stinking blood. It is there that he appears only to his most favoured. The Champion of the Void, some speculate that Vangual is the Void, while others claim he is no more than a slave to its desires. Puppet or not, Vangual places his home directly upon the heart of the Void and has terrible powers indeed.

Vangual has followers on many worlds, with the majority made up of evil clerics, sentient undead and foul persons that cling to the night. Many vampires revere him and he grants powerful spells to his faithful. He has been known to ally himself with gods of darkness, decay and death. The lord of vampires has no regard for mortal existence and desire nothing more than the total subjugation of all life on all the mortal worlds.

Vangual's touch can slay any living being in an instant, devouring their life force with no possible chance of resurrection. He can cause any mortal to rise up as a vampire of any race with but a moment's thought. This transformation is both permanent and irreversible, but is seen as a blessing rather than a curse in the eyes of his devoted.

Vangual's favoured weapon is a wicked looking knife, designed for gutting and causing the most vicious wounds imaginable. He commonly appears as a skeletal raven with burning crimson eyes, a patch of utter blackness or a glowering and massive vampire lord that attacks with a giant blood-drenched sword.

WORSHIP

Vangual demands screeching litanies, regular blood sacrifice and absolute loyalty. Those who sway from the black path are instantly destroyed. He promotes torture, self-fulfilment and favours those who would become undead themselves. Those who do so to stave off death, disease or old age are his particular favourites.

Clerics vie for supremacy. Those who perform well are promoted and given even greater power, those who fail are relegated to lesser undead - mindless servants under his absolute command.

Around the realms there are many churches dedicated to the god of vampires, and a cleric whose heart is black does not need to look very far to find a home in one of them. Vampiric churches can be found in hidden places, dank and foreboding, bloodstained and filled with the lingering remnants of terror. They are sinkholes of evil, and are often located surprisingly near churches of the *Powers of Light*, where they can keep an ever-vigilant eye on the actions of their enemies.

VAMPIRE CLERICS OF VANGUAL

A large portion of the undead that revere Vangual are part of the Devoted Incarnate. Those that do not meet the demanding entrance requirements can still be among his faithful, and Vangual blesses all of his worshippers equally.

Vampire clerics of Vangual are amongst the most evil beings imaginable. They have hearts of ice and the *Chill* around them is dark and malevolent. Vangual places a great demand upon his black clerics and regularly seeks fresh blood sacrifices and total devotion from those who take him as their patron deity.

A growing number of feral vampires have begun to revere Vangual as their one true deity. The god of blood is not so foolish as to turn any away; he bathes all of his worshippers in unholy darkness, living, dead or undead.

Mortal Clerics of Vangual

Clerics of Vangual are often emaciated, sun fearing creatures. Typically *thrice touched*, these mortals have been sorely afflicted by necromancy, yet not quite enough to drag them over the brink and into undeath. A vague glimmer of mortality still flickers within them.

Mortal clerics gain the domains of Black Pallium, Faithful Undead and Harm. Followers must drink fresh blood at least once per month and are driven to commit many despicable acts in their unholy service. Many study under the tutelage of a vampire cleric of the Devoted Incarnate. The most favoured are always *thrice touched*. Mortal clerics carry out many of the functions of vampire society during the hours of daylight.

Clerics of Vangual try to imitate the god of vampires at all times. Rituals involve human sacrifice and the drinking of fresh blood. Many avoid the sun at all costs and when they must travel during the day, do so heavily cloaked and hooded. The sun beats down upon the *vampire touched*, draining their strength and clouding their judgement. They quickly grow tired and out of breath when exerting themselves.

Those blessed by Vangual have parchment-thin, pallid skin. Their flesh becomes ever more clammy as they gain favour with the god of vampires. Most have pronounced canines or a strange and unpleasant odour about them. Most clerics have spent so much time donating their own blood to the church that they have a fine scar across their palms. Others have permanent bite marks upon their bodies; signs of frenzied feasting when they were lower down the order's ranks.

All potential clerics of Vangual must seek out a black cleric or member of the Devoted Incarnate for recruitment into the black clergy. On entrance, they are granted a vampire patron who gives them their orders. Aspirant clerics are tested to prove their merit. Those that succeed are eventually made into vampires, those that fail become Vampire Scion, or worse, slain and raised as lesser undead under the command of their vampiric masters.

Churches to Vangual are dark and evil affairs. Set in crypts or places of death, clerics revere their god, following his edicts and practising their dark magic in secret. Altars are sinister yet functional, draped with gore stained velvet covers that can quickly be removed in times of discovery.

Rituals

Vangual demands the drinking of blood at least once per month. All acolytes must slay and devour the heart of an innocent before being accepted into the order. Clerics must have some skill in necromancy and know the ways of the undead with absolute familiarity.

The unholy sacrament is held on the last day of the week, at the dead of night. There, from the Black Chalice, clerics take a mouthful of still warm blood and re-swear their allegiance to the god of vampires. This blood affects them in various ways. It keeps them vampire touched, as well as a means to prove their eternal loyalty to the god of the undead. The faithful of Vangual are slavishly obedient to their vampire masters, as well as dedicated to the destruction of all things good.

Damnation

Mortal clerics of Vangual are amongst the most despicable clerics in the realm. They are soulless, dark and often desperate people, with hearts of absolute pitch. They will do whatever they must to advance themselves in the eyes of their deity, even slaying their own kind, should the opportunity present itself. They are completely without morals or compassion and show no mercy to their victims.

Mortal clerics have sold their souls to the Void and there is precious little chance of salvation for those that seek it. Those clerics that find a glimmer of humanity within them realise that they must walk the path set out for them by fate or be destroyed by Vangual's ever-vigilant army of clerics. There is no escape from Vangual's clergy; the black path is a route that leads directly to the Void.

Advancement

Talented clerics are brought to Avystervan and turned into vampires. Those who fail or have anything but the darkest hearts are summoned to the *City of Graves* to face their crimes. A cleric rarely knows whether he has favoured or displeased his god, and so a calling to Avystervan is a time of much uncertainty for the faithful. Those who fail either become food for the populace, or are sent to the Negative Energy Plane to be added to Vangual's undead army. The remaining faithful may find themselves summoning the undead, to be faced with a previous member of their own order amongst the ranks of the conjured skeletons and zombies.

Attire

Clerics wear black robes stained with the blood of the innocent during important ceremonies. They typically keep the vermilion teardrop icon of their deity well hidden, although some have tattoos branded into their flesh as a sign of their unswerving loyalty to the Lord of Suffering.

Clerical Powers: Rebuke the undead.

Hit Dice: d8

Alignment: Evil only.

Domains: Black Pallium, Faithful Undead, Harm

Immunity to Energy Drain

The faithful of Vangual can resist up to their cleric level in energy drain attacks per day. These are individual levels, so an *energy drain* spell that drained 6 levels, would count as 6 of the cleric's levels of protection per day. This resistance can be voluntarily lowered as a move-equivalent action. Additionally they gain +4 to all negative energy saves.

Blessings of the Faithful

Once per day, a cleric in good standing may invoke a prayer to Vangual. This will render them wholly impervious to the attacks or spell-like effects of the undead for 1 round per level.

Note: This power does not protect the cleric against actual spells cast by the undead. A cleric would be immune to a ghoul's touch-based attacks, but not from a *fireball* spell cast by a lich.

CHURCHES IN THE MORTAL REALMS

THE CHURCH OF THE IMMORTAL CORPUS

The Church of Vangual: the Gore Tainted. This is the church the Devoted Incarnate seeks to promote throughout the civilised world. There are many chapters living in secret in the largest cities, many in the same neighbourhood (or even the same street). Members of these churches are always wicked persons who will do anything to reach their dark goals of becoming a true vampire (or simply gaining ever-greater wealth and power).

APPLICATION

The church demands a great deal from its mortal supplicants before they are accepted into its ranks. A member has to prove their value and dedication before the vampire elders will even consider their application. A standard requirement is to slay a cleric of the *Powers of Light* of at least the supplicant's level. Churches trade in blood, slavery, gold and information.

THE CHAPEL OF THE MERCIFUL HEART

Not really a church at all, this order of physicians and doctors is just one of the ways vampires gain access to fresh supplies of blood. The Merciful Heart with its humble appearance move across the world offering aid to those in need. They carry black bags, filled with alchemical equipment and odd black phials designed for storing blood.

Their surgeons have great skill and considerable understanding of mortal anatomy. On the surface, this is just another benevolent organisation. The Merciful Heart has great open hospitals where anyone with any injury can go to be healed. In return, the clerics take blood from every patient - siphoning it off for the vampires in their order. Those too ill or dangerous are placed in isolation where only the Merciful Heart know what happens to them then...

Although the Heart does much good. It is all done in the name of evil. Many who seek aid never walk from their doors, and many bodies are never again found. The black robed clerics are found everywhere, offering a healing hand to those in need - but always at a price - a sample of blood...

CHURCH OF THE STIRGE

The Stirge is the sacred animal of Vangual. Or at least, history says that Vangual was obsessed with stirges when he was mortal.

The ancient texts in the Obsidian Towers make mention of an ancient cult dedicated to the Stirge - the mythical bird of death and blood. Cultists in their crimson robes would command huge flocks of stirges, stealing blood and causing terror wherever they went. So foul and powerful were they that the forces of good focused all of their efforts on eradicating them.

They have not been seen for centuries, so even the Children of Vangual believe they have been lost to history. But perhaps, just perhaps Kynosh has uncovered the resting place of one of these ancient vampires and perhaps this church will live once again...

Or it is just possible that its clerics are already aroused and moving across the mortal realms, awaking their long slumbering stirges and preparing to reaffirm their allegiance to the god of blood....

THE CHURCH OF THE VERMILION HEART

There are a number of growing churches across the realms preaching self-fulfilment and offering release from sickness and protection against the corruption of the world. These clerics that dress in brilliant crimson robes are appearing in ever-increasing numbers, spreading their doctrine and helping wherever they can. Many say they have a heavy hand, that they do what they must to achieve their ends. If this results in violence, then so be it.

This church has Vangual at its head, although the clergy believes its god is called Incaron. They are unaware that their god is the evil deity of blood and suffering and their representative is the evil Ishtyx, who appears in the guise of a powerful and mysterious shadow - the emissary of Incaron - who passes on words of 'wisdom' to the clerics of this order. Ishtyx personally grants spells to the followers of Incaron. This church is considered a rival religion to the Church of Vangual.

The holy symbol of Incaron is a black raven with glowering crimson eyes. As blood is sacred to the church of Incaron (see below), clerics may not draw blood directly in battle. They are restricted to hammers, maces, staffs, clubs and any other non-standard bludgeoning weapons.

INTRODUCTION TO DARKNESS

First clerics are brought into the fold. They are required to give a fresh sample of their blood in the holy sacrament once per week. The arch cleric stores this blood in the sacred vessels. This blood always vanishes - further evidence that Incaron has 'faith' in his followers.

Followers are indoctrinated with continuous reinforcement that strength is advisable when all else fails, that there are those who deserve to be slain, and that evil is just another facet of life. Seek to understand evil before judging it.

The Tenets of Incaron

1. Blood is life incarnate. Treasure it above all other gifts.

2. Thy body is thine own temple. Pollute neither thy flesh or thy mind.

3. Eat not of the flesh of the living.

4. Shed not a drop of blood from thine enemies.

5. I am both life and death. Give up thy life blood in sacrifice to me and I shall bless thee highly. I shall guide you to the highest planes of celestial glory.

CHAPTER TEN: THE FIRST

The First are the original Children of Vangual. They are powerful and ancient. Once numbering eleven, they now total eight. Their history is dark and filled with violence, but history remembers them as a noble party of adventurers given to protecting the land and defeating evil. As is the way with such things, there is a fine line between justice and persecution, and left unchecked, the eleven of the *Ordo Nobilis* plunged headfirst into darkness. They shattered a temple to a band of necromancers and routed the evil. But they were not merely content with bringing an end to the necromancers' threat. They desired nothing more than their total extermination. They pursued the necromancers as they fled back to their home city. There, standing upon their home soil it is said the necromancers begged for forgiveness, pleading to the members of the shining *Ordo Nobilis* for mercy, exclaiming that they had seen the error of their ways and would embrace the light. Yet the members of the *Ordo Nobilis* were resolute. Acting as judge, jury and executioner, they razed the city to the ground, killing all that could not escape, slaves, peasants, innocents, everyone.

The heavens thrashed with crimson lightning as flames ruined the skyline. But it was not the necromancers who called down this fire; it was the *Ordo Nobilis* as purity turned to corruption and light turned to darkness.

It is said that the dread god Vangual manifested amongst the burning buildings, ready to cast sentence upon those who had slain his faithful. Vangual's wrath was terrible, he called for justice and the other gods turned away. They knew there was enough darkness festering in the hearts of the *Ordo Nobilis* to punish each of them forever. They had shown neither compassion nor wisdom in destroying so many, so very willingly. As the god of blood had lost his chosen, so the *Ordo Nobilis* became his new family. They became vampires - the Children of Vangual…

That was a very long time ago. The *Ordo Nobilis*, struggling to come to terms with their new found exile into darkness, returned to civilisation, hoping that someone would give them aid. But the people were afraid, fearful of the human seeming monsters that stood beyond the city walls, stained with the blood of the innocent. Although the *Ordo* begged for aid, the people would not listen. The high cleric whispered a prayer and the gods heard, turning away the eleven (hence it was called 'turning' from that day on).

Furious at being denied, the *Ordo* retaliated. There was a great battle in which many were slain. The powers of the eleven were great, but even they could not stand against a city that had the sun on its side. One of the *Ordo* was slain and the rest fled into the night, defeated solely by the dawn. The *Ordo* knew humanity had turned their backs on them, and that they were forever denied sanctuary in the cities of men. Faced with no other choice, the remaining ten returned to the place of their second birth, the smouldering ruins of the city they had so naively destroyed. Now a place of ghosts and endless dead, they made a new home in the sprawling caverns beneath its blackened streets. This undercity they named Avystervan, *Place of Dark Solitude*, and forming the Black Council, they hid from the world, fermenting in shadow and growing in hate for the mortal races.

Appearance

The passing of time has made the First far from human. They are greater in stature than even the largest mortal, each standing well over eight feet in height. Some have liquid, blood filled eyes, while others have scales, claws or even flesh the colour of amethyst.

About the First

The First are powerful. They have existed for two thousand years. Some of their plans are far beyond mortal comprehension. They have been plotting for centuries; who knows what they have in store for humanity? Slowly but surely, the Black Council seeks to take back the darkness, extending their malevolent grip ever further into the mortal realms. Some scholars speculate that they desire nothing more than to extinguish the sun and create a black Eden, a world of total night where vampires can exist without terror of the sun.

Two Thousand Years

The unlives of the remaining eight First have not been without incident. The Black Council lost a second of their number a thousand years ago. Avystyx, the vampire bard allowed himself to be destroyed. Some say he was summoned by Vangual and never returned, while others claim that he grew weary of living and allowed the sun to take him. Only Vangual and the Black Council know the truth.

Loss of an Ancient

The First lost another of their ranks a decade ago. Salvatorian Vanadayne vanished from the Citadel and has not been seen since. Many whispers fill the night: Salvatorian is dead, slain by the *Powers of Light;* Salvatorian destroyed himself; Salvatorian fell into the *eternal quiescence* and is slumbering under the earth. The rumours are endless, but whatever lesser vampires may think, the Black Council spent considerable physical and magical resources in locating him. Quite suddenly, they called off all searches and placed one of their elders at the head of the house of sorcery in Avystervan. His name has not been mentioned since.

Skills and Powers

The First shall not be quantified here. They are simply too powerful. They have the powers and skills of an epic level character, as well as **all** of the Dark Gifts listed in this book.

Using the First in your Campaign

The First can be used as high-level bad guys in any campaign. They should be used sparingly. Their motives and actions should be kept secret, and a party should rarely encounter them, and if they do, it should never result in the death of one of the First. They have been around for thousands of years; it would take a very powerful party indeed to slay even one of them. Additionally, Vangual keeps a close eye on his favoured; he would look unfavourably on any group of mortals who managed to destroy one of his creations.

The PCs could aim to thwart a major scheme of the Black Council, but only the most powerful groups should encounter any of the First directly. It might make for dramatic effect if the PCs tracked down one of the First - only to find themselves hopelessly outmatched. They would be lucky to escape with their lives.

THE BLACK COUNCIL

The Black Council is made up of the eight remaining First plus at least one member of each vampire race. They reside in the Citadel, a towering fortress of sprawling black rock on the Negative Energy Plane. Access to the Citadel is by planar shifting spells or via the portal on the Plaza in Avystervan.

THE NEGATIVE ENERGY PLANE

The Negative Energy Plane is typically a featureless place filled with endless night and howling swirls of necromancy. While this is still true, there are some differences where the First are concerned.

In their personal region of the great plane, there is both gravity and substance. Perhaps this suits their black moods, for looming out of the darkness, an obsidian plateau stretches on for thousands of miles in all directions. Towering mountains and deep ravines, winding gulleys and endless tunnels from which nothing but blackness glowers are the sights a visitor will encounter. The ever-crumbling rock echoes through the silence.

This place means instant death to mortals that find their unfortunate way here...

Few things live on the Negative Energy Plane, mainly a rare few sentient undead and mindless ghosts. Most creatures find their way to other, more inhabited places; only those mortals who are slain here find themselves trapped for all eternity in the barren and black wasteland. Occasionally, an Ash Dragon will drift through the skies, but mostly the realm is a place of empty, endless darkness and deadly torrents of necromancy.

At the center of the obsidian plateau, the sprawling Citadel of the First stands on a pinnacle of smooth stone several thousand feet high. Two thousand years ago, countless dwarven hands painstakingly carved out the gothic castle, with its intricately carved towers, runes and angular features.

GETTING TO THE CITADEL

A narrow track winds its way around the outside of the column that supports the citadel. The path is treacherous; necromantic winds threaten to cast any that make the ascent into the depths of the Negative Energy Plane. Some carriages do make the journey, and can be seen winding their way around the column, up towards the citadel where the path opens into a large underground chamber where carriages can be parked in safety.

THE CITADEL

The Citadel's entrance hall is a great black marble lobby that stretches off into the distance. Bloodlight orbs line the walls in great sconces. The polished floor is so black as to be almost mirrored.

The air rings with the faintly eerie sound of the Void as it whispers down the corridors. A visitor gains the distinct feeling that they are never alone while in the Citadel.

The exit portal from Avystervan is tied to this chamber. A vampire can step from the Plaza to the Citadel in a moment, although any of the Black Council can close the gateway with but a single thought.

SEAT OF THE BLACK COUNCIL

Through the many rooms and winding corridors of the Citadel, the Black Council hold their meetings. There are countless rooms for guests and a contingent of Blood Guard stand on duty at all times.

Vast metal doors carved with the faces of children and intricate scenes of death; arched ceilings and wide stained glass windows are the norm. A visitor can stand in many of the rooms, overlooking the swirling, necromancy-fuelled storms and peer out into darkness and into the Void itself.

There are thousands of rooms in the Citadel. Some have not been used for more than a thousand years. Some have never been used at all. Many stand as they did the day they were completed, the furniture lying wrapped in protective cloth.

Time does not pass in the Citadel. Everything hangs as if motionless in time. Living things seems to erode in moments, yet stone, metal and glass remain intact, as though the ages move around them, unwilling to disturb the peaceful quality of death that fills the air.

THE BLOOD VAULT

Far beneath the citadel lies the Blood Vault: a labyrinth of corridors where the Void does not reach. The only place in the Citadel that casts back the flows of Necromancy, it is here that mortals are kept as food for the inhabitants of the Citadel. Vampire chefs prepare feasts of elven flesh on a daily basis, and the Blood Vault is place of bloody halls and gore stricken mortals.

THE RESTING PLACE OF THE ELDERS

The resting-place of the elders lies at the very heart of the Citadel. A place of extreme serenity and silence where the oldest and most powerful vampire elders sleep when they grow too weary of unlife. Guarded by the Arcane, this is where the most ancient vampires slumber away the centuries when they are no longer content to live amongst the living or the undead.

THE HEART OF THE COUNCIL

At the top of the Citadel beyond a maze of black stairwells and opulent carpets lies the Heart - the seat of the Black Council; a vast hemispherical chamber with a breathtaking stained glass window encircling it. The room looks up into the heart of the Void, a swirling maelstrom of blackness and swirling winds of necromancy. The gateway to the *Black* lies just behind this room in a small and subtle chamber. The chamber itself has a polished black floor and is filled with huge black thrones set around a vast obsidian table. Each throne is individual to the elder that built it. The throne of Toth is a simple slab-like affair standing over twelve feet high. The throne of Moloch is an ornate bejewelled throne of gold, with rich satin seat and plush (fireproof) arms.

The Citadel is a terrible place. It is darkly oppressive and there is precious little illumination. The flows of necromancy can strip a mortal of their vitality in moments and few can withstand the powers of the Black Council. Those who visit the Citadel should have important business there, or face a sudden death at the ends of the terrible evil that lies within.

MEMBERS OF THE BLACK COUNCIL

The current members of the Black Council are:

LORD MELANCH ABRAXIA

Lord of the Blood Knights of Avystervan, Melanch Abraxia is an imposing figure. Dressed in an immaculate black velvet coat, he stands well over ten feet tall, with glowering blood filled eyes and powerful hands. His sword Korthax, a barbed and evil weapon is never far from his side.

Abraxia has little tolerance for fools or for those who think of nothing but their own petty schemes. He rarely comes to the mortal realms and when he does, rarely leaves Avystervan.

It is said that Abraxia leaves a wide trail of bleeding mortals in his wake and that a low vibration accompanies his movements.

AGORAVAAL

Agoravaal 'The Damned' is a vampire Mage. Master of the Black Cabal, he is one of the smallest (though no less imposing) of the First. Standing at just seven feet tall, Agoravaal has inky black eyes and dresses in a black velvet robe that contrasts starkly against his pallid complexion.

The 'damned' was a brilliant mage and scholar in life, and is ten times the wizard in undeath. It is said his magical ability is unsurpassed, and that he sold his soul to the darkest powers in order to gain command of both life and death, earning him the sobriquet 'the damned'. His only passion is the Black Cabal, which he rules both as a father and intolerant master. He personally oversees the recruitment of each new member, who learn to revel in his praise and fear his dissatisfaction.

It is said that Agoravaal leaves bloody footsteps when he walks.

ISHTYX

Leader of the Devoted Incarnate, Ishtyx is perhaps the most evil of all the First. In life she was an elf maiden who followed the god of wisdom and healing. Whether there was a glimmer of darkness in her heart, or whether Vangual utterly subjugated her will, Ishtyx took swiftly to undeath. Truly despicable, she favours capricious death, slow and painful torture and has an absolute and unquenching love for Vangual.

Ishtyx appears as a tall alabaster skinned woman of about eight feet in height with liquid blue eyes and platinum hair. It is said that she bathes in the still-warm blood of children and takes many mortal lovers. Those that can endure the night are turned into vampires, although she quickly grows tired of her conquests and regularly casts them aside for more interesting diversions. She wears robes of the finest velvet, and has a penchant for jewels and fineries.

She has a terrible thirst for vengeance against the *Powers of Light*. She particularly despises clerics of gods of learning and wisdom and savours the worst of her tortures for them alone.

Ishtyx has spent many years studying the Avystyx Prophecies, and has recently become obsessed with them, to the exclusion of all else.

KYNOSH

Kynosh the 'blood-stained' druid is never seen in Avystervan. He is out in the mortal realms creating new vampiric creations, twisted monsters that are abominations of all that is good and wholesome.

Kynosh maintains relationships solely with black druids and Blood Mages, many of whom spend decades learning his secrets. Kynosh has many homes. Surrounded by twisted blood creatures, he favours deep swamps and blood filled forests where he can work in secret away from the prying eyes of the mortal races.

RAXX

Raxx, is a black rogue and leader of the Black Eye. He spends much of his time in the mortal realms where he gathers information on the *Powers of Light*. He controls a vast network of lookouts, thieves, beggars and urchins in his organisation that spans several of the largest cities. Indeed, only the highest-ranking members of the Black Eye are aware that Raxx is a vampire.

Raxx appears much as he did in life, standing just over six feet tall, with thick brown hair and exceedingly pale features. He dresses in finery and indeed thinks nothing of obtaining the rarest jewels and magical treasures the world across. His presence on the Black Council is a great asset, for his ability to gather information is second to none, and his personal order of vampires, the Shadow are both feared as information gatherers and murderous assassins.

TOTH

The barbarian Toth stands over twelve feet tall and is almost as wide. He commands the precious few Vangaard that remain, and has large lion-like golden eyes and leathery skin the color of parchment. He wears the pelts of animals across his massive body and rarely enters melee with anything other than his hands, which are capable of tearing lesser beings in two in an instant.

Toth is utterly faithful to the Black Council, yet the creation of the Cruentus Vangaard has greatly angered him. He is fully aware of the decline of the Vangaard and of their diminishing capacity to protect the Black Council.

VATHAN GELLEAN

Vathan 'the hunter' is an amethyst skinned vampire with baleful crimson eyes. He is the leader of the black ranger organisation and spends much time beyond the environs of Avystervan in the mortal realms. The Black Council only recall Vathan on matters of extreme emergency, and only then to pursue the most hated vampires.

Vathan is a tall vampire with long fingers and a powerful lower body. He favors flowing black cloaks with deep hoods through which his eyes glimmer brightly.

VOLIK

Volik is the leader of the Blood Guard and commands his order with an iron fist. Over ten feet in height with long flowing hair the color of midnight, Volik wields twin swords, Aarikosh and Varl; one burns with a brilliant bloodlight, the other with an frigid darkness. It is said Volik has no equal in battle, having spent two millennia learning his art from the greatest swordsmen that ever lived.

Non-First Black Council Members

Agan Ravaar

Agan Ravaar is one of the *mocked*. He has greenish flesh and small pointed ears. He wears fineries, and always appears hooded to hide his disfigurements. His eyes blaze vengeful scarlet, tiny pinpricks of malice in the folds of his hood.

Ravaar rarely attends Black Council meetings. His uncommon intelligence has done little to still the attitude towards his kind. The *mocked* will always be considered second class vampires. Ravaar has publicly spoken out against the treatment of the *mocked* on many occasions, directing this anger firmly in the direction of the Black Council. Some whisper that the *mocked* may soon abandon Avystervan in favour of finding a new unlife free from the prejudice of the Black Council.

Avernuus

This ebon-skinned elf is the leader of the drow House *Avernuus*. With long black hair and pale yellow eyes, Avernuus commands his Shadow Vampires with an indomitable grip. He wears black robes of rich velvet and carries a long smooth stave, the *Staff of Ochre Shadow* that he himself crafted centuries ago. He has a white goatee and long tapered ears. Standing over seven feet tall, Avernuus is an imposing figure, and has amazing skill in melee with his staff. He is devoted to the Black Council and has seen his drow rise to greatness over the centuries. He despises mortal drow, seeing them as weak and afraid to make the transformation into undeath and greatness.

Corth

Corth 'the grey' is an Ash Vampire. With liquid grey eyes, he stands over eight feet tall, slender with sloping bald head. He rarely speaks unless he has something to say and when he does, pronounces every syllable, speaking slowly so all can hear. With a heart of ice he is eager to begin the destruction of the mortal races. He favours knives and wicked implements of torture and regularly visits the mortal cities to indulge in acts of wanton torture and destruction.

Malik Faldein

Malik is the grotesque member of the Ravenous on the Black Council. A hideous and towering creature, Malik has deep emerald, sinewy flesh and stands over nine feet in height. He wears finery and is fond of rare toxins and ancient mystical poisons.

Moloch

Moloch is a bitter vampire. Horribly burned in the fires that ravaged Veil he was not one of the First. He fell in the great melee that destroyed the city. After his death, necromantic energies seeped into him, perhaps with a blessing from Vangual and he awoke at dusk the following night as the first Fire Vampire.

Moloch is a bitter and vengeful vampire. He wears hooded vermilion robes that are enchanted to resist the transformation into flame. A powerful wizard, he works solely for the Black Council and is considered one of the most learned scholars and elementalists in the realm. He runs the Scorched Hand, a powerful order of vampiric elementalists who have mastered control over their positive energies of fire and flame.

Other Notable Characters

Arikostinaal

This lich is both ancient and powerful. One of the first liches, Arikostinaal oversaw the creation of Avystervan, offering assistance to the newly created Children of Vangual more than two millennia ago.

Over the centuries, Arikostinaal's studies have taken him away from the Black Council and off on some strange and secret quest. Now, the Black Council no longer fully trust their ancient advisor and his motives are in question. Once Arikostinaal's eyes blazed a vengeful crimson, now they simmer with radiant azure.

Where does the ancient lich really place his allegiance and what powers are behind his mysterious transformation?

Avystyx

This ancient bard and prophet was slain long ago. Many say he allowed himself to be slain, that he found within himself a fragment of mortality and it pained him so much that he forced himself to sit out the dawn. The Black Council are in possession of his ashes, yet even they have been unsuccessful in restoring him to unlife.

The Devoted Incarnate believe that he will return one day to decipher his prophecies written in a language none can understand. Only Avystyx can lead the Children of Vangual to their black Eden…

Ket uth Makkar

This ancient mind flayer is the leader of the Union, the house of vampire psychics. It is said that Ket uth Makkar has mastered the sun and that even when he sleeps, his mind is free to roam the mortal realms. It is said he can teach this power to others for a price, but that he does not charge mere gold.

The Union are powerful, focusing their efforts on watching Avystervan for intruders as well as searching the mortal realms for promising new recruits.

Phillian Artus Alucidan

Phillian is the *vigilant*, the watcher of the City. He has been in existence for well over a thousand years. He keeps to himself, having kept his mortality, perhaps on a whim of the gods. While he is evil, he is certainly not despicable, finding no pleasure in destruction or causing senseless agony to those upon whom he feeds. He knows many things, having seen vampire society form over the last millennium.

That he is the only descendant of Avystyx is perhaps the only reason the Black Council keep him alive. Many of the Council have demanded his destruction, but Arikostinaal has commanded that Phillian be kept alive, at least for the moment…

Salvatorian Vanadayne

Until recently, Salvatorian was leader of the guild of sorcerers in Avystervan. He has disappeared and his whereabouts are unknown. The Black Council has appointed the highest-ranking member of the order Sorcarae to continue his work during his absence.

Chapter Eleven: Vampire Broods

A brood is a group of vampires that make their home in one particular location. Broods typically consist of a 'family' of vampires, one master and his Scion, although this is not always the case. There is greater strength in numbers and often a brood has good relations with vampires of other races. Many broods try to ensure that they have at least one Vangaard or Ravenous close by at all times.

Broods can be found in remote locales, close to several villages or towns (where the feeding is good), in crypts or *places of rest* or most commonly in cities. Some even make their bases in town houses where the most civilised (and daring) vampires live.

The Black Council is careful to maintain a presence in every city where a brood exists. Every major town has at least one residence owned by the First, locations wrapped in darkness and magic and sealed away from the prying eyes of the *Powers of Light*. These ancient vampires usually have their own broods that are information gatherers and have their own agenda. These broods are the eyes and ears of the Black Council.

Surviving in a City

City broods must be more cautious than their rural counterparts. They must be careful to avoid the ever watchful gaze of the *Powers of Light*. They cannot afford to take risks with their kills. While they know the *Powers of Light* have their eyes scrutinising the night, they know they cannot be everywhere at once. A cautious brood can exist for centuries without being discovered.

Other Dangers

The *Powers of Light* are not the only worries for a city brood. Random elements can prove to be their undoing. A passing paladin or a wandering band of adventurers can prove to be the ruin of a brood that has existed for centuries. Of great concern are good Dhampyre and vampire hunters who actively seek out and destroy vampire broods across the realm (see Vampire Hunters, **Powers of Light**).

How do Vampires hide from the Powers of Light?

The Children of Vangual are careful. They loom out of the shadows to feed, then vanish back into the darkness once again. They use their dominate powers when they can to feast freely, and are careful not to feed from the same mortal too often.

It is conceivable that there are more evil things in a city than vampires. Vampires certainly aren't the greatest of a clerical order's worries (although they are high up the list). Most religions do not have the resources to investigate an order of powerful vampires and the ones that do are fully aware of the dangers of confronting a brood of ancient vampires on their own territory.

Elder vampires have the power to mask their aura, hiding their presence from the holy senses of the *Powers of Light*. Additionally, many vampires employ high level wizards to erect wards to guard against detection. Many buildings have *nondetection* wards in place, while others rely on liberal use of the *aura of tranquility* spell. Clerics using their *sense* powers typically overlook the presence of vampires using these powerful spells.

Many vampires have preferred hunting grounds; areas from which they regularly feed. Most rely on mortal servants to aid them in large cities, having broods that consist of a number of slaves, aids and worshippers. These vassals plus vampire simulacrum go a long way to protecting sleeping vampires during the day and providing an excellent cover against their nightly activities.

When things are going well, a vampire brood can have an idyllic life in a city. Many such broods have feasted upon the residents of the most heavily populated cities for hundreds of years. They have their choice of mortals from which to feed and can move about at their leisure, unseen in general by the populace.

Making a Living

Vampires have many powers at their disposal to make money. Their powers of domination are considerable and they can easily force a mortal to hand over their riches and 'forget' about the incident.

But vampires typically do not use their powers for petty larceny. A vampire merchant can ensure a trade goes in his favor without the mortal ever suspecting anything is amiss. A vampire can get an incredible deal on collectibles and works of art, as well as lowering the price on anything they buy. Those that can mingle with the gentry use their powers to their advantage, stealing the hearts and passions of the ladies and capturing the minds of the rich gentlemen.

Of course, theft and deception aren't the only ways a vampire can make money. They can *thrice touch* various folk around a city, making powerful allies and increasing their network of contacts. But there are better ways for any vampire to make money…

Blood

The Children of Vangual trade primarily in blood. Whether fresh or bottled, vampires need blood to survive and they will go to great lengths to obtain it. With the Black Cabal creating all kinds of magical containers to capture fresh blood, vampires have an easier time of storing it for future use.

Blood is considered one of the major vampiric currencies. Of course, many vampires trade in mortals, keeping slaves for the purposes of siphoning blood for trade.

It is considered customary to 'sweeten' a deal by adding some fine blood to any transaction.

Considered particular delicacies are:

* Wizards. Spellcasters are considered particularly delectable. Very high-level wizard blood can sell for a considerable sum. Sorcerers do not have the same taste and their blood is not as desirable.
* New-born babies - those no older than seven days.
* Blood from virgins, particularly women/girls in their early to mid teens.
* Clerics, particularly goodly aligned, high level priests.
* The blood of avatars, solars and powerful religious figures.
* Dhampyre blood, particularly that of the goodly aligned.
* Goodly aligned, hero vampire blood.

SAMPLE BROODS

These are just some of the types of broods a character may encounter in a city. There are many others, the Children of Vangual are cunning and foul creatures.

THE HOUSE OF HEALING

The House of Healing is a poor house located in the slums of any city. Offering food, a warm bed and comfort to those in need, the house is a façade for the vampires that lurk within. Evil and neutral clerics masquerading as good healers lure travellers, the impoverished and the homeless within its doors. Once inside, the vampires feast on their blood when they sleep. Many folk vanish over the course of a year, but no one complains. Some speculate that the authorities are aware of the vampires, but as they are doing the city a 'service' they have not yet chosen to act against them.

Note: In situations where the House of Healing has dealings with the public, only the neutral clerics deal with paladins and representatives of the *Powers of Light*.

THE POOR HOUSE

On the surface the Poor House looks like a place of warmth and life, a cheery home for the orphans of the city. Underneath it is a place of terrible sickness and despair. Run by the Ravenous that control *thrice touched* mortal wardens, the Poor House is careful to maintain a flawless façade. They spend much time maintaining their image. They help the community, offering services, money and assistance to those who need it. They are careful to have 'front' children, those who are kept away from the diabolical acts that occur when evening comes… When darkness falls, the Poor House sells blood to other vampires and provides a service where a vampire can feast upon a chosen child for a fee.

THE BLACK EYE

A group of elite vampire rogues and bards. The Guild of the Black Eye pose as travellers, gathering information from across the realm and feeding it back to the guild that operates in the largest cities across the realms. Created from the most skilled thieves and bards, these vampires are typically elder vampires that steal purely for their own intellectual purposes. They steal from the powerful or from those who are magically protected. They are controlled by Raxx who actively controls many of the thieves' guilds across the mortal realms. The Black Eye targets treasures and items of great power and steals them for the Black Council. It is said that when the Black Eye is upon you, nothing is safe, or sacred.

VAMPIRE SAFE HOUSES

Run by those mortals in the employ of the Black Council, a safe house is a place where a travelling vampire can find sanctuary during the day. They can be found in many of the largest cities in the realm, and also in some of the smaller towns.

Each safe house has a name, and a Blood Gate to which a vampire can link. All are protected against scrying by powerful Wards of Tranquility (see 'Wards' - **Powers of Light**). Some vampires have safe houses that are designated for use by the various vampire races. These buildings are typically located in the seedier parts of town, although some daring safe houses are located in plain view of the *Powers of Light*.

THE DARK ICON

A brood in the largest of cities. They gather in the shadows, typically in the slums where they offer money to those who would offer them fresh blood.

The Dark Icon pays very well for the fresh blood of children - taking advantage of the poverty in an area to gain the willing services of the impoverished masses. Some even pay for their first born to be sacrificed so a family can get out of the slums. And the Dark Icon pay very well indeed for this service - in the region of several hundred gold coins, although whatever they can pay, they will. All mortals are charmed to forget their transactions, or at least never to speak of them again. Many families escape the slums, but they carry a terrible secret with them to their graves.

THE ORDER OF THE NECROMANTIC VESTIBULE

The Necromantic Vestibule consists of necromancers and sages wishing to study vampirism and death. They are almost exclusively mortal and are funded by the Black Cabal to continue important research into the fields of the dark arts.

The order knows many of the magical happenings in the mortal realms and has a great understanding of the ways of life and undeath. They have dealings with both vampires and liches on a daily basis, and many are specialists in all manner of fields of necromancy. While they are not entirely evil, many have little regard for mortal life, and they do not socialise well with other wizards.

THE ORDER OF THE RAVEN

This order of cruel black fighters make their home in the docks area of one of the largest cities. Over a century old, it was founded by a Vangaard who was both cruel and exceptionally brutish. He was finally slain, but his brood continued. Now consisting solely of Black Bloods and an Ash Vampire, the Order of the Raven uses extortion and fear to establish a reign of terror over the local merchants. Few are even aware they are vampires, only that they are powerful warriors of incredible strength and skill. They have great sway over the docks and aid the Black Council in bringing vampires into the city by sea.

THE IMMORTAL MNEMOSYNE

A guild of vampire bards that seek to capture the greatest living minds the world has to offer and preserve them for all time.

This rich guild funded by House *Sonoruus* travels the world, seeking the greatest athletes, warriors, bards and artists and offering them eternal life in exchange for a set period upon the earth to finish their mortal affairs.

NEVER MAKE A DEAL WITH A VAMPIRE!

An artist and scholar called Algenon Faustus decided that after ten years of being given all the money, health and power he could ever want, that he would renege upon his agreement with the Immortal Mnemosyne. The Black Council sent a party of Ash Vampires to claim him at the temple to the sun god where he took up residence…

Doctor Faustus was never seen or heard from again.

CHAPTER TWELVE: MONSTERS

BLOOD HOUND

Large Undead
Hit Dice: 6d10+12 (45 hp)
Initiative: +0
Speed:. 30 ft., 60 ft.
AC: 19 (-1 Size, +2 Dex, +8 Natural)
Attacks: Bite +8, Claws x 2 +8
Damage: Claws 1d6 +2, Bite 1d4 +2
Face/Reach: 5 ft. by 5ft./5 ft.
Special Attacks: Blood Drain
Special Qualities: Damage Resistance 5/+1, Scent, Sense Prey
Saves: Fort +7, Ref: +4, Will +1
Feats: Improved Initiative, Multiattack, Track
Abilities: Str: 14, Dex: 15, Int: +3, Wis: +12, Con: 15, Cha: 8
Skills: Intuit Direction +15, Listen +15, Move Silently +10, Search +10
Climate: Any
Organisation: None
Challenge Rating: 5
Treasure: None
Alignment: CE
Advancement: None

Blood Hounds are hulking monstrosities formed from blood. Transformed from the worst performing vampire clerics in Vangual's service, they are vaguely dog shaped, but with long crimson covered bodies and scarlet matted fur and piercing vermilion eyes. A mass of sinews and tendons, they leave b l o o d y footprints as they move.

They have the mystical ability to track blood. So long as they have the original trail, they can track blood, even when the victim has transported themselves over great distances. Given enough time, a blood hound can track any prey.

COMBAT

Blood Drain (Ex): A Blood Hound can drink the blood of the living by making a successful grapple check. If it pins the foe, it inflicts 1 point of temporary Constitution damage per round through its bite attack and heals 1d12 hit points per point of blood drunk.

Note: Magically preserved blood can be used by a Blood Hound to track its prey, so long as the blood is not 'physically' more than a single day old.

Sense Prey (Su): A Blood Hound can sense blood. Providing it has a fresh sample of a person's blood (no more than twenty four hours old), the Blood Hound can track its target so long as it has a physical trail to follow. A Blood Hound can track any character that has moved through an area. It cannot track a character that has transported by magical means (unless it can first pick up their trail).

BLOODLING

Small Undead
Hit Dice: 1d8 (8 hp)
Initiative: +0
Speed: 20 ft.
AC: 11 (+1 Size, -1 Dex, +1 Natural)
Attacks: Slam attack +3
Damage: 1d4
Face/Reach: 5 ft. by 5ft./5 ft.
Special Attacks: Blood Drain
Special Qualities: Blood Strength, Immunity to Bladed Weapons, Merge
Saves: Fort +1, Ref: +1, Will +1
Abilities: Str: 9, Dex: 9, Int: 3, Wis: 3, Con: 9, Cha: 3
Skills: Listen +3, Spot +3
Climate: Any
Organisation: None
Challenge Rating: 1 (special)
Treasure: None
Alignment: CE
Advancement: 2-6HD

Bloodlings appear as vaguely humanoid masses of clotted blood, sinews and organs. They are favoured by Vangual and are said to be the transformed remnants of his enemies. They reek of blood and leave oozing trails of gore as they move. They are always found within pools of blood, from which they stretch themselves out forming their undulating mass from the greatest concentration of gore.

To be called into being, a bloodling needs to be given at least 8 hit points worth of blood. This blood is absorbed into the bloodling and gives it 8 hit points (one point of vampire Blood is worth 12 + *age* hit points).

COMBAT

Blood Drain (Ex): Physical damage caused by a bloodling can be used to heal it if is has sustained any damage. Blood is absorbed for the purposes of augmenting their abilities or creating new bloodlings (see below).

Blood Strength (Ex): Bloodlings can choose to form new versions of themselves, or to advance their own abilities. Bloodlings can choose to advance from 1 to 6 HD, needing an equivalent amount of blood (8 hits points of blood) to do so. They gain +1 to hit, damage and Strength when they gain a HD as well as an additional 8 hit points.

Immunity to Bladed Weapons (Ex): Bloodlings are wholly immune to bladed weapons and only take half damage from other physical attacks.

Merge (Ex): This ability is opposite to *Split*. Bloodlings can merge together to form even more powerful creatures. They add their HD and powers, taking a full round action to do so. Bloodlings that do this become one entity, to a maximum of 6HD.

Blood Ooze

Medium-Size Ooze
Hit Dice: 5d12+10 (42hp)
Initiative: -5 (Dex)
Speed: 10 ft., climb 10 ft.
AC: 5 (Size +0, -5 Dex)
Attacks: Slam +6 melee
Damage: Tentacle 1d6+1
Face/Reach: 5 ft. by 10ft./10 ft.
Special Attacks: Blood Drain, Tentacle
Special Qualities: Blindsight, Multiattack, Ooze, Split
Saves: Fort +5, Ref: -4, Will -4
Abilities: Str: 12, Dex: 1, Int: 1, Wis: 1, Con: 11, Cha: 1
Feats: Improved Grapple
Climate: Any
Organisation: Solitary
Challenge Rating: Special (or 4)
Alignment: Always Neutral
Advancement: Special

The Blood Ooze is the creation of the Blood Mage and given life by Vangual. They appear as shifting pools of inky black blood, almost invisible in areas of darkness. They seep along, seeking living flesh that they can sense within a 1000 yards radius. They are typically conjured by vampire mages who bolster their abilities with their own Blood. A point of attuned Blood gives the Blood Ooze hit points equal to 12 + the vampire's *age* category.

A Blood Ooze is typically stationed at the entrance to a dungeon where it provides excellent protection against any low level characters that might come its way

COMBAT

Tentacle (Ex): A Blood Ooze can extend a tentacle for every two of its hit dice. These tentacles have a reach of 10 ft. and can inflict 1d6 +1 damage per attack. They will attempt to drag a character into the main body of the ooze with a successful grapple attack. A blood ooze gains 1 hit point for every 2 it inflicts with its tentacle attacks.

Immunity to Bladed Weapons (Ex): Bloodlings are wholly immune to bladed weapons and only take half damage from other forms of physical melee attack.

Split (Ex): A blood ooze can chose to split itself at any time. When a blood ooze reaches 10 hit dice, it immediately splits into two separate oozes of 5 hit dice each.

Blood Drain (Ex): A blood ooze will drain the blood of those trapped within its main body. It will attempt to drag victims into itself, or will hurry to envelop those it senses are prone. It will drain one point of Constitution per round, gaining hit points equal to the character's hit dice. For every additional 12 hit points the blood ooze absorbs above its maximum, it gains an additional hit die, increasing both in size and ability (gaining +1 to hit, damage and Strength for every hit die it advances).

Lesser Blood Ooze

A vampire that has a blood ooze as a familiar will conjure a lesser Blood Ooze. Lesser oozes have 2 hit dice and are small creatures with only 15 hit points.

Children of Vangual

(Based on a 6th level, age 1 black fighter)
Medium-size Undead (Black Blood)
Hit Dice: 6d12 +24 (63hp)
Initiative: +9 (+5 Dex , Improved Initiative)
Speed: 40 ft.
AC: 17 (+0 Size, +5 Dex, +2 Chaimail)
Attacks: Slam attack +12/+7
Damage: 1d6+6 plus energy drain
Face/Reach: 5 ft. by 5ft./5 ft.
Special Attacks: Energy Drain, Blood Drain, Domination
Special Qualities: Damage Reduction 15/+1, Fast Healing 5, Resistance: Cold/Electricity 20
Saves: Fort +9, Ref: +7, Will +4
Abilities: Str: 22, Dex: 20, Bld: 19; Int: +15, Wis: +14, Cha: 15
Skills: Concentration +15, Hide +12, Intuit Direction +7, Listen +14, Move Silently +11, Search +10, Sense Motive +12, Spot +15.
Feats: Alertness, Cleave, Combat Reflexes, Dodge, Great Cleave, Improved Critical, Improved Initiative, Lightning Reflexes, Power Attack, Weapon Focus (longsword)
Weaknesses: Allergy: Garlic, Allergy: Iron, Allergy: Silver, Cannot Enter Holy Ground, Cannot Enter without Invitation, Chill of the Grave, Fear of Fire, Fear of Sunlight, No Reflection, Stench of the Grave, Water Vulnerability.
Dark Gifts: Blood Agility, Blood Armor, Blood Strength, Blood Speed, Blood Vault, Claws, Gaseous Form, Turn Resistance.
Climate/Terrain: Any land and underground.
Organization: Solitary, pair, gang (2-5), or troop (1-2 plus 2-5 Vampire Scion).
Treasure: Double standard
Alignment: Chaotic Evil
Advancement: By character class

Black Bloods are the most common of all the vampires. They make up over 80% of all the Children of Vangual and can be found everywhere across the mortal realms. They integrate the most easily into mortal society - finding it easier to hunt in populated areas where they might be noticed. The *Chill* is never quite as strong in a Black Blood as it is in many other vampires and they have the most mortal seeming appearance. Black Bloods are made up of nearly every race, from elves to orcs, and even the more exotic races, such as Mind Flayer and Troll.

Black Bloods form broods in cities, or hide in crypts in remote areas close to several towns or villages where the feeding is good. Many have lived for hundred of years and are crafty and powerful beings that are not easily slain.

COMBAT

Undead: Immune to mind-influencing effects, poison, sleep, paralysis, stunning and disease. Not subject to critical hits, subdual damage, ability damage, energy drain or death from massive damage. The Will save against this vampire's charm and the Fortitude save to regain lost levels to its energy drain have a DC of 16.

Black Fighter Skills: Magical Weapon +1

Magic Items Carried: Blood Pearls 3, +2 Longsword, +2 Chainmail Armor.

Challenge Rating: 9

CONSANGUINEOUS VAMPIRE

Medium-size Undead

Hit Dice: 1d12 (6hp)
Initiative: +0
Speed: 30 ft.
AC: 13 (+0 Size, +2 Dex, +1 Natural)
Attacks: Bite +1, 2 x Claws +0
Damage: Bite 1d3, Claws 1d2
Face/Reach: 5 ft. by 5ft./5 ft.
Special Attacks: Drain Blood
Special Qualities: Undead, Spider Climb
Saves: Fort: +2, Ref: +4, Will +0
Abilities: Str: 10, Dex: 14, C: -, Int: 11, Wis: 11, Cha: 10
Skills: Hide +4, Listen +4, Move Silently +4, Search +4, Spot +4
Feats: Multiattack
Climate: Any
Organisation: Solitary or pack 1- 12
Challenge Rating: 1/2
Treasure: Standard
Alignment: CE
Advancement: 2HD

Consanguineous vampires the 'least of vampires' were created by the Black Cabal. A punishment inflicted upon their greatest enemies, consanguineous vampires are ravenous creatures tormented by madness and hunger. Created in a special ritual, the procedure of which is known only to members of the Black Cabal, the process transforms a mortal (or a vampire) into a consanguineous vampire. When used upon a vampire it is considered a terrible curse. Consanguineous vampires exist solely on blood (see below). They have few powers of their own but have *all* the weaknesses of a vampire. They have soft pulpy bodies and none of a vampire's strengths. They are often indistinguishable from true vampires.

A consanguineous vampire must feed daily. Although they only require two points of blood to satisfy their craving, they must feed or grow increasingly weak. They lose a hit point for every day they cannot gain their full quota of blood. A consanguineous vampire that falls to 0 hit points is instantly destroyed. They can drink from the blood of the dead or the dying, but only obtain half the normal sustenance from such sources.

Consanguineous vampires are completely under the dominance of their master and will obey *any* order from any member of the Black Cabal (although they will only destroy themselves on an order from their creator).

COMBAT

Drain Blood (Ex): A consanguineous vampire can drink the blood of the living by making a successful grapple check. If it pins the foe, it inflicts 1 point of temporary Constitution damage per round through its bite attack.

Spider Climb (Su): Consanguineous Vampires gain the Dark Gift, Spider Climb.

ADVANCEMENT

A consanguineous vampire is created with 1 HD for every 5 levels it had when it was alive (to a maximum of 4 HD). They retain their original feats although they lose all abilities not applicable to a creature of their new HD. Some retain very basic spellcasting abilities.

WHY DON'T VAMPIRES CONTROL THE WORLD?

Vampires are arrogant and solitary. They like their own broods and their own feeding grounds.

When it comes down to it, vampires are exceedingly petty creatures. They like their own evil schemes, devising their own plots without having to listen to any other voices. They don't like being told what to do or when to do it. Joining a group of vampires for any kind of concerted attack on the mortal realms would be near impossible.

Additionally, the Children of Vangual are powerful - but they have their limits. A vampire can only dominate so many. Even an army of vampires could not control enough of a city to bring it to its knees. The disadvantage of having to sleep through they day is a terrible weakness, and as past history tells, those vampires who try to enslave even a small town fail. They may have command over the night but when dawn comes...

Regardless of their failings, vampires have been successful in enslaving remote villages in the past - at least for a short time...

The Town of Gethin was one that must have been just that little bit too close to the city of Veil. The vampires decided they would enslave it. There, the food was good and what militia the town had could be easily overpowered.

Or so the Black Bloods thought...

The Children of Vangual were successful. They dominated, controlled and killed enough of the town's guards to take command of it. But a single cleric sent a message to a nearby town before he was slain.

He sent just one word 'vampires!'

The Children of Vangual managed to hold the town for five whole days before reinforcements arrived. Armed with stakes and powerful holy magic, the militia swept through the city breaking through any resistance and shattering the vampires' defenses.

A shame really. One could almost feel sorry for the vampires.

Almost...

Phillian

ELEMENTAL, BLOOD

Blood elementals appear as a swirling mass of blood and gore. They typically leave a trail of crimson behind them as they pass. Conjured from the realm of Vangual they are neither alive nor dead, but have a vague sentience that ever seeks fresh blood. Blood elementals can appear as a puddle of red-black blood or appear as an undulating mass. They commonly appear as a column of dripping gore. Blood Elementals are of similar size to water elementals and have approximately 25% additional weight for their size.

	Blood Elemental, Small Small Elemental	Blood Elemental, Medium Medium-size Elemental	Blood Elemental, Large Large Elemental
Hit Dice:	2d8+2 (11hp)	4d8+12 (30hp)	8d8+32 (68hp)
Initiative:	+0	+0	+0
Speed:	20 ft. Climb 20 ft.	20 ft. Climb 20 ft.	20 ft. Climb 20 ft.
AC:	17 (+1 size, +6 natural)	19 (+1 Dex, +8 natural)	20 (-1 size, +2 Dex, +9 natural)
Attacks:	Slam +3 melee	Slam +6 melee	Slam +13/+8 melee
Damage:	Slam 1d6+1	Slam 1d8+2	Slam 2d8+3
Face/Reach:	5ft. by 5 ft./5 ft.	5ft. by 5 ft./5 ft.	5ft. by 5 ft./10 ft.
Special Attacks:	Blood Drain	Blood Drain	Blood Drain
Special Qualities:	Elemental	Elemental	Damage Resistance 10/+1 Elemental
Saves:	Fort +4, Ref +0, Will +0	Fort +7, Ref +2, Will +1	Fort +10, Ref +4, Will +2
Abilities:	Str 12, Dex 10, Con 13, Int 4, Wis 11, Cha 11	Str 14, Dex 12, Con 17, Int 4, Wis 11, Cha 11	Str 16, Dex 14, Con 19, Int 6, Wis 11, Cha 11
Skills:	Listen +5, Spot +5	Listen +7, Spot +7	Listen +11, Spot +11
Feats:	Power Attack	Power Attack	Cleave, Power Attack

	Blood Elemental, Huge Huge Elemental	Blood Elemental, Greater Huge Elemental	Blood Elemental, Elder Huge Elemental
Hit Dice:	16d8+80 (152hp)	21d8+105 (199hp)	24d8+120 (228hp)
Initiative:	+0	+0	+0
Speed:	20 ft. Climb 20 ft.	20 ft. Climb 20 ft.	20 ft. Climb 20 ft.
AC:	21 (-2 size, +4 Dex, +9 natural)	22 (-2 size, +5 Dex, +9 natural)	23 (-2 size, +6 Dex, +9 natural)
Attacks:	Slam +19/+14/+9 melee	Slam +20/+15/+10 melee	Slam +25/+20/+15/+10 melee
Damage:	Slam 2d10+4	Slam 2d10+5	Slam 2d10+6
Face/Reach:	10ft. by 5 ft./15 ft.	10ft. by 5 ft./15 ft.	10ft. by 5 ft./15 ft.
Special Attacks:	Blood Drain	Blood Drain	Blood Drain
Special Qualities:	Damage Resistance 10/+2, Elemental	Damage Resistance 10/+2, Elemental	Damage Resistance 15/+3, Elemental
Saves:	Fort +15, Ref +9, Will +5	Fort +17, Ref +12, Will +7	Fort +19, Ref +14, Will +8
Abilities:	Str 18, Dex 18, Con 21, Int 6, Wis 11, Cha 11	Str 20, Dex 20, Con 21, Int 6, Wis 11, Cha 11	Str 22, Dex 22, Con 21, Int 6, Wis 11, Cha 11
Skills:	Listen +18, Spot +18	Listen +23, Spot +23	Listen +26, Spot +26
Feats:	Cleave, Great Cleave, Power Attack, Sunder	Cleave, Great Cleave, Improved Critical, Power Attack, Sunder	Cleave, Great Cleave, Improved Critical, Improved Initiative, Power Attack, Sunder

Climate/Terrain: Any land and underground
Organisation: Solitary
Challenge Rating: Small 1, Medium 3, Large 5, Huge 7, Greater 9, Elder 11
Treasure: None
Alignment: Neutral
Advancement: Small 3 HD (Small), Medium 5-7 HD (Medium-size), Large 9-15 HD (Large), Huge 17-20 HD (Huge), Greater 22-23 HD (Huge), Elder 25+HD (Huge)

COMBAT

Blood Drain (Ex): The blood elemental can drain hit points from its foes. When fighting living enemies the blood elemental can heal itself by draining up to its HD in hit points per round. Excess hit points are lost; it cannot have more than its maximum number of hit points. The blood elemental causes painful welts as it attacks with its flailing gore drenched limbs.

VAMPIRE GHOUL

Medium-size Undead
Hit Dice: 6d12 (39hp)
Initiative: +7 (+3 Dex, +4 Improved Initiative)
Speed: 30 ft.
AC: 19 (+0 Size, +3 Dex, +6 Natural)
Attacks: Bite +11 melee, 2 x Claws +6 melee
Damage: Bite 1d6 +5 (plus energy drain), claws 1d6+5
Face/Reach: 5 ft. by 5ft./5 ft.
Special Attacks: Devour Flesh, Domination, Energy Drain, Paralysis
Special Qualities: Create Spawn, Fast Healing, Undead
Saves: Fort: +0, Ref: +7, Will +4
Abilities: Str: 20, Dex: 16, Con: -, Int: 6, Wis: 10, Cha: 10
Skills: Hide +8, Listen +8, Move Silently + 6, Search +6, Spot +6
Feats: Alertness, Dodge, Improved Initiative, Multiattack, Weapon Finesse (Bite)
Climate: Any
Organisation: Solitary, Pack 1-4
Challenge Rating: 5
Treasure: Standard
Alignment: CE
Advancement: None

Created by the twisted diseases of the Ravenous and the sorceries of the Black Cabal, vampire ghouls are twisted versions of vampires. Part vampire, part ghoul, they must eat the flesh of the living in order to survive.

They have partially rotted, green skin with filthy claws and pointed teeth. Their eyes glow a nacreous green in darkness.

Normally indistinguishable from ghouls. These creatures rarely exist anywhere other than Avystervan or in regions where a vampire master desires a particularly nasty end to his enemies. They are vicious and nearly mindless, bestial creatures incapable of proper thought. A rare few have the ability to communicate, muttering and growling in an almost incomprehensible tongue. Even fewer gain full sentience and have formed their own society, but there are only a handful of these every century.

Vampire Ghouls need to inflict their HD in hit points damage per day to survive. A vampire ghoul loses 1 HD per day in which it cannot get its full quota of flesh. Although they can live upon the dead, they gain only half the sustenance from carrion (a corpse is worth its original Constitution (-1 per day) in hit points).

Vampire Ghouls do not tend to live in places where food is scarce. They can be found hidden in places of death where they can feast upon the remains of the living. Some live in crypts, others close to small towns or villages. Many are kept as pets by evil vampires, a particularly efficient method of ending the lives of their foes.

COMBAT

Create Spawn (Su): Mortals devoured by a vampire ghoul rise up as vampire ghouls in 1d4 nights time.

Devour Flesh (Su): A vampire ghoul can devour the flesh of the living by making a successful grapple check. If it pins the foe (or the foe is already incapacitated), it inflicts 1d4 points of damage per round. Damage inflicted by a vampire ghoul in this way is lost. Although the wounds can be healed, the hit points cannot be restored until the vampire ghoul has been destroyed. Powerful magical restoratives will increase the healing process, but neither can work until the vampire ghoul is dead. Hit points return at a rate of 1 per week.

Domination (Su): As the vampire power *domination*.

Energy Drain (Su): Vampire Ghouls drain 1 level upon the successful delivery of a bite attack.

Fast Healing (Su): Vampire ghouls heal at a rate of 5 hit points per round.

Paralysis (Ex): Those hit by a vampire ghoul's bite or claw attack must succeed at a Fortitude Save (DC 15) or be paralysed for 2d4 minutes.

PLAYING A VAMPIRE GHOUL

Vampire Ghouls are typically blood-crazed monsters that are kept in the sewers under Avystervan or in crypts as powerful guards.

Those that elevate themselves from the Void gain the ability to speak with reasonable clarity and a modicum of intelligence. They gain powers and abilities as a standard Black Blood (but do not gain any additional Dark Gifts at creation or due to each new age category they gain).

Vampire Ghouls are mistrusted by vampire society and those that are fully capable of independence are rare. There are a small number that live in Avystervan, but they keep to themselves. Most free willed Vampire Ghouls form broods in cities, where they can exist in secrecy, close to crypts or where the feeding is good.

ECL: +1 (per age category)

> *"The foulest stench is in the air,*
> *The funk of forty thousand years*
> *And grizzy ghouls from every tomb,*
> *Are closing in to seal your doom..."*
> Vincent Price, Black Cabal

VAMPIRIC SIMULACRUM

Medium-size Construct
Hit Dice: Increases to d12
Initiative: +4
Speed: Same as the base creature
AC: The base creature's natural armor improves by +6
Attacks: A Simulacrum retains all the attacks of the base creature and gains a slam attack if it did not already have one
Damage: Standard
Face/Reach: 5 ft. by 5ft./5 ft.
Special Attacks: None
Special Qualities: Construct, Damage Reduction 20/+2, Fast Healing (5), Magic Immunity
Saves: Fort +6, Ref +5, Will +6
Abilities: S: +6, Dex +4, Int: +0, Wis +0, Con (Blood) +6, Cha +2
Skills: As base creature
Feats: As base creature, plus Alertness , Combat Reflexes, Improved Initiative
Climate: Any
Organisation: Any
Challenge Rating: Same as base creature +2
Treasure: Standard
Alignment: Neutral
Advancement: By class

Vampire simulacra are a vampire's link to the mortal world. Created by powerful magic, they are typically kept as the head of a household where they are used to conduct matters in a city or place where the vampire has dealings with mortals. They look and seem completely mortal in every way.

A vampire simulacrum retains all the knowledge it had in life, all feats and powers. A vampire can only have one simulacrum at any one time and should his current creation be destroyed, must wait a full month before beginning the preparations to create a new one.

Simulacra have tremendous powers, they can suffer terrible wounds, have near limitless stamina and live for hundreds of years. They are to a greater extent, mortal, although they radiate powerful necromantic magics and detect as magical creatures. They do not need to sleep or rest and burn just one point of Blood per week (unless they consciously chose to expend their resources of Blood on their abilities). Simulacra suffer no ill effects from sunlight or holy spells, and are the ideal creatures to act as bodyguards, merchants or those who deal with intruders, visitors or the public.

Simulacra are powerful creations. They are wholly subservient to their masters, but do not have will beyond that specified in their creation. A vampire typically has an excellent relationship with their simulacrum.

Simulacra are powered by attuned Blood. If they run out of Blood, they simply stop working until they receive a fresh supply. They do not age during this time and many remain dormant for centuries with the unexpected deaths of their masters.

When a simulacrum is reduced to 0 hit points it instantly turns into a greenish goo that quickly dissolves into a steaming puddle of nothing but the clothes it was wearing.

Simulacra advance as a standard character, retaining all their skills and powers they had in life. In addition, they can buy the vampiric Dark Gifts: Blood Agility, Blood Speed, Blood Stamina and Blood Strength as if they were fledgling vampires.

A vampire can scry through the eyes of his simulacrum if he knows the spell *eyes of the damned;* otherwise he must rely solely on a telepathic link between the two. This link allows the two to communicate regardless of distance but does not work across planes or in magically warded locations.

A simulacrum can attempt to raise their master from sleep during the day, if he needs to by telepathically calling him. The master immediately gains a Rousing check with no penalty. The vampire simulacrum can only do this once per day.

COMBAT

Construct: Vampire Simulacrum are immune to mind-influencing effects, poison, disease, and similar effects. They are not subject to critical hits, subdual damage, ability damage, energy drain, or death from massive damage.

Fast Healing (Su): A vampire simulacrum heals at a rate of 5 hit points per round.

Magic Immunity (Ex): Vampire simulacra are immune to all spells, spell-like abilities, and supernatural effects, except as follows: cure spells inflict one point of damage per spell level upon the target. A *neutralise poison* spell drains the simulacrum of 4d6 hit points and a *heal* spell inflicts 8d8 points of damage. The simulacrum can make a Fortitude save to take only half damage from these spells.

ECL: +3

SIMULACRUM

Good day to you:...

No. I'm afraid Mr Deludigan is out of the city right now. But if you would like to leave your name and address, I'll make sure that he contacts you upon his return.

Where is he?

Out of town, on business. But he will be back after sundown.

Do I know what he wants with you?

I can but guess. You are a cleric of the Auraran are you not? I think then that it's quite clear what his desires are.

Mr Deludigan is expanding his religious tastes...

I believe he would like to have you over for dinner.

THE BLACK CABAL'S CREATIONS

MONSTER VAMPIRES

The Black Cabal have experimented with the undead for centuries. They have created just about every form of vampire imaginable, from celestial beings to the infernal. What follows is a list of the most common.

UNIQUE MONSTER VAMPIRES

SPELLMITE - TINY UNDEAD

Spellmites, or *Arcanus Phagum* are tiny vampiric creatures created by the Black Cabal. Invisible and near insubstantial, they are transmitted to a suitable host where they feed upon their arcane spell energy. Each day the spellmite resides within an arcane spellcaster, the spellmite will randomly absorb any one spell that the spellcaster knows, of any level. At the end of every day that a spellmite has drained a spell, the spellmite has a cumulative 1% chance per spell level absorbed of creating another spellmite.

Detection is very difficult. Physical assessment will not detect the presence of a spellmite, however magical discernment *may* uncover the parasite (*detect magic* will reveal some unusual magical energies but that is all). The spellmite can only be negated with a *cure disease* spell cast by a cleric of no lower than 9th level. Additionally, a spellcaster can wholly cure themselves by purging every spell they know and remaining without spells for a total number of days equal to their level, by which time, all spellmites will have died. Spellmites are highly contagious. An infected spellcaster must have no contact with other spellcasters as the spellmites can transfer from one host to another in a very short space of time

The Black Cabal have been creating ever more powerful spellmites, and are in the final stages of creating a spellmite that can absorb two or even three spells of varying levels from an arcane spellcaster per day.

BLOOD LEECH - TINY UNDEAD

Blood leeches are pale wormlike creatures. Vampiric in nature, they are about 6 inches long and cold to the touch. They are typically conjured by the Black Cabal to obtain a sample of a target's blood.

Blood leeches have 1 hit point. They can attach themselves to a target and drain 1 point of Blood (Constitution) in 1 minute (10 leeches will therefore drain 1 point of Constitution in 1 round). They are relatively harmless alone, but in great numbers, can quickly overwhelm an opponent.

A blood leech can drink up to 3 points of blood at which time it becomes swollen and engorged and transforms to a brilliant crimson color.

Detecting the presence of a blood leech is very difficult. They have an anaesthetic quality that affects both humans and vampires. A sleeping mortal may make a Will check (DC 25) to detect a feeding leech (DC 30 for a vampire). The difficulty drops (DC 20) for a waking mortal (DC 15 for a vampire who is more able to detect the depletion of their blood supplies).

COMMON MONSTER VAMPIRES

GOBLIN VAMPIRES

Small, and numerous, goblin vampires are evil and wicked. Gathering in broods, they attack in numbers, swarming their prey and devouring their fill before vanishing back into the night. Goblin vampires are often subjugated by their more powerful orc brethren. Goblin vampires can only inflict a single negative level per attack on a victim. The DC to resist their energy drain attacks is 5 + 1/2 HD + *age* + Charisma modifier. They can only inflict one negative level per energy drain attack.

Mortal goblins typically have red blood although some have green.

LIZARDMEN VAMPIRES

There is rumoured to be a clan of lizardmen vampires in the great swamps, where the mists obscure the sun and daylight never comes. There are many rumours about these ancient creatures. Some say they are so old they have passed through the Void and have some semblance of good in them. Other say that the deepest regions of the great swamps are places of utter evil where dark and ancient powers covet the souls of the good and the pure.

Lizardmen always have green blood.

OGRE VAMPIRES

Ogre vampires typically are bound to their *place of rest*, but are powerful and fearless in battle. They are frequently used as bodyguards and protectors to vampire elders.

Almost as large as the Vangaard, ogre vampires are terrible opponents and have limitless vampiric strength and stamina. Their vampiric powers are weak. The DC to resist their energy drain attacks is only 5 + 1/2 HD + *age* + Charisma modifier.

Mortal ogres have red blood.

ORC VAMPIRES

Orc vampires are evil and bloodthirsty. They enjoy death and destruction and will always slay a victim after feeding. They delight in torture and dismemberment and in causing as much physical damage as possible. They are frequently led by a powerful master who typically commands a great number of orcish vampires.

Mortal orcs can have either green or red blood.

TROLL VAMPIRES

Fearsome, troll vampires typically are bound to their *place of rest*, but are powerful in battle. They are frequently used as bodyguards and protectors to greater vampires. Troll vampires are terrible opponents indeed, they heal their wounds at an incredible rate, far more than even the most powerful elder vampires. Their vampiric powers are weak, the DC to resist their energy drain attacks is only 5 + 1/2 HD + *age* + Charisma modifier.

Mortal trolls have green blood.

Exotic Monster Vampires

Beholder Vampires

Not much is known about beholder vampires except that somehow, the transformation to undeath is possible. These creatures are powerful and live mainly in secret in Avystervan, hidden away even from other vampires. They radiate powerful necromancy and have the power to transform their targets into vampires with the use of their central eye.

Even amongst vampires there is much mistrust about the possibility of beholder vampires. They are seen as evil and capricious, and few want anything to do with them. Those that do not know better speak about strange floating shadows moving silently through the darkness.

Whispers abound of beholders created by Vangual known only as Blood Tyrants, evil and wicked creatures conjured by dark magic and filled with bloodlust for the mortal races.

Beholder vampires have utterly alien minds to mortals; the transformation into undeath makes them strange and often incomprehensible creatures, with goals and desires far from those of typical vampires.

Beholders have syrupy yellow blood.

Demons

Demons and outsiders typically can not be made into vampires. Only the greatest powers have the might to strip the divine energies from outsiders and transform them into vampires. The Black Cabal has had some minor success with lesser demons and devils, but on the whole, demonic blood will never support vampirism.

Demons typically have thick black or grey blood.

Dragons

A dragon's great size is more of a weakness than a strength in undeath, and few places are large enough to hide a dragon completely from the sun. That said, the Black Cabal have made a handful of dragons that now reside on the Elemental Planes of Ash or Negativity, allies and minions of the Necromancers that live there.

Ash dragons are fully detailed in **The Lords of the Night: Liches**.

Dragon blood is typically highly toxic to a vampire and varies greatly in color, depending on the dragon type.

Drider

Drider vampires become either clerics or mages, or a combination of the two. They are the elite guard to House *Avanaar*, where the old enmity between drow and drider stands forgotten, the ties of necromancy more powerful than any mortal hatred. With heightened senses and tremendous strength, drider vampires are fearsome indeed. Many have learned the art of *Shadowdancing* from their vampire elders, the fabled ability to cast spells and attack both in the same round. The most powerful drider, the *Crucio* sect accompany Shadow Vampires on missions of great importance.

Drider have toxic black blood.

Drow Vampires

Drow are perfectly at home with the transformation to undeath. They view it as the perfect change for those who desire eternal life or great power. Most drow seek out the black curse when they sense their youth is fading. These vampire drow are filled with knowledge and blackness and quickly become powerful indeed.

Many drow vampires become wizards or clerics. Drow sorcerers are eagerly sought by House *Avanaar* and the Black Cabal, and paid very well for their services.

Drow Powers: Drow retain the powers they had in life (as detailed in the MM). Their innate spell-like abilities are changed to casting either *bloodlight* or *darkness* up to a total of three times per day. Additionally, drow vampires gain the Move Silently feat as standard.

Drow have red blood.

Giants

There are few places giants can hide during the day with any security. Although the Black Cabal have successfully made a number of vampire giants, they do not adapt well to the change. Those that have survived now live on the Elemental Plane of Negativity in the care of the Black Council in the vast halls of the Citadel.

Whispers have been heard of towering creatures of the night storming remote places, but these stories could as easily have been the great Vangaard as much as undead giants.

The Denthalus clan are a group of vampire stone giants, powerful and massive who live in remote places in the mortal realms. When they must, they travel in massive crates on ships run by the *vampire touched*. They are seen as gods by the primitive locals who leave tributes to appease the great deities of blood and darkness.

Giants have red blood.

Mind Flayer Vampires

Mind Flayers make excellent vampires and their mind powers are greatly enhanced through the transformation to undeath. The Mind Flayers of the Union are faithful to the Black Council, although they work for no one unless it suits their ultimate goals.

Mind Flayers are typically wizards or sorcerers, although many have powerful psychic talents that make them invaluable to Avystervan. The Union teaches the ancient school of Telepathea, the mystical discipline of the mind although little is known about this beyond the confines of Ast Ath Kavaar. What is known is that only Mind Flayers can master the discipline. The silence of the dead mind considerably increases a Mind Flayer's link to their telepathic abilities.

Mind Flayer vampires must drain mental energy as well as needing to drink mortal blood to survive. Their attacks drain both Intelligence and Wisdom and they frequently devour the minds of their victims before drinking their blood.

Mind Flayers have thick grey blood.

CHAPTER THIRTEEN: DM'S NOTES

INJECTING DARKNESS INTO YOUR GAME

There are many ways to use **The Lords of the Night: Vampires** in your game. Much depends on your personal play style. A campaign can focus on powers and skills just as much as it can be about suffering and personal loss.

This book can be used on many different levels:

* It can be about salvation, a race to find redemption or to find a cure for the most terrible curse the mortal realms have ever seen.
* It can be about dark heroes or shining examples of purity despite the sinister tarnish of undeath. Being a vampire does not mean you have to be evil - nor does it mean you must abandon your old life - although maintaining it is very difficult indeed.
* It can be about the *Powers of Light* struggling to destroy evil in a city packed with vampires.
* It can be about evil and becoming a Servant of the Void.
* It can focus on maintaining your mortality, even in undeath, or picking up the mantle of black avenger and remaining a hero, despite passing into the realm of the dead.
* It can be about manipulation, about the newly created vampire realising there are powers at work in the universe that are far beyond mortal comprehension.
* It can be about finding the truth. About exploring the new dark world of vampires.
* Or it can focus on the story - that the Lords of the Night are planning something terrible for the mortal realms…

RUNNING THE LORDS OF THE NIGHT: VAMPIRES

Here are some suggested types of vampire-based campaign:

NORMAL MORTALS

The PCs are (unless transformed through play) mortal. They never become vampires, instead this source material is designed for the DM to give the players a new enemy to fight against. Darkness is rising in the mortal realms. Great heroes will be needed to stop it.

Notes: The PCs may be vampire hunters, or clerics of the *Powers of Light*. They may hunt vampires or simply seek revenge against the undead. They may be necromancers researching powerful rituals, or scholars studying the Children of Vangual. There is enough information in **The Lords of the Night: Vampires** to give DMs a huge boost in the unpredictability of their vampire monsters for months of play.

VAMPIRE MAGICAL ITEMS

The PCs come into possession of one or more vampiric magical items. The PCs can discover new spellbooks or even ancient vampiric weapons, and through their actions uncover a campaign in which they discover the extent to which vampires really have integrated themselves into the mortal realms.

Notes: While powerful, vampiric items might be sought by their original vampire masters, making the bearer a danger to himself and others while he wields the item.

MORTALS TOUCHED BY VAMPIRISM

Slightly more in depth, the PCs are actually part vampiric. The PCs begin play as powerful mortals, whether a group of Dhampyre, *thrice touched*, or even vampire simulacra.

Notes: PCs could play a guild of mortals desiring nothing more than to become vampires, or they could use their vampiric powers to seek out and destroy the undead. There are plenty of options here for a campaign enjoying high levels of combat and increased power levels.

MORTALS MASQUERADING AS VAMPIRES

For a temporary storyline, PCs could masquerade as vampires. There are enough spells, powers and magical items to allow this, but the risks are great. Not only does a mortal risk discovery, the energies of necromancy that conceal a mortal's true form are dangerous, and can be deadly when abused. PCs could be asked to infiltrate a brood, discovering the master and destroying him. This would add a change of pace to a campaign and would add an element of terrible danger, for discovery could mean the loss of everything.

Notes: The Arcane have magic far more powerful than even that of the Black Cabal. A magical 'benefactor' could manipulate a group of PCs for his own gain while allowing them to masquerade more completely as vampires. PCs could utilise powerful magical protections that could allow allow them to remain hidden under even the eldest vampire's magical scrutiny. For more information on the Arcane, consult **The Lords of the Night: Liches.**

VAMPIRE CAMPAIGN

The PCs are vampires that are part of a brood. They were either created at or around the same time. They should have similar starting alignments. This type of campaign has the greatest number of options from high combat, to constant struggles against the Void.

VAMPIRES ARE WHOLLY GOOD

A vampire brood has been created by a powerful entity for purposes unknown. They are granted their mortal alignments without fear of the Void, due to powerful Arcane magic (detailed in **The Lords of the Night: Liches)**. They are heroes without the Void ever pulling them towards darkness. This is a very high power campaign with all the abilities and few of the disadvantages of being vampires.

SERVANTS OF THE VOID

PCs are vampires who have chosen or fallen to darkness. They are evil and are no longer subject to the Katharein. Any campaign involving such characters would involve a high level of death, destruction and hatred of the mortal races.

Note: Here the PCs have turned against the *Powers of Light* and for them, there is no little or no chance of redemption. This campaign is hardest to play as all the characters are evil and therefore have little or no loyalty to each other and will act in their own selfish interests. PCs will typically be part of a brood under the command of a powerful NPC master. They will have their group objectives and must have a good reason to work (and stay working) together.

Game Themes

There can be many styles of vampire based campaigns. Here are just some suggested ideas:

❋ **The Cure:** The vampires desperate to find a cure for their curse. They will spend their first years seeking a cure, or someone with the knowledge to restore them to life.

❋ **Heroic:** Vampires given new powers struggle against a darkness that threatens the land. The darkness could be other vampires, or any evil that they can uncover.

❋ **Internal:** Vampires struggle to comprehend who and what they have become (high role-playing).

❋ **Diabolical:** Evil Vampires do what they like. They can amass wealth, create broods or continue to adventure, gaining power and wealth in the process.

❋ **Strife:** Vampires struggle to create a brood in a new city, or are part of a brood whose territory overlaps another. They struggle to defeat their opponents while carrying out their normal unlives.

❋ **Divine Conflict:** The PCs fight for - or even against - the *Powers of Light*.

Crossovers

There may be times when a player wants to create an evil vampire in a game of good characters. Generally this is just about impossible. An evil vampire is a monster, whereas good vampires are heroes (or are struggling to become heroes). They can rarely mix without conflict. To avoid such incidents we suggest that there are no crossovers between alignments. The PCs should create entirely good/neutral or entirely evil vampires.

It is possible, although difficult for differing alignment groups to mix and only recommended for very advanced DMs and players.

Additionally, campaigns involving vampire and mortal characters can be unbalancing. While some players are unconcerned with the power levels of other characters in their game, having one or more vampiric players can create problems with a group and can have other effects (like the vampire characters being unable to act during the day).

Playing Older Vampires

Older vampires can be very powerful. Too many Dark Gifts can be unbalancing. A DM should be certain of his actions before he allows very high *age* category PC vampires into his game. Of course role playing is all about fun and being an elder vampire can be a great deal of fun indeed. While we recommend that most PCs begin play as fledgling vampires, there are no specific rules on selecting the *age* of a vampire; this is for the DM to discuss with his players.

Note: It is recommended that PCs play the events leading up to their *Second Waking*, but advanced players and DMs may want a more powerful campaign where their vampires have been around for hundreds, or perhaps even thousands of years.

ECL and CR Comments

We have included the ECL and CR ratings (on p. 127) only as a guideline. If you want to make your PC vampires gain levels more slowly, or feel that these ECLs are too high, feel free to increase them accordingly. Vampires should gain experience more slowly than standard characters, and an ECL of at least +1 is recommended for every fledgling PC vampire.

A Note on Vampire Weaknesses

As a way to mitigate the great power of vampires, remember that while they have amazing strengths, they also have considerable weaknesses. It is only as a vampire gains in *age* and begins to shed their weaknesses do they truly become formidable.

❋ The greatest weakness - sunlight - can kill in a matter of rounds, regardless of how many hit points or powers a vampire has.

❋ A vampire is all but powerless between the hours of dawn and dusk. Nearly all vampires must sleep during the day, this can be in excess of twelve hours on the longest days of the year (although in winter it is considerably shorter).

❋ Fledgling vampires that are still bound to their *place of rest* cannot journey far from their home. This means for at least the first year of their unlives, they are limited to a city based campaign (unless they have some means of travelling great distances in a very short space of time).

❋ Being unable to enter the home of a mortal makes adventuring tough. There will be many times when a vampire cannot go where they want (which can be frustrating).

❋ Not being able to cross running water or enter holy ground can be extremely limiting.

❋ A vampire can only use their Dark Gifts while they have a supply of attuned Blood. Once that is depleted, they lose access to most of their vampiric powers.

Add the mass of vampire hunters, adventurers and orders of the *Powers of Light*, and vampires have a hard time of things.

To survive, vampires must live an unlife of secrecy and stealth. Active vampires that draw attention to themselves may find more than just clerics after them. Wizards seek their flesh for experiments, necromancers seek ichor for mystical transformations. Would-be liches seek out vampire dust for components in their rituals and for every vampire in existence, there are a hundred who would pit their might against them for sport, pleasure or simply for vengeance.

If you feel your vampire characters are too powerful, use their weaknesses against them. Remember, the *Powers of Darkness* have not yet managed to dominate the world (and they have been trying for two thousand years). Vampires are powerful, but it is their weaknesses that have proved to be their downfall time and time again. Further help on dealing with overly powerful vampires can be found in **Powers of Light.**

Beyond the Veil

There are many changes to being dead...

First shuddering exhalation. The last breath of life. Open eyes, darkness...

Fear. Panic. Darkness...

Always darkness.

Your flesh is cold, your body inert. Blood no longer flows through your veins. The chilling realisation that you no longer move by control of your own muscles, but by conscious thought alone. Only your will compels your body into action.

And the sun. You can sense it always, feel it as it moves across the sky. It burns into your mind, a terrible blazing orb of fire. As it rises, it compels you to slumber, and you cannot deny it. Of course, every one of us gathers our resolve and steels ourselves for the sun at some point in our unlives. We sit on a rooftop and dawn approaches. But even as the first rays of copper line the horizon, our eyes bleed and our skin burns, and we must retreat into darkness, defeated, knowing that we can never again see the sun.

But there are many advantages to being dead...

Just being a part of the night, experiencing the world for the first time. Your eyes casting back the darkness with absolute clarity, your senses taking in everything, from the whisper of the wind to the flows of life force as it surges through the land. You gain the feeling that you can do anything, that raw power lies just beneath your fingertips.

The night has become the best friend you never knew you had. And even time has become an ally. You have conquered the one great mortal barrier; you no longer get sick, grow old, and barring any unfortunate accidents, will never die.

You are unchanging.

You fall asleep during the day although you no longer or rarely dream. A vague blackness (the Void) writhes at the edge of your vision - a constant reminder of the transformation you have undergone. But these changes are greatly outweighed by the vampiric powers, the endless strength and boundless stamina that you now possess. Necromantic energy fuels your body. You do not grow tired, can run or toil all day, and you heal at an amazing rate.

You truly are a creature of the night.

Blood becomes the sweetest nectar. Drinking from the living is hard at first, an act akin to cannibalism and seemingly against all the laws of nature. But once you cast back your mortal doubts and accept what you have become - you will experience a joy unlike no other...

To drink directly from the source of all life is the greatest sensation. The taste, every sip carries with it the life force, the personality of the mortal from which it came. It is intoxicating, an experience unlike no other. It sates your desperate hunger, quenches the Void driven thirst that burns inside. It is a sensation the mortal races will never come to know...

In the end - is losing the day really such a high price to ask?

CHAPTER FOURTEEN: ROLE-PLAYING A VAMPIRE

ROLE-PLAYING

If you want to play a game filled with angst where you have become a vampire and must spend every night struggling against the evil within, that's fine - but there are other games (and worlds) for that.

This is D&D. It's about epic adventures, about choosing sides, about being a hero. Even as a vampire you can still bring light to darkness (metaphorically). You can still remain true to your mortal self, even in undeath. Darkness may glimmer on the horizon, but on the whole, you remain the same as you were when you were alive.

You no longer fear death or old age. Instead you have a new enemy…

The Void.

The Void is your new master. It is ever vigilant. It threatens to drag you down to the depths of darkness. It is judge, jury and executioner. There is no escape or release from its endless pressure. Every power you use increases its hold over you, and even feeding takes you one step closer to shadow.

Will you accept Vangual's darkness and destroy all that is good within you, pick up a black class and become more than you were? Or will you turn away from Vangual and try to remain pure against darkness, even though the shadow constantly threatens.

These choices are yours alone to make.

Your actions will influence everything…

SUGGESTIONS ON ROLE-PLAYING A VAMPIRE

What follows are some tips on discovering what it is to become a vampire, to be cursed by darkness and the powers of shadow.

Leaving your mortality behind can be a frightening business, but it can open your game to new and terrifying possibilities.

VAMPIRES ARE ONLY HUMAN TOO…

Many games about vampires focus on darkness; on being damned by the gods and cursed to live in shadow. While there's certainly an element of that in **The Lords of the Night: Vampires** - we believe that it's far more fun to take your character on a journey into shadow than it is to treat vampirism as an excuse to gain even greater power.

Becoming a vampire is a descent into darkness, not necessarily the blackness of the soul, but certainly into a darker world, where vampires live in fear of the *Powers of Light* and where even more sinister creatures lurk, feasting upon the blood of the living.

> *"Any man's death diminishes me, because I am involved in Mankind; and therefore never send to know for whom the bells toll; it tolls for thee."*
> **Phillian Artus Alucidan**

BREAKING THE STEREOTYPE

With all the movies and books about vampires, it's easy to base your vampire on an existing concept. D&D vampires are very different to classical vampires. Vampires are driven by darkness; they are not living creatures, they are necromantic monsters that radiate the *Chill*.

But despite the physical changes, a vampire has desires other than just drinking blood and killing the living. They carry a portion of their mortal mind with them - even when long dead - and they retain many of the drives they had in life.

A great number of vampires spend long years trying to continue their old lives. Many use their great wealth to create elaborate scenarios where they are still mortal, surrounding themselves with mortal followers and vassals. Over the years, this facade gradually fades until the vampire realises there is no point in pretending to be mortal, the Void takes over and all scenarios become necessary only for the purposes of feeding and surviving.

AWAKING AS A VAMPIRE

Because you are a vampire does not mean you instantly become a blood crazed monster with delusions of grandeur. You have awoken into a dark world with your mortal mind intact.

Many fledgling vampires believe the *Powers of Light* can save them, that they can be restored to mortality only if they can find a cleric with the power to restore them. Many spend their first years seeking a cure. But a cure is not so easily found…

Some mortals never overcome their loathing for what they have become - but few characters can overcome their desire for self-preservation. Few newly created vampires destroy themselves; their vampire masters go to great lengths to ensure that any vampires they create are as prepared for the transformation as possible.

SAMPLE CHARACTER IDEAS

The following are just some of the types of vampire you could play:

✳ **Avenger:** You seek to use your powers to protect the helpless.

✳ **Beast:** You prey on those weaker than you.

✳ **Revenge:** You seek revenge on the one that transformed you.

✳ **Cure:** You desperately seek a cure to the curse of undeath.

✳ **Deceiver:** You use your powers to gain wealth and power.

✳ **Desperation:** Self loathing - you have fallen into despair.

✳ **Hero:** Despite the adversity you struggle to remain a hero.

✳ **Pretense:** You seek to maintain the facade of your old life.

There are many different ways to play a vampire. How you choose to accept unlife is entirely up to you.

A Treatise on the Void

It is time to discuss the Void. The source of all darkness, the driving force that gives life to the undead and caresses their flesh with soothing hands of shadow. I may speak lightly, almost fondly of the Void, but it is a powerful ally and a deadly enemy. It is lord and master over us all, ceaseless in its desire to drag every last fragment of mortality from our souls. Brought into the world by Vangual and his terrible *curse of retribution*, the Void has great power over the Children of Vangual and few can resist its effects for very long. I have seen my master's progeny grow as cold and dead as their flesh in a matter of nights, heady on the intoxicating power granted to them by the Void. In a naive frenzy, these fledgling creations move swiftly toward darkness, losing more and more of their mortality with each night that passes.

I recall at first that my master could not fathom what had brought about this change in his creations. Certainly then, I was as dark and wild as they were, filled with immortal courage and a desperate longing to feast upon the gore of the living. How I rose from those black times, I will not write here, for I should certainly incriminate those who have helped me along the way. I shall instead comment on the Void, and how to avoid the worst of its evil.

What is the Void?

The Void is pure darkness. It is the force that drives the undead, the power of evil and shadow. It corrupts the mind and slowly destroys the soul.

When a vampire first opens his eyes, the Void is present to a lesser, or greater degree. It is a glowering mote of darkness, a smouldering shard that irrevocably strips away a vampire's mortal resolve and replaces it with evil. The Void is stronger in some undead than others. A person who held many of the Void's qualities in life will find the Void an indomitable master in undeath.

The Void strips away at the conscience, making a vampire less human. As the years pass and the Void grows, a vampire will find that they care less about the world around them. Things they once held dear no longer have any meaning. Friends and family, even lovers become things of mental stimulation. The mind is still active, even if the heart no longer functions. Emotions diminish - everything is darkened by the touch of the Void.

Without the constant whisper of the mortal conscience, a vampire moves steadily towards evil. The goodly emotions of justice, honor and kindness vanish. The eldest vampires can no longer love. They can only covet that which they see, and desire.

Gaining Void

As a vampire uses their necromantic powers, they accrue Void until they can either purge it through the Katharein, or succumb to its influence. A vampire can tolerate as much Void as their alignment will allow. A good character suffers greatly from the over use of their vampiric powers

Preventing the Void

There are a number of ways to slow the incessant pull of the Void. The most well known is to refrain from using your vampiric powers. The forces of necromancy are intrinsically linked to the Void; frequent use of your abilities will speed you along the road to darkness. If you desire to keep your mortal soul, then use your powers sparingly. You will still travel down the path the Void has set out for you, but you will do so much more slowly.

Secondly

Perform good acts. Do not allow the Void to take hold. Every action you allow to go unpunished, or worse, that you perform yourself is another step you have taken towards darkness. Remember who you were at all times and strive to uphold the qualities you held dear in life. Stick to your mortal routine and you will distance yourself from the Void.

Third

There are spells and powers created that will allow you to stave off the Void. I have heard of philtres and magical items that can restore the mortal mind, but these are rare and expensive, the province of the Black Cabal. I do not trust them. Trust only in the spells and powers you know. Seek solace in the comforts of the living, remind yourself always of what it meant to be alive.

Fourth and most importantly

Do not drink the blood of the living. A dark and despicable act, at least from a mortal's perspective. All vampires need to drink blood to exist, but to do so is to speed you along the path to darkness. Drink from the blood of animals or even the recently dead if you have to, but mortal blood is precious and valuable and the darkness will quickly gather if you drink from the well of vitality.

Of course, my words are meaningless.

Over time, everything falls to the Void.

Phillian

CHAPTER FIFTEEN: THE VOID

The Void score is a measure of evil's hold on a vampire. Everything a vampire does, every power they use, every time they drink from the blood of the living will increase their Void score. The quicker they use their powers, the more swiftly they descend into darkness.

A character awakens as a vampire with a variable amount of Void dependant on their first Katharein. They can tolerate only so much Void before it begins to drag them slowly towards evil. Each alignment has a Void Threshold, the total amount of Void a character can endure before slipping one step closer to darkness.

Descent into Darkness

The Void score is kept secret. A player should never know the *exact* amount of Void their characters have. If a vampire reaches their Void Threshold, they must make a Will save (DC 10 + amount of Void over their Void Threshold) upon waking each night. Failure drops their alignment one step and their Void score resets to 0. Success indicates they can continue to act for another day without penalty. A Neutral Good character that shifts one step towards evil becomes Neutral (see Vampire Void Table, below).

When a character gains twice their Void Threshold they *immediately* move one step towards evil. This move is permanent; the Void has whittled away at a character's mortal conscience, draining their mortality and filling them with darkness.

Example: Perrin the Lawful Good cleric of Auraran becomes a vampire. He is slain in his Katharein, immediately becoming Lawful Neutral. Although he is still a cleric of Auraran, he no longer has quite the same outlook on the world. The Void has touched him and he now places much more emphasis on himself than he does on helping others. After all, he has died and the world hasn't exactly shown him any favours.

The power of undeath goes to his head and in a burst of vampire might reaches twice his Void threshold. Perrin's alignment immediately slips to Neutral. Now he doesn't particularly care about his former life or his undeath. He just doesn't care about anything. He falls from Auraran as he is no longer neither good nor lawful, but he doesn't care about that either. In his eyes, Auraran was a charlatan, a deceitful god who cared only about his followers and didn't help him in his darkest hour.

Perrin can find his own way, seek out a deity more agreeable to his needs (this change happens literally overnight. There's no soul searching or angst involved). The Void has insinuated itself into his mind and while he may know something has changed within him, he may not necessarily care enough to do anything about it.

Finally Perrin's devotion is picked up by Vangual, who willingly reinstates him as a black cleric. Another liberal use of his powers and he is well on the way to utter darkness (slipping to Neutral Evil). In Perrin's case, the Void has swiftly wrapped itself around his mind, and its victory is almost assured. Unless Perrin's situation quickly changes, he is certain to fall entirely to absolute evil.

Vampire Void Table

Lawful Good > Lawful Neutral > Neutral > Chaotic Neutral > Chaotic Evil.

Alignment	Void per Action	Void Threshold	Void Cost (XP)
DRINKING BLOOD (per mortal)			
LG	5	50	20
LN	4	75	30
LE	2	100	40
NG	4	75	50
N	3	100	60
NE	2	125	70
CG	3	100	80
CN	2	125	90
CE	None	The vampire no longer accrues Void. They are permanently a vampire with little or no chance of redemption (see Servants of the Void, p. 112).	
OTHER ACTIONS			
Vampiric Power	2	Per use of each Black Class power.	
Dark Gift	1	Per use of each Dark Gift.	
Prestige Class Power	3	Use of any Prestige Class power	
Energy Drain	1	1 per level drained	
Killing a mortal	1-9	Based on alignment of mortal slain. Lawful Good = 9 Void / Chaotic Evil = 1 Void	
Creating Vampire Scion	5	-	
Creating a true Vampire	10	-	
Vampire touching a mortal	5	-	

Notes: A paladin that drinks from the lifeblood of a mortal immediately loses their paladin status.

BECOMING EVIL

The first step on the path of evil is the detachment from the goodly emotions: love, compassion, kindness, honesty. While these things do not diminish immediately, they matter much less to a vampire than their own selfish needs.

As a vampire accrues Void and shifts down the alignment scale, he begins to grow further away from his mortal emotions. He starts to think only of himself. He may have family and loved ones that want to protect him or even to restore him to mortality, yet he will seek only to further his own desires and care less about regaining his mortality.

As a vampire moves towards evil, activities that would once abhor him become unremarkable. Where once he might balk at drinking blood, the act now becomes commonplace, even enjoyable. Beyond neutral, he has no problems with slaying mortals to feed.

A chaotic evil vampire is fully devoid of their human emotions and feels only the evil desires of the Void. They are incapable of feeling love or passion. Those emotions have long faded, replaced with desire, avarice and greed. They have become wholly enslaved by the Void...

EVIL AND THE VOID

A vampire that is evil (but not Chaotic Evil) still has some modicum of free will. Only a Chaotic Evil vampire has fully succumbed to darkness and become a Servant of the Void (see below).

STAVING THE VOID

A vampire can use their own inner strength of will to fight the Void. While they might not be able to fight it forever, there are actions they can peform to lessen the Void's hold over them.

✳ Characters can purge their character level in Void per month at an XP cost as determined by their current alignment (see Void Cost on the Vampire Void Table, p. 111).

✳ A vampire can reduce their Void score by 1 by abstaining from using any Dark Gifts or vampiric abilities for twenty four hours. This excludes automatic powers like fast healing but does include Blood Strength or Invisibility.

✳ A vampire can reduce their Void score by 1 by not drinking the blood of the living for 1 day +1 day per *age*.

✳ A vampire can purge their Void through the *eternal quiescence* at a rate of 1 point of Void for a number of days equal to their *age* + 1 days. *Example: An age 3 vampire will lose 1 point of Void for every 4 days they remain in the black sleep.*

Note: A vampire cannot have a Void score of lower than 0, nor can they (easily) move up the Void Chart (moving from Neutral to Neutral Good). A vampire may only retain their mortality through Holy or divine influence, powerful rituals or Arcane magic.

> "The only difference between saints and sinners
> is that every saint has a past
> while every sinner has a future."
> Oscar Wilde - House *Sonoruus*

SERVANTS OF THE VOID

Characters who choose (or fall) to the Void have left their mortality far behind them. The Void controls their actions and they have fully shed what remained of their mortal essence. Many say that Vangual collects the souls of previously good vampires and jealously hoards them in his Fortress of Shadow. What he does with them is unknown, even to the Black Council.

Servants of the Void are evil, unfeeling monsters. They have no positive emotions of any kind. Desire, hatred, fear, envy and jealousy are the only emotions they know, for they are the only emotions mirrored by the Void. Darkness is reflected in their eyes and for them, any chance of redemption is slim indeed. These are the creatures of myth, despicable bloodsucking fiends (one step away from their feral cousins).

Any vampire that becomes Chaotic Evil can no longer continue to play their character. There is little, if anything heroic about them. They are feral and bestial creatures, dominated by their instincts and desires. They see living beings as nothing but food and do not integrate well with any part of mortal society. The *Chill* is powerful in them and darkness surrounds them.

A Servant of the Void always has d12 for their hit dice.

DESCENT

I remember caring once. Caring about the world, friends, lovers. Emotions.

I remember feeling invulnerable...

In fact I still do.

Only I was mortal then. And naive.

Foolish.

My mortality was stripped from me. Stolen when I was in the prime of my youth. I passed beyond the Veil.

And I remember that there was a time when I cared about that. Cared about life, about finding my way home.

But instead I found the Void.

It was there for me in the darkness, whispering soft words of comfort when I was alone.

After that I was never alone. The Void carried me.

Into darkness...

The Katharein

Unconsciousness. Your vision narrows to a single point of light, then flickers out.

You remember the jaws of the monster clutching at your throat, rasping as it fed upon your lifeblood...

But you are not dead.

Not entirely.

You wake, a prisoner in a realm of nightmares and endless screams. Through the one window in your tiny black cell you can see an endless shadowy landscape where the sun never rises, a sickly haze of swirling silhouettes and inky blackness.

Redemption and sunlight are far away from this realm. Your soul languishes in shadow - until it is summoned by the dark powers.

Only the dead live here...

On occasion, you might not be alone, but it is on the whole, a realm of cold, fearful darkness, of knowing you have been abandoned by your gods and are about as far from the realms of goodness and protection as you can ever be.

So you wait, believing that the nightmare will soon end and that you will waken back to the brightness of life and the warmth of the sun.

You will waken, but it will not be to the warmth of the sun.

Suddenly, it could have been minutes, hours or days since you awoke in the timeless dream, an arch appears. Sickly green light and swirls of ashen mist pour from it.

You must venture beyond the Arch to whatever fate awaits you, choosing your own path and forging your own destiny. The *Powers of Darkness* will attempt to thwart you, but the battle is fair, or at least it seems to be. Your mortal flesh is cold and tired, but how you act from then on is up to you. You must fight for your life or at least for your mortality.

You do not know it - yet, but you have already lost your first life.

Your greatest battle lies ahead...

I can give you no advice but trust your heart and instincts, for you are in Vangual's realm, and here the path of darkness is always easiest.

Here alone do your decisions have lasting repercussions, for here, a permanent choice is made. Side with shadow and become like darkness. Side with good and forsake the blessings of Vangual.

Step through the Arch and forge your destiny.

But choose wisely. The choices you make will stay with you for a very long time indeed.

Phillian

CHAPTER SIXTEEN: KATHAREIN

When a mortal is slain by a vampire, their soul does not go to the outer planes; it is instead swept in a swirling miasma of darkness to the Negative Energy Plane where it passes beyond the Necrotic Arch and into the *Black*, the domain of Vangual. The *Black* is filled with storms that can sweep a soul away into oblivion. It is here in the treacherous realm of night that a vampire must fight to decide the fate of their mortality. Will they lose themselves in darkness, or remain true to what they once held dear? Accept evil or struggle forever against it. This is their curse.

KATHAREIN SUMMARY

Katharein (Kath-a-Rane) is a means to purge the Void. A vampire is subjected to their first Katharein on the death of their mortal body. There, they are subjected to Vangual's will, but can fight to retain their mortality. They will find themselves trapped in the Necrotic Crypt, a magical holding cell from which there is no escape. When the Arch appears they will encounter whatever 'quest' Vangual has laid out for them. A vampire must complete their Katharein and find the exit without being destroyed (if they wish to retain their mortal minds). Characters reaching the exit will retain their mortal alignments with whatever Void they have accrued along the way. But the quest is not without temptation. Vangual will grant treasures in the form of riches or Dark Gifts during the quest. Although the Katharein must be fair, Vangual gets a certain amount of leeway. While he can not cheat, he often gives characters boons that are too enticing to ignore.

As a character fights in their Katharein they may kill both good and evil creatures. Every good creature they slay or accidentally allow to be slain results in them gaining Void. The amount of Void they accrue is the Void score they retain upon waking. If they go over a threshold they awaken as a vampire one step closer to evil.

Katharein quests take many forms, depending on the role-playing level of a group. The most commonly encountered Katharein take the form of a dungeon filled with creatures both good and evil, traps and terrible dangers.

A character will appear mortal in the Katharein, with maximum hit points, restored powers and his full contingent of spells.

BACKGROUND TO THE KATHAREIN

The Katharein did not exist before the arrival of Vangual. Some say the Katharein came directly from the *Powers of Light*. The Gods gave those slain by the Children of Vangual a means of stalling their descent into darkness, and in return, Vangual tempts those newcomers with ever-greater power. He may have captured their souls, but he does not yet have their minds…

It was said the First were not granted a Katharein; that their hearts were too filled with darkness to be granted even a chance of redemption. Although they themselves were damned, the *Powers of Light* granted their progeny a choice. Although they too were cursed by the foulest darkness, every mortal soul has the chance to seek redemption, to fight against the Void and to retain their mortality. Those that were successful were blessed by the *Powers of Light* and granted the strength to elevate themselves beyond the monsters that are the Children of Vangual. Those that failed succumbed to the curse and fell to evil.

THE NECROTIC CRYPT

The room in which the recently deceased will awaken is a large cell-like chamber. Cold black stone walls; dripping water. The clanking of chains and screaming; hellish noises are many of the sounds that will assail the ears of the newcomer. This is limbo for vampires, a realm of uncertainty and terror. There are times when the most favoured are escorted from the Crypt by glorious creatures of brilliance that burst forth from shadow. In a coruscating wash of incandescence they carry the soul back to its rightful heaven, leaving behind a more palpable darkness for those that remain. Luckily for those that are left behind, such times are rare indeed.

THE NECROTIC ARCH

The Necrotic Arch (or more commonly just 'Arch') is a gateway that appears in the wall of the Crypt. Beyond the towering arch of black stone lies a tunnel that plunges into blackness. A nacreous green light emanates from the darkness; a warning that something wicked lies in wait for the adventurers ahead…

DREAMS AND REALITY

Any PC will no doubt believe they are dreaming (and indeed the DM should play on this). They certainly appear mortal and unharmed in every way. Attempts to flee the Crypt result in failure. No spell or power will grant them exit, nor can they communicate with the outside world. Escape is impossible. The walls are impenetrable.

THE FLEDGLING QUEST

Beyond the Arch lies a spiritual quest. While this can take many forms, it most commonly appears as a dungeon filled with many different types of creature both good and evil. The PCs must fight for their freedom. Somewhere within the dungeon lies the exit. Characters must reach the exit to awaken to unlife. The exit will be guarded by the most powerful monsters in the Katharein.

The fledgling quest could be a treacherous dungeon or take some other form entirely. Some Katharein consist of a maze of rooms each littered with encounters designed to trick the unwary. Others take the form of memories or places known to the questing mortals.

ENCOUNTERS

Encounters in the Katharein are not real. They are creations forged from negative energy. They are entirely controlled by the minions of Vangual and everything is an elaborate ploy to drive those questing further into darkness. A character will encounter friends and allies along the way who may try to hinder, trick or even aid them. Characters may even face themselves, encountering a mirror of their mortal likeness on the quest. Their evil selves will always be their vampire equivalents. They may be attacked by goodly aligned creatures that see them as the monsters they *will* become. They can choose to fight or use some other method of incapacitating good opponents.

> *Webster's was much possessed by death and saw the skull beneath the skin; and breastless creatures underground, leaned backwards with a lipless grin.*
>
> T. S. Eliot, Black Sorcerer

Group Katharein

A vampire need not undertake a Katharein on their own. Katharein can be completed solo or in a group. All characters that pass beyond the Arch as a group undertake the Katharein as a group. Katharein Challenge Ratings are based on the party's current mortal level.

Note: A character may magically journey to the Arch to aid another, but if they are **not** undead they are **forever slain** by the necromantic forces of the *Black* should they die on the Katharein.

Calculating Void

An encounter's Challenge or Encounter Rating during a Katharein is the amount of Void a character can gain or lose in that encounter.

A character gains twice a good creature's CR in Void (minimum base CR of 1) for slaying or failing to protect good characters, the CR in Void for neutral creatures and only half the CR in Void for slaying an evil creature (round down).

Example: On their Katharein a party accidentally slay two good clerics (CR 5). They immediately gain 20 Void points each. If they then slay two evil trolls CR 6, they will reduce their Void total by 6. If they then allow an evil vampire to slay a group of five good virgins in front of them, they will each accrue 10 Void (as the base CR for each virgin is 1).

Results of a Katharein

Whatever the outcome of the Katharein, the changes to a character's alignment are permanent. The character will awaken, a fledgling vampire touched by necromancy. They are now bound to their alignment and must adhere to its restrictions. In the character's minds, they have been transformed; the change is instantaneous and permanent. Of course the Void tugs at the mind of a vampire even then, pulling them ever down towards evil.

Notes:
* A character can never have a Void score lower than 0.
* Characters that were Chaotic Evil in life do not suffer a Katharein. They are automatically transferred to their black class variants and awaken as a Servant of the Void with two free Dark Gifts.
* A character slain during their Katharein awakens with his alignment moved one step toward evil (see Vampire Void Table on p. 111).
* A character slain by their good self awakens as a Mock Vampire.
* A character that destroys or allows their mortal 'good' form to be slain will immediately move one step towards evil.
* If a character takes more than 4 days to complete their Katharein (and many of the creatures will not give them proper resting time). They have a 10% chance per day that when they complete their Katharein they will awaken as a Mock Vampire.

Creating Katharein

A Katharein should be a carefully created quest designed to test the players' mettle. It should involve monsters, heroes and characters from their past and all manner of torments to best manipulate them towards darkness. The players should be able to trust nothing; the dark powers cannot interfere directly, but they can tempt and confuse along the way. Vangual will not let his 'children' leave the Katharein without a fight...

Playing Fair

Katharein quests should be fair. Vangual has great power in the *Black*, but the forces that set the Katharein in motion do not allow him to twist it utterly. The quest cannot be unfair. It must be able to be completed by those on the Katharein. It is designed to confuse and manipulate, but it is never impossible, nor can it cheat.

Example: The questing party should not encounter a group of vampires behind a wall of force that slay a group of good clerics in front of them. If the PCs have no way to get to the vampires before they do their evil deed, this is not fair. However, if the entire scene was an illusion designed to trigger something even more devious...

DMs Note: Earning Trust

Although Katharein can take any form - continually tricking characters into slaying good creatures by masking them as evil monsters quickly gets old. If you intend to use this method, do it once, or do it for a very good reason. The PCs will quickly feel duped if you take advantage of them in this way. They might not be able to trust their senses - but they should be able to trust the DM.

The Katharein can be as role-play intensive as the DM likes. Any physical rules can apply depending on the Katharein. The PCs may believe they are dreaming, or that they have been captured by vampires and forced to endure some surreal challenge.

The following are some suggestions on running Katharein:

The Gauntlet

The PCs must battle ever more difficult monsters in an attempt to find the exit. Along the way they will face both good and bad monsters, memories of their past and other challenges.

Low Role-Play - High Combat

Finding themselves in the Necrotic Crypt, the characters must face a dungeon together. This quest will consist of good and evil monsters and magical traps designed to fool or force the party into making rash decisions that will push them towards evil. There will be 'scripted' scenes where good creatures are preyed upon by monsters, and the characters must do all they can to protect them.

Moderate Role-Play - Moderate Combat

The characters find themselves passing beyond the Arch to a familiar tavern. There they must choose power over the innocent. They may have to protect the powerless or side with the forces of darkness. All the time, the powers of necromancy will tempt them into joining, giving up their mortal classes and joining the black classes. They may face hideous monsters tortured by the *Black*. Creatures that were previously slain by the PCs.

High Role-Play - Low Combat

The characters will find themselves sorely tested by the dark powers. They will enter a situation where they must bargain for their souls, finding themselves in a court of law or even their home town. They may even have the appearance of strangers. They may be on trial and pleading for their innocence. How their enemies will pass judgement upon them - depends on the actions of the players.

Other Rewards

Vangual will offer those on the Katharein incentives to move towards evil in the form of free Dark Gifts. If it is in his power to tempt the PCs, he will do so. These temptations will always be designed to manipulate the questing party down a particular route, ie. to the most powerful creature or most dangerous encounter in the Katharein.

Example: Vangual may tempt a player with a magical sword. When one of the PCs takes it, the owner of the sword will appear, a powerful paladin, furious that the 'evil' character has stolen his weapon. He will not stop until the 'thief' is dead (unless the PCs can deal with him in a non-aggressive manner).

A magical item may become a Dark Gift upon the vampire's successful exit from the dungeon - or it might remain a valuable magical sword. Jewels, spells and secrets have been granted to vampires that converted to their Black Class equivalents in their Katharein.

Vampires who do not convert to evil find that their granted rewards do not pass from the Katharein into the real world.

REVERIE

I thought I was dead. I fell from the monster's arms and plunged into darkness. Death came - and with it - dreams.

I dreamed I was standing before a monolithic, mist enshrouded archway that rose up before me like the jaws of a great beast. There was nowhere else to go, so I stepped beyond the threshold and into the eerie green haze. Darkness seemed to surround me. I wandered for hours, finding nothing but strange ghastly faces that looked up out of the mist and did nothing but stare back at me.

Then I awoke to brilliant sunlight. The dream was over. Feeling groggy, I sat up and gazed around.

I was in a huge bright field with flowers everywhere. Poppies and violets surrounded me in a blanket of color, and in the distance rich stalks of corn rose up into the afternoon sky. I picked myself up and started walking, moving through the flowers, trying to get my bearings and work out exactly where I was.

I came in time to the flat surface of a sawn-off tree stump. It seemed strangely small. But strangely familiar.

I remembered thinking *that tree stump used to come right up to my chest*. Then I realised. This field, this valley. This tree stump. I used to play here when I was a child. But I don't recall it having any undead in it back then. And I never had to fight for my life...

Pouring through the trees were the dead: zombies, skeletons and worse. They were surrounding me, rising up from the earth on all sides. Everything seemed unreal, perhaps I was still dreaming...

I used to play here as a child. It's my earliest memory...

I wouldn't want to die here...

Future Katharein

All non-evil vampires automatically undergo a Katharein Quest when their Void score reaches its Void Threshold. Different from the Fledgling Quest, Katharein take a similar form, but through it, a vampire gains the ability to purge their Void, risking a portion of themselves in an attempt to purge the darkness that grows within.

A vampire has no little or no choice in their Katharein Quest. They will see the Arch appear as dawn comes and will pass beyond it as they fall into slumber.

Resisting

A vampire that does not wish to endure a Katharein may make a Will save (DC 10 + total over Void threshold) to resist the effects of a Katharein for that night. The difficulty increases by +1 for every additional night they resist. They can only resist for so long before they finally find themselves trapped in the Crypt.

Katharein Quest

In this quest the PCs are not fighting for their unlives, but to shatter the darkness that gathers in their souls. They will face vampires, undead and other monsters spawned by the Void. Creatures they have recently vanquished may return to face them, ghoulish spectres long thought defeated. The more undead they slay, the more Void they negate.

They lose Void as before, slaying increasingly more powerful creatures as they venture through their quest. They can choose to exit the Katharein at any time by retreating back to the Arch. They gain a considerable bonus by fighting their way to the exit and completing the quest.

A character who is slain on a Katharein immediately slips one rank toward evil upon waking and instead of resetting at 0, his Void score falls to half way to the next Void level.

Notes on Katharein Quest

* Characters cannot accrue Void in the Katharein Quest, they can only lose it by battling ever more powerful creatures. Some encounters are locked; a group cannot leave certain encounters until they have solved them. The last encounter in a Katharein is always like this.
* The further the PCs get before returning to the Arch is the amount of Void they remove. Each encounter is worth its CR in Void points.
* The spell *call necrotic allies* allows a vampire to take a group through a Katharein Quest. The vampires can journey together, destroying evil in an attempt to purge their own evil.
* The CR for every Katharein a vampire experiences beyond the first in the same month increases by +2.
* For the purposes of negating Void only - the CR for every monster in the Katharein Quest is reduced by 1 per additional Katharein per month. If a monster would be worth 6 Void Points (CR 6), on the second Katharein in a single month it would be only worth 5 Void points (even though it would still be CR 6).
* A completed quest (slaying the end of Katharein monster) is worth anything from -5 Void to reducing the Void total to 0.

CHAPTER SEVENTEEN: REDEMPTION: A CURE FOR VAMPIRISM

The Children of Vangual have sought a cure for vampirism for two thousand years. Newly created vampires search desperately for a way to be restored to life, yet only the rarest of rituals and divine forces have the power to rekindle the flicker of life-force and restore the mortality. Vangual's curse is too potent for mundane magic to unweave.

The most common misconception is that a *resurrection* spell or similar will restore a vampire to life. This is wholly inaccurate. Attempts to restore a vampire to mortality sever a vampire's connection to the Negative Energy Plane, destroying the vampire immediately. A vampire's soul languishes in Vangual's realm. The soul must first be released before the flesh can be resurrected.

Despite the difficulties, a rare few vampires *have* been restored to life over the centuries. More myth than reality, the Black Cabal has records of missing vampires found moving once again amongst the living. How these vampires found release from the curse is still unknown.

What *is* known is that once a vampire has aged beyond his first year or become fully evil, the chances of restoration are slim. Nothing short of a divine power (or the Arcane) can restore a Servant of the Void to mortality. If a vampire is to seek their mortality, they must do so immediately following their *Second Waking*. They must pursue this above all else, for as time passes the Void gains an ever-greater hold over them. Their chances of restoration diminish with every point of Void they gain. Many vampires that truly seek restoration journey first to Kethak, where it is said the answer to every mystery can be found.

RESTORATION

There are several ways that the Children of Vangual can find release from the curse of undeath, each of them as dangerous and complex as the last.

SPELLS

The divine spells *restore the shattered spirit* and *ritual of the veil* may restore a vampire to life (detailed in **Powers of Light**). Other more specific spells exist; yet these are the domains of the Arcane, and liches do not willingly grant vampires restoration without good reason. Few are prepared to anger the god of vampires, and Vangual does not take kindly to losing his children.

RITUALS

It is said that there are some mortal rituals allow the restoration of a vampire. Ancient, they require rare and hard to obtain components and their results are uncertain. Many of these spells are beyond the power of even the Black Cabal and are only used in the most desperate of circumstances. The Black Cabal destroy these spells whenever they find them.

The Arcane have many powers, the greatest of these is their command over life and death. It is said that there are some liches who can grant life to the undead (or at least a general approximation of it). These rituals are fully detailed in **The Lords of the Night: Liches**.

RESTORATION QUESTS

A vampire can seek redemption through a deity or specific Power. This can be difficult as many gods are unwilling to become embroiled with the Children of Vangual. Some gods will allow their devoted a chance to prove themselves before condemning them to unlife - but such quests are complex and dangerous and the *Powers of Light* demand great sacrifices on the part of the vampire before they will even hear their plea. Before a vampire can be restored to life, they must first become hero vampires and prove their worth to the *Powers of Light*. Restored mortals forever earn the enmity of the Children of Vangual for finding release from the curse. Many are destroyed in the trying. Few ever find the solace they desire...

QUEST FOR THE HEROIC RESOLUTION

The quest for mortality begins with the quest to become a hero. The vampire must risk all by sacrificing their Katharein and moving down a path which will result in them gaining hero status and becoming free from the Void (or falling to absolute darkness). While these vampires do not regain their mortality, they retain their mortal minds and can become heroes, free from the taint of the Void.

Restoration Quests will be fully detailed in **Powers of Light.**

RESTORE THE MORTALITY

When a PC vampire falls to the Void, his unlife is literally in the hands of his friends. Even though his mortality is lost, it is not forever destroyed. Willing PCs have one option:

Recover the good portion of a vampire's soul from the *Black*. This lies directly in Vangual's inner sanctum and would be a near insurmountable task for any group of adventurers. Infiltrating Vangual's Fortress of Shadow alone would be an almost impossible quest, it is guarded by bloodlings and terrible shades twisted the darkest forces of necromancy.

Needless to say, determined heroes have recovered souls, on more than one occasion. But when journeying to the *Black*, a group may have much to gain, but they have far more to lose...

THE PATH OF LIGHT

Some say there is another, even *more* dangerous path for the walking dead to follow. The Iliari, the mysterious 'bright' vampires offer an alternative path to redemption (although finding them is in itself a quest). The price they ask for redemption is considerable, and those who claim to have seen them have been unable to pay their price.

> *"My soul was shattered to the four winds when I became a vampire. But I was not a monster. At least not yet.*
>
> *In those early days I searched long and hard for a cure. I spoke with wizards, alchemists, sages, seers, healers and clerics...*
>
> *Then I met him. The lich. I didn't know he was a lich at the time, and I could never have imagined the price he would have asked. But it was there, in front of me, ready for the taking - restoration..."*

CHAPTER EIGHTEEN: ENERGY DRAIN

Most vampires (though not all) possess some form of energy drain attack: the power to strip the living of their vital energies by touch alone. Whether this drain steals levels, health, mental or physical abilities, these powers are a vampire's greatest strength.

HOW DOES ENERGY DRAIN WORK?

Attuned to necromancy, a vampire's cold and dead flesh radiates the *Chill*. Upon contact with a living being, positive and negative forces clash. Life energy is violently drained from the mortal and absorbed by the vampire (stolen by the Void).

EFFECTS OF ENERGY DRAIN

Energy drain negates the vital forces of the living. Accompanying this theft is a weariness, a lethargy that usually passes with time and rest. The weakness, shivers and chills that accompany an energy drain attack eventually fade, but with them the victim will have lost a portion of their life-force. Powerful mortals have the ability to resist the drain, or at least mitigate its effects. In these cases the drain still manifests but the lost energy recovers over time.

With the many forms of energy drain are many different ways in which that drain manifests. Some complain of memory loss, others, a drop in their physical abilities, others experience chills and shakes. While a casual encounter is typically insufficient to snuff out a mortal's existence, it is enough to temporarily deplete their life-force. Whether this drain is permanent depends on the *age* and power of the vampire and the inner strength of the affected mortal.

HOW TO HANDLE ENERGY DRAIN

The effects of energy drain can manifest in various ways.

STANDARD ENERGY DRAIN

The least severe is that the character gains one or more negative levels with no adverse effects (other than those penalties listed for standard energy drain). Other, more potent effects may be:

THE CHILL

A vampire's touch freezes a mortal to the core. Trembling, chills and fever accompany the drain that may last for minutes, hours or days. These penalties can effect a character in many ways, from suffering a penalty to each of their actions, to a penalty to specific ability scores.

Age	Duration	Penalty
0	*age* +1 Rounds	-1
1	*age* +1 Minutes	-2
2	*age* +2d4 Minutes	-3
3	*age* +1 Minutes	-4
4	*age* +2d4 Hours	-5
5	*age* +1 Days	-6

As energy drain is individual to each vampire, penalties imposed can vary greatly. An *age* 2 Black Blood could confer a penalty of -3 to all actions, while another could strip a character of -3 to their Strength for a short period. Powerful vampires could impose a penalty to physical abilities AND a penalty to all actions.

JUSTIFYING ENERGY DRAIN

What follows are some of the reasons why a character may have lost some of their levels due to energy drain.

LOSS OF CONFIDENCE

The character has lost a portion of their life-force and is not the hero he once was. Battling vampires can take its toll and a character may feel unsure of his abilities. In this way, a he loses the ability to master his most powerful skills until he has regained his confidence.

Disadvantage: A character could suffer a penalty of -2 to their actions when dealing with the undead until they have regained their lost levels.

LOSS OF LIFE ENERGY

Vital energies drained, the character feels weaker. Negative energy has reduced their abilities, diminishing them in some way. It will take time for a character to fully recover their strengths and regain the levels stolen by necromancy.

Disadvantage: A character can suffer a permanent or temporary reduction to their abilities until the lost experience is recovered or the levels have been regained.

MEMORY LOSS

The character has had their memories sucked from them. The DM can deem that the vampire drained some of the memories from the PC, ranging from a few moments, right up until the point where they last gained a level. Varying vampire races have different energy drain powers with very different effects. A character may simply forget how to use a skill, the negativity clouding their ability/ reasoning. They will have to relearn their skills as they did before. Memories can occasionally be regained through hypnosis or magic, but only a *restoration* spell (or similar) can restore lost levels.

UNCONSCIOUSNESS

The DM can rule that when a character is drained of more than a quarter of their levels in any set period (twenty four hours), the necromantic stresses placed upon them are so great that they fall into unconsciousness for a period (as determined under the *Chill*). This is a particularly nasty attack and can be used with exceptionally powerful vampires to add that extra kick to their energy draining abilities.

PERMANENT ENERGY DRAIN

There are some vampires that are so old or powerful that they do not need to use their Dark Gifts to permanently drain the energy from the living. Some vampires can do this automatically. This is a harsh attack and can be mitigated by allowing the PCs to recover their lost levels when the vampire is slain.

BONUSES TO RECOVERING FROM ENERGY DRAIN

Benevolent DMs can give their players a bonus to regaining lost experience. As the character has previously earned those levels, a DM can rule that a character earns between 10% to 50% additional experience until he is again restored to his original experience total.

CHAPTER NINETEEN: STORY AND ADVENTURE HOOKS

These story ideas are plot hooks designed to be easily inserted into any campaign. They are for vampire use only where mentioned.

CORPUS HUNT (VAMPIRE)

As an initiation, a new vampire must obtain a sample of blood from an important person in the city. This can be as hard or as difficult as the DM wants to make it. The vampire will have to use all his new-found powers and will be given a *Phial of the Stable Pabulum* in which to collect the blood.

✳ ✳ ✳ ✳ ✳

ASSASSINATION ATTEMPT (VAMPIRE)

An Ash Vampire must infiltrate enemy lines. A particular high cleric is causing the First some trouble. He must be eliminated. The Ash Vampire is slain, transformed into ash and transported through the holy wards into the temple via unsuspecting merchants from a nearby town. The temple's magical wards of protection do not register the inanimate ash as being a vampire and so the PC is left in the storeroom, waiting to reform. The vampire must slay the high cleric without being discovered or slain.

To adjust the difficulty of this mission, the DM could rule that the Ash Vampire takes damage from the holy wards of the temple once back in vampiric form, thus adding another element of risk. With the holy wards detecting evil, the vampire risks discovery - adding a sense of urgency and a time restriction to the mission.

✳ ✳ ✳ ✳ ✳

LOVE AND UNDEATH

Two lovers met while they were mortal. Born of rival merchant families, Ariella and Cellium were kept apart once their family knew of their relationship. Unable to stand any more of the agony of being apart, Ariella vanished one night. Yet she returned to her love, a vampire. Even in undeath, she still loved Cellium, and he in turn loves her.

The heroes are hired by Cellium's family to protect Cellium from the 'monster' that is Ariella.

When they meet Cellium, he is practically a prisoner. He wants to join Ari - to spend eternity with her. He can't think of anything better, to spend all of unlife with the one he loves. Cellium's family want her dead - again. They are offering a substantial amount of money for her death.

What do the PCs do when Ariella visits?

The Twist: In order to prove her love, Ariella sacrificed much to receive the blessings of the lich Dormalian who performed the *Ritual of the Eternal Resolution* upon her (see **The Lords of the Night: Liches**). She still has a good soul. But she is bound to the lich for a hundred years.

✳ ✳ ✳ ✳ ✳

THE GREATER OF TWO EVILS

A Vampire Scion comes to visit the PCs. He informs them that he is the slave of a great and powerful vampire, and desires nothing more than to be free from his tyranny and to become a vampire in his own right. He says that if the PCs agree to slay his master and allow him freedom, he will show them where his master lives. They will never find him on their own. He agrees to leave the city and never return if they do as he asks.

The PCs must decide what they will do about the Scion. Will they destroy it or do as it asks? Do they slay the Scion in the hopes that they can find its master on their own? The master lives in the sewers in a bricked off area, only accessible either by breaking down a wall, or by magical entry.

Twist: The Vampire Scion is actually the slave of an evil master that is having his minions slowly destroyed by a good vampire. The PCs are being manipulated into slaying the 'evil' vampire, but will they realise the truth in time?

✳ ✳ ✳ ✳ ✳

BLIGHTED HEART

PCs are called to investigate the local sanatorium where the clerics and healers cannot cope with the fatality rate. It seems many of the patients are growing weaker and dying over the course of a few weeks. There is no explanation, the healers are working as fast as they can but the hospitals are becoming overrun with the dead. The PCs are called to investigate, as the healers are concerned about the rise of some kind of new plague. Victims, already weak yet showing no signs of immediate death are deteriorating over the course of a few nights. Others are simply losing the will to live and are allowing wounds that would normally be treatable to become fatal.

The *Blighted Heart* is behind this. A group of Ravenous have made a brood in the cellars beneath the hospital. There they rise every evening to feast upon the vitality of the living. They typically choose the most healthy, but drain the essence from anyone suitable. They prefer the injured who are normally strong and healthy, perhaps those adventurers who suffer magical wounds.

Alternative Scenario: One of the PCs is hurt and taken to the hospital. Awaiting a cleric, they hear the rants of a 'madman', who is suffering from a feverish delirium. He cries out for help, whispering of a darkness that rises at night to feast upon the living. Terror abounds in the hospital, can the PCs uncover the Ravenous' secret?

✳ ✳ ✳ ✳ ✳

CONTESTED OWNERSHIP

The PCs buy an abandoned tower or keep very cheaply. The original owner vanished without a trace some years before. When the PCs have moved in, the original owner (a powerful vampire) awakens from his *eternal quiescence* - and wants his residence back!

✳ ✳ ✳ ✳ ✳

DOUBLE-EDGED SWORD

The PCs discover an ancient vampiric sword long thought forgotten. It could be anywhere, while they are clearing out the lowest vaults of a temple, in a ruin or even on a quest or dungeon, long forgotten. The sword seems rusty and worthless, but magical. As they get it home, it activates, draining blood from whoever carries it. Bound to the sword is a long lost and important vampire from Avystervan. Disappearing centuries ago, he was long thought destroyed. Sensing his presence, the vampires will come to realise that his essence remains and that he has been found.

They will come looking…

❋ ❋ ❋ ❋ ❋

ONCE, TWICE BITTEN

An elder vampire is using his powers to dominate the PCs. If they are staying at an inn, he will have ensured each PC drinks some of his blood in their evening meal before attempting to charm them. While they sleep, they are visited by his brood, who will bite each of them once on the first night and again on the second. Weakened greatly and each in possession of several negative levels, the PCs wake on the afternoon of the second day, weak beyond imagining, and not any the wiser as to what has happened (although clever PCs may realise what has occurred)

That afternoon, a visitor comes to their inn, a simulacrum of a powerful vampire. He tells the PCs that he needs their help. His master is in a war with another vampire who has been encroaching upon his territory for years. It is this new brood that has *twice bitten* the PCs.

The simulacrum has been granted the power to assist the PCs as best he can. He will be able to negate their negative levels up to this point and offer some assistance against the blood loss affecting them all.

Twice bitten, the PCs find themselves searching out the new vampire brood in an desperate attempt to destroy them. The brood is warded against intruders, yet, because the PCs share some blood with the brood, they can pass the wards unharmed. The *twice touched* must slay the vampire master or become vampires themselves.

❋ ❋ ❋ ❋ ❋

LONG TIME DEAD

The PCs find a tomb and a section blocked by a rock fall. Within they find one (or if the DM is feeling particularly malevolent) or many corpse, each one ancient and desiccated. Some of them may be wearing rich jewellery (to entice the players to remove them).

The corpses are actually vampires in the *eternal quiescence*. Contact with their dead flesh may rouse some of the vampires to waking. The Waking Check is DC 20 + *age* category minus the level of the character touching the vampire. These vampires will awaken to come hunting the PCs when the sun goes down.

❋ ❋ ❋ ❋ ❋

VISITATION

The PCs find themselves staying at an inn where a vampire has previously bitten one of the residents the night before. That day, the bitten character is out of action, in bed with a fever. Ideally this would be an out of the way, rural place where the PCs won't have much backup or access to greater firepower. That night, the vampire returns, this time the act is discovered yet the vampire escapes. The PCs may suspect the vampire will return a third time, or decide to hunt it down and destroy its evil.

The DM should choose the victim carefully and decide the vampire's motives beforehand. Is it seeking a beauty to be one of its many slavish brides, or a sage/wizard to add to its defences?

Alternative Scenario: The PCs may have come to the vampire's knowledge and it could desire one of them greatly. It is possible the vampire had already bitten one of the PCs on the first night of them coming into its territory. If this were the case - the vampire could be returning to claim what it *believes* is its rightful property…

❋ ❋ ❋ ❋ ❋

DESPERATION

The party go to a new city, where they have been sent to give aid and materials to the PC cleric's new temple. The cleric wakes in the middle of the night, to sense an unholy presence close by. If they go to look, they will find the Arch Cleric doing deals with a vampire. If they stay to watch, the cleric gives the vampire a number of glass phials containing what looks like blood. In exchange the vampire gives the cleric a great deal of money.

The temple isn't doing very well. Funds have been limited and there is much poverty and problems for the hard-pressed clerics to deal with. On the surface, the temple appears to be doing very well, but has in truth been struggling. So the Arch Cleric was approached by a local vampire. All the cleric has to do it to take blood from his clerics in exchange for gold. He has been doing this for some time.

Twist: The Characters can decide what to do. The vampire lives close by, with a small brood. The Cleric is of course deeply shamed by his actions, and the characters may decide what to do with him, once his secret is revealed. Of course, he is openly worried about the consequences. He wants to be free of his dark actions, but he does not want to lose the money he is making. Because of it, the church is doing a great deal of good for the community.

❋ ❋ ❋ ❋ ❋

TREASURE MAP

The players find a mysterious treasure map with directions to a city that is not detailed on any chart or map in the kingdom. The map is hundreds, if not thousands of years old. The map leads to the city of Veil and has been planted by vampires to bring mortals to the city of their own volition. They use the upper city as a distraction. No one suspects that the evil *City of Graves* lies far beneath the city of necromancers.

❋ ❋ ❋ ❋ ❋

CHAPTER TWENTY: DARKNESS RISES

THE FIRST TRUTH

The world is changing. The darkness grows; some say the nights are a tad longer, the days that little bit darker. Even the sunniest of summer mornings no longer seem quite as bright.

Creatures loom out of the night. Growing bolder, they move ever closer to civilisation, the long forgotten places of darkness are once again rife with evil. Once solitary creatures are working together, united by unseen hands.

Darkness gathers its strength, and the *Powers of Light* begin to feel the first glimmerings of fear.

Vampires are moving across the world in ever-greater numbers. The *Powers of Light* have encountered vampires bolder and braver than ever before, forming broods in cities and feasting greedily upon the lifeblood of the living.

The wise warn that creatures that have long slept are being woken, and deep within the bowels of the earth, fires once again stir, the rousing flickers of evil.

The world turns, and with it, the *Powers of Light* know their self-assured millennia of comfort is over.

THE RISING FEAR

Although the general populace do not yet suspect, a darkness *is* rising. Vampires are making their homes in major cities; ancient vampires are being awoken from their *black sleep* and are moving once again across the realms.

Vampires gather for purposes unknown. They are meeting in remote places, gathering, discussing. They are preparing themselves and with their presence the darkness takes on a more tangible shadow.

Rumours whispers that a dark god has arisen and that a storm comes. But it is not an earthly storm, for forces beyond those of mortal comprehension are ready to battle for possession of the earth...

WHISPERS OF DARKNESS

The levels of fear rise slowly, almost imperceptibly in remote places as the creatures of the night encroach steadily upon mortal territory. People mutter that it is more dangerous to walk the streets at night, or to travel unarmed. Merchants take on guards and folks no longer walk alone. Many say that murderers freely walk the streets and deaths in the poorer parts of town are on the increase. No one notices, or if they do, they say little about it. Doors are kept locked and windows firmly shuttered.

The local militia are being increasingly hard pressed to handle the mysterious threat.

Every day the town criers list the murders of the previous night, of mutilated, agony stricken bodies and wide-eyed corpses drained of blood. The orders of goodness have hired heroes to uncover the new threat that faces the mortal realms.

Someone or something is feasting upon the living in the poorer parts of town. A great fear is beginning to stir. The fear of the unknown. Although no one says anything openly, there is just one word whispered behind closed doors - "Vampires!"

Few say anything, yet fear of the night increases hour by hour, day by day.

The *Powers of Light* speculate about the state of the world. They have their suspicions.

The truth is far more terrible...

They have no idea what is to come...

Darkness rises.

EPILOGUE: CHOICES

I returned to the temple of Auraran, the package clutched under my arm. The golden sunrise holy symbol above the altar burned as I passed, and for some reason, I felt ashamed.

Steeling myself, I crossed the temple floor, avoiding the gaze of the other clerics. I retreated to my cell, lit a candle and rammed a shoe under the door. Satisfied that I would not be disturbed, I threw myself down upon my cot, and with trembling fingers, unwrapped the package.

I don't know why I shook so; perhaps my soul knew what lay within. My heart fluttered and beads of sweat formed on my brow. As I rolled back the velvet, a large black book fell out onto the sheets. Bound in strange sinewy material that looked like lizard skin, the book seemed ancient. I was almost afraid to breathe, lest I contaminate it, or worse, cause it to turn to dust.

After a few moments I found the strength to turn the book the right way up. I stared at the cover for a long time. The candle had burned low before I found the courage to look at the first page. I simply spent the moments running my fingers across the rough cover, as if I could read the words within by touch alone.

Someone knocked on the door and my heart skipped. Alain whispered if I would like to accompany him to midnight prayer. I stammered that I was feeling tired and that I would join him the following night. My voice sounded hollow and strange, and for a moment, his shadow lingered beyond the door, uncertain, then he vanished, his footfalls fading back into silence.

I exhaled deeply. Then turned back to the book. I opened the cover and gazed at the first page. I knew what I would find. Somehow, my soul knew.

There, written in a scrawling crimson script, were words that I could not understand. I knew the ink was human blood, but I dared not consider it. This abomination was my darkest heart's desire, my destruction, and salvation both. My heart was panicked yet overjoyed. Perhaps with this tome I could decipher the scriptures sealed deep within the temple's vaults. Historian and linguist, translating the texts had become my life's work, but without a translation key on which to rely, I had made few successes.

All that was about to change…

I had in my hands an original of what I believed to be the works of the ancient demon Avystyx. For whatever reasons the dark powers had seen to give this book to me, I did not know, but possibilities ran through my mind. Although I knew I should tell, should run screaming to the elders for redemption, the book had me transfixed. My soul belonged to it entirely. I could no longer flee, or protest. I was powerless to fight.

I read the book all night. It was only when I looked up and the candle had long burned down that I realised I had read the book in complete darkness. Sunrise was not far distant, and a great lethargy filled me. I knew I must race downstairs, to the vaults where the fragments of the ancient prophecies lay, but I could not, the sun burned in my mind, and my body slipped into darkness.

When I awoke. It was night again. I had slept with the book clutched against my chest throughout the day. I rose quickly, moving unseen through the temple like a shadow. I made my way into the vault, where I spread out the ancient scriptures around me. Now they made sense. Somehow, I could decipher their meaning. Words seemed to flash out at me. Hate, blood, darkness, vengeance. I could understand them all. Still clutching the tome, I began to scribble down passages, neither pausing for breath or for food.

I did this for days, stopping only to sleep when the sun was in the sky.

Finally I was done. A week had passed while I concealed myself in the temple vaults working feverishly on the translation.

I picked myself up from the floor and stretched. Strangely I did not feel the elation I believed I would, only a gnawing darkness that festered within. I needed air; the temple felt stifling, stuffy, strange to me as if I had wandered aimlessly into a strange part of town and only now realised that I was out of place.

I wandered down the alley behind the temple. I had not gone far when a dark shape loomed forth from the blackness.

It was the stranger. His eyes blazed before me like burning coals. I was powerless to resist and stood motionless, waiting for him to speak.

"Greetings once again, Devin." I didn't move. I stood mutely watching as other figures appeared behind him. A tall man draped in grey with a sloping bald head, a figure dressed entirely in a flowing crimson robe, a green skinned creature with rising mist pouring from its body. The others blurred as I gazed back at the tall man. "We welcome you as a friend." He said, his accent as thick as I remembered. "You have done us a great service."

I nodded vaguely. My soul screamed to flee, to call out for the assistance of Auraran. I realised dimly that I wasn't even wearing my holy symbol. The icon that had been with me for over ten years was lying forgotten beside my cot, relegated to mere trinket as the book dominated all of my passions. The man spoke again, bringing me back to reality,

"You have done what we could not." He said, smiling wickedly. "In only a week, you have managed what the greatest of us could not do in a thousand years."

I remember nodding, feeling pride at my accomplishment, yet fear at what I knew I had unlocked.

"We have a proposal for you." The tall man said, his eyes burning. "That tome you had, the fragments in your temple. They were nothing compared to what we have to show you."

His words drifted through my skull. *More texts, more ancient tomes?*

"What do you mean?" I managed to stutter. The tall man gave a low barking laugh and darkness seemed to fall down around him like midnight.

"The writer of these tomes penned a much larger volume. Long ago. Parts of it were copied and were passed down through the generations. Your temple has some of them and *you* managed to translate them." He paused as if for breath, then continued. "But none of them are the *true* version. Words have been misspelled, entire passages incorrect."

His eyes flashed a baleful crimson.

"Devin. We have the original volume. You could help us decipher it."

My mind reeled. The chance to take a look at such ancient texts. It was a dream come true. A dark and terrible dream, but I was prepared to face the nightmare for the chance to know the truth.

My soul spoke for me. I remember taking an uncertain step forward. The stranger nodded wickedly, his sharp teeth flashing in the darkness.

"Think of it, Devin." He said. "This will be your life's work. To unravel the impossible." He reached out his pale hand.

I remember glancing back at the temple, tracing the lines of the stained glass windows with a pang of regret. Then biting my lip, I took the tall man's hand. The other sneered and his eyes glimmered with hellfire.

"Well done, Devin." He hissed. "You will not be sorry."

"I'm already sorry." I whispered as we vanished into darkness, leaving nothing behind but the wind and silence.

✳ ✳ ✳ ✳ ✳

In the shadows, Phillian Artus Alucidan watched unobserved. His face was grave as he stared at the fading vampires, and with them, Devin.

He had watched the young priest for years. Watched as his mortal mind unravelled the incredible writings of the vampire, Avystyx. He had barely believed it possible. Devin was a genius. But how had the Black Council discovered his talents?

It didn't matter anyway - they had found the means to translate the Avystyx Prophecies. All was lost…

"Darkness is coming." He said grimly, fading into shadow.

AFTERWORD

If you thought this was the end of The Lords of the Night – it's not.

Powerful forces of light and dark are about to collide.

This is only the beginning…

LEXICON

age: The amount of time a vampire has been in existence. As they age, their powers grow.

Arcane: The guild of ancient liches whose power lies in the mythical city of Kethak on the Ash Plane.

Arikostinaal: One of the Arcane. Arikostinaal is the vampire advisor to the Black Council.

Ash Vampires: Vampires joined with the powers of ash, entropy and decay. Their touch drains life energy.

Attunement: The act of magically transforming mortal blood into Blood that a vampire can use to fuel his Dark Gifts.

Avystervan: The *City of Graves*. Located several miles under the ruined city of Veil — Avystervan is the seat of the Children of Vangual's power and is carefully hidden from the *Powers of Light*.

Avystyx Prophecies: The cryptic warnings and secrets of the vampire race. Written by Avystyx two thousand years ago, the prophecies are said to be indecipherable.

Black: Vangual's realm beyond the Negative Energy Plane. He resides there in his Fortress of Shadow.

Black Bloods: The name for vampires that look most like mortals.

Black Cabal: The vampire wizards of Avystervan.

Black Council: The ruling council of elder vampires.

Black Kiss: The ritualistic act of turning a mortal into a vampire.

Blood Gates: Magical portals of shimmering blood that connect with a network of exit portals in Avystervan and across the mortal realms.

Blood Guard: The protectors and warriors of Avystervan.

Blood Knights: Vangual's unholy anti-paladins.

Blood: Vampiric essence. Vampires need mortal blood to survive and must feed almost every day. Also the ability score Blood.

Children of Vangual: The collective term for all vampires under Vangual's control.

Chill: The icy cold that surrounds every vampire. It strikes terror into animals and sends a shiver down the spines of even the hardest mortals.

Citadel: The home of the Black Council on the Negative Energy Plane.

City of Graves: See Avystervan.

Consanguineous Vampire: Created by the Black Cabal, Consanguineous Vampires are the least of vampires.

Dark Gifts: Vampiric powers and magical abilities fuelled by Blood.

Death State: The form a vampire assumes when reduced to 0 hit points or lower (usually ash, blood, or mist). These forms are almost utterly impervious to physical harm.

Devoted Incarnate: Black Clerics of Vangual.

Dhampyre: Half-vampires. Mortals touched by necromancy.

eternal quiescence: The *black sleep*. A slumber into which vampires fall when they run out of Blood.

Feral Vampires: The oldest vampires — those not created by Vangual.

Fire Vampires: Vampires born of fire. Badly disfigured they have complete control over flame and fire, but their constant pain drives them insane.

First: The first of the Children of Vangual. They formed the Black Council and created Avystervan over two thousand years ago.

Good Standing: The Term 'Good Standing' refers to a cleric who is in favour with his god. See **Powers of Light**.

Iliari: Elusive vampires that have aligned themselves with sunlight and goodness.

Katharein: The spiritual quest by which a vampire can retain their mortality and stave off the effects of the Void.

Kethak: The *City of Lost Souls*. Found in a crater on the Ash Plane, Kethak is home to the Arcane, the wicked council of Liches.

Kethax: Mythical vampire demons as mentioned in the Avystyx Prophecies. Beings of brimstone and darkness.

Lost: Fallen divine beings stripped of their power and cursed to live as vampires.

Mock Vampires: The degenerated mongrels of vampire society, the *mocked* live in the sewers under Avystervan.

Mortal Realms: The kingdoms of men and elves and all the living races.

Necrotic Arch: The spiritual domain in which all mortals find themselves upon their first death.

Occularum: Magical eyes of darkness that observe Avystervan and the underworld.

Once Touched: A mortal bitten once by one of the Children of Vangual.

Powers of Darkness: The collective term for the forces of darkness, decay and destruction. The mortal enemies of the *Powers of Light*, they represent vampires, liches and all things evil.

Powers of Light: The collective term for the forces of good. They represent light and life. They are detailed in *Powers of Light*.

Ravenous Vampires: Green skinned vampires with a desperate craving for blood.

Shadow Vampires: Shadow bound vampires that exist primarily on the Shadow Plane.

Simulacrum: Mortals enslaved by vampires and transformed into living automatons.

Stench of the Grave: The stench of death and air of rot that surrounds a vampire.

Thrice Touched: A mortal bitten thrice by one of the Children of Vangual. The vampire has greater control over the victim.

Twice Touched: A mortal bitten twice by one of the Children of Vangual. This is traditionally part of the Visitation, where on the third night, the vampire will either *thrice touch* the mortal or bring them into undeath

Va'Vash: A black magical mineral that is found only on the Negative Energy Plane and mined by Ash Vampires.

Vampire Scion: Lesser vampires under the control of a vampire master.

vampire touched: Those bitten by a vampire and placed under their control.

Vangaard: The defenders of the Black Council. Huge, hulking vampires with tremendous strength.

Vangual: The God of vampires who lives in his Fortress of Shadow in the *Black*.

Veil: Vangual's ancient city from which he rose to power and became the god of vampires.

Visitation: To visit a mortal on three or more occasions with the intention of turning them into a vampire or binding them to darkness.

Void: The force of darkness and entropy that drives all vampires towards evil.

INDEX

Advanced Energy Drain: 56

age: 29

    Vampire Age Table: 29

Anatomy of a Vampire: 6

Arikostinaal: 85, 95

Ash Vampires: 5, 9-10

Attunement: 30

Avystervan: 4, 80-88

Avystyx Prophecies: 6

Black: 89

Black Barbarian: 37

Black Bloods: 4, 11

Black Cabal: 5, 47-48

Black Classes: 36

    Black Barbarian: 37

    Black Bard: 37

    Black Cleric: 38

    Black Druid: 39

    Black Fighter: 40

    Black Monk: 41

    Black Paladin: 42

    Black Ranger: 43

    Black Rogue: 43

    Black Sorcerer: 44

    Black Wizard: 45

Black Council: 93-95

Blood: 7, 25, 30, 96

    Blood Drain: 30

    Drinking Blood: 25, 30

    Monster Blood: 104-105

Blood Gates: 88

Blood Guard: 40, 87

Black Kiss: 6, 29

Blood Knights: 51-52

Blood Mage: 49-50

Children of Vangual: 4, 99

Chill: 6, 35

Dark Gifts: 7, 55-63

Death State: 31

Devoted Incarnate: 53-54

Dhampyre: 2, 26-27

Energy Drain: 118

Fast Healing: 31

Feral Vampires: 4

Fire Vampires: 4, 12-13

First: 92-93

Gravebound/Unbound: 31

Holy: 31

    Holy Ground: 31

Iliari: 5

Katharein: 113, 114-116

Lost: 5, 14-15

Master Age Table: 128

Mock Vampires: 5, 16-17

Occularum: 81

Place of Rest: 31

Prestige Classes: 46

    Black Cabal: 47

    Blood Knight: 51

    Blood Mage: 49

    Devoted Incarnate: 53

Waking Checks: 32

Ravenous Vampires: 4-5, 18-19

Servants of the Void: 31, 112

Shadow Vampires: 5, 20-21

Simulacrum: 103

Sleeping: 32

    eternal quiescence: 7, 32

    Penalties for Not Sleeping: 32

    Second Waking: 6

Stench of the Grave: 6

Sunlight: 33

    Sunlight Damage Table: 33

Va'Vash: 79

Vampiric Familiar: 45

Vampire Scion: 5, 24-25

Vampiric Traits: 34

Vampiric Weaknesses: 35

Katharein: 113, 114-116

Vampire touched: 5, 28

    Once Touched: 28

    Twice Touched: 28

    Thrice Touched: 28

Vampire Shadow Armor: 77

Vampiric Weapons: 78

Vangaard: 4, 22-23

Vangual: 4, 89

    Mortal Clerics: 90

Visitation: 29

Void: 7, 110-111

    Vampire Void Table: 111

VAMPIRE MASTER AGE CHART

ASH VAMPIRE	STR	DEX	INT	WIS	CHA	AC	Spd	DR	TR	FH	ECL	CR
Age 0	+2	+1	+1	+1	+1	+3	+0	10/+1	+2	3	+3	+2
Age 1	+4	+2	+2	+2	+2	+6	+5	15/+1	+4	5	+4	+3
Age 2	+6	+4	+3	+3	+3	+8	+5	20/+2	+6	6	+5	+4
Age 3	+8	+6	+4	+4	+4	+10	+10	25/+2	+7	7	+6	+5
Age 4	+10	+8	+5	+5	+5	+12	+10	25/+3	+8	8	+7	+6
Age 5	+15	+10	+6	+6	+6	+15	+15	30/+3	+10	9	+8	+7
BLACK BLOOD												
Age 0	+3	+2	+1	+1	+2	+2	5	10/+1	+2	3	+2	+1
Age 1	+6	+4	+2	+2	+4	+4	10	15/+1	+4	5	+3	+2
Age 2	+8	+6	+3	+3	+6	+6	15	20/+1	+6	6	+4	+3
Age 3	+10	+8	+4	+4	+8	+8	20	20/+2	+7	7	+5	+4
Age 4	+12	+10	+5	+5	+10	+10	25	25/+2	+8	8	+6	+5
Age 5	+15	+12	+6	+6	+12	+12	30	25/+3	+10	10	+7	+6
FIRE VAMPIRE												
Age 0	+1	+2	+1	+1	+1	+2	5	10/+1	+2	3	+2	+1
Age 1	+2	+4	+2	+2	+2	+4	10	15/+1	+4	5	+3	+2
Age 2	+3	+6	+4	+3	+3	+6	15	20/+1	+6	6	+4	+3
Age 3	+4	+8	+6	+4	+4	+8	20	20/+2	+7	7	+5	+4
Age 4	+6	+10	+8	+5	+5	+10	25	25/+2	+8	8	+6	+5
Age 5	+8	+12	+10	+6	+6	+12	30	25/+3	+10	9	+7	+6
LOST VAMPIRE												
Age 0	+1	+2	+2	+2	+6	+2	5	5/+1	-	3	+1	+0
Age 1	+2	+4	+4	+4	+8	+4	5	10/+1	-	4	+2	+1
Age 2	+3	+5	+5	+6	+10	+6	5	15/+1	-	5	+3	+2
Age 3	+4	+6	+6	+8	+12	+8	10	15/+2	-	6	+4	+3
Age 4	+5	+7	+7	+10	+14	+10	10	20/+2	-	7	+5	+4
Age 5	+6	+8	+8	+12	+16	+12	10	20/+3	-	8	+6	+5
MOCK VAMPIRE												
Age 0	+3	+2	-6	+1	-8	+2	5	10/+1	+2	3	+2	+1
Age 1	+6	+4	-4	+2	-6	+4	10	15/+1	+4	5	+3	+2
Age 2	+8	+6	-2	+4	-2	+6	15	20/+1	+6	6	+4	+3
Age 3	+10	+8	-0	+6	+0	+8	20	20/+2	+7	7	+5	+4
Age 4	+12	+10	+1	+8	+2	+10	25	25/+2	+8	8	+6	+5
Age 5	+15	+12	+2	+10	+4	+12	30	25/+3	+10	9	+7	+6
RAVENOUS VAMPIRE												
Age 0	+3	+2	+1	+1	+1	+4	5	10/+1	+2	3	+3	+2
Age 1	+6	+4	+2	+2	+2	+6	10	15/+1	+4	5	+4	+3
Age 2	+7	+6	+3	+3	+3	+8	15	20/+2	+6	6	+5	+4
Age 3	+8	+7	+4	+4	+4	+10	20	25/+2	+7	7	+6	+5
Age 4	+9	+8	+5	+5	+5	+12	25	25/+3	+8	8	+7	+6
Age 5	+10	+10	+6	+6	+6	+15	30	30/+3	+10	9	+8	+7
SHADOW VAMPIRE												
Age 0	+1	+2	+1	+1	+2	+2	10	10/+1	+2	3	+2	+1
Age 1	+2	+4	+2	+2	+4	+4	15	15/+1	+4	4	+3	+2
Age 2	+4	+6	+3	+3	+6	+6	20	20/+1	+5	5	+4	+3
Age 3	+6	+8	+4	+4	+8	+8	25	20/+2	+6	6	+5	+4
Age 4	+7	+10	+5	+5	+10	+18	30	25/+2	+7	7	+6	+5
Age 5	+8	+15	+6	+6	+12	+12	35	25/+3	+8	8	+7	+6
VANGAARD												
Age 0	+8	-2	+0	+1	+1	+4	5	10/+1	+1	4	+3	+2
Age 1	+12	-1	+1	+2	+2	+8	10	15/+1	+2	6	+4	+3
Age 2	+14	+0	+2	+3	+3	+10	15	20/+2	+3	8	+5	+4
Age 3	+16	+2	+3	+4	+4	+12	20	25/+2	+4	10	+6	+5
Age 4	+18	+4	+4	+5	+5	+14	25	30/+2	+5	12	+7	+6
Age 5	+20	+6	+5	+6	+6	+20	30	30/+3	+6	15	+8	+7

AC:	Bonus to Natural Armor Class
Spd:	Bonus to Speed per round
DR:	Damage Resistance
TR:	Turn Resistance
FH:	Fast Healing
ECL/CR:	Equivalent Character Level/Challenge Rating

OPEN GAME LICENSE

This printing of **The Lords of the Night: Vampires** is done under version 1.0a of the Open Game License, the D20 System Trademark License, D20 System Trademark Logo Guide and System Reference Document by permission from Wizards of the Coast. Subsequent printings of this book will incorporate final versions of this license.

Designation of Product Identity: The following items are hereby designated as Product Identity in accordance with section 1(e) of the Open Game License version 1.0a. Any and all Bottled Imp Games logos and identifying marks; all text under the Description header of any new creature, spell, magical item, vampire race, dark gift, any elements of **The Lords of the Night: Vampires** setting, including but not limited to any and **all** items listed in the Lexicon on page 125 of this book, capitalized names, characters, creatures, geographic locations, gods, historic events, magic items, organizations, spells, any and all stories, storylines, plot and artwork, symbols, designs, depictions, illustrations, maps and cartography, likenesses, logos, symbols or graphic design, except such elements that already appear in the D20 System Refence Document and are already Open Game Content by virute of appearing there. The above is **NOT** Open Game Content

Designation of Open Game Content: Subject to the Product Identity designation above, the following portions of **The Lords of the Night: Vampires** are designated as Open Game Content: all creature statistics, all skills, feats, special attacks (SA) and special qualities (SQ), all text under the Combat section of a creature's listing, all magical item and spell statistics and abilities, vampiric weaknesses, anything else contained herein which is already Open Game Content by virtue of appearing in the System Reference Document or some other Open Game Content source; and all text contained herein that is already public domain.

All contents of this book, regardless of designation are **copyrighted Bottled Imp Games 2003.**

OPEN GAME LICENSE Version 1.0a. The following text is the property of Wizards of the Coast, Inc. and is Copyright 2000 Wizards of the Coast, Inc ("Wizards"). All Rights Reserved.

1. Definitions: (a)"Contributors" means the copyright and/or trademark owners who have contributed Open Game Content; (b)"Derivative Material" means copyrighted material including derivative works and translations (including into other computer languages), potation, modification, correction, addition, extension, upgrade, improvement, compilation, abridgment or other form in which an existing work may be recast, transformed or adapted; (c) "Distribute" means to reproduce, license, rent, lease, sell, broadcast, publicly display, transmit or otherwise distribute; (d)"Open Game Content" means the game mechanic and includes the methods, procedures, processes and routines to the extent such content does not embody the Product Identity and is an enhancement over the prior art and any additional content clearly identified as Open Game Content by the Contributor, and means any work covered by this License, including translations and derivative works under copyright law, but specifically excludes Product Identity. (e) "Product Identity" means product and product line names, logos and identifying marks including trade dress; artifacts; creatures characters; stories, storylines, plots, thematic elements, dialogue, incidents, language, artwork, symbols, designs, depictions, likenesses, formats, poses, concepts, themes and graphic, photographic and other visual or audio representations; names and descriptions of characters, spells, enchantments, personalities, teams, personas, likenesses and special abilities; places, locations, environments, creatures, equipment, magical or supernatural abilities or effects, logos, symbols, or graphic designs; and any other trademark or registered trademark clearly identified as Product identity by the owner of the Product Identity, and which specifically excludes the Open Game Content; (f) "Trademark" means the logos, names, mark, sign, motto, designs that are used by a Contributor to identify itself or its products or the associated products contributed to the Open Game License by the Contributor (g) "Use", "Used" or "Using" means to use, Distribute, copy, edit, format, modify, translate and otherwise create Derivative Material of Open Game Content. (h) "You" or "Your" means the licensee in terms of this agreement.

2. The License: This License applies to any Open Game Content that contains a notice indicating that the Open Game Content may only be Used under and in terms of this License. You must affix such a notice to any Open Game Content that you Use. No terms may be added to or subtracted from this License except as described by the License itself. No other terms or conditions may be applied to any Open Game Content distributed using this License.

3. Offer and Acceptance: By Using the Open Game Content You indicate Your acceptance of the terms of this License.

4. Grant and Consideration: In consideration for agreeing to use this License, the Contributors grant You a perpetual, worldwide, royalty-free, non-exclusive license with the exact terms of this License to Use, the Open Game Content.

5. Representation of Authority to Contribute: If You are contributing original material as Open Game Content, You represent that Your Contributions are Your original creation and/or You have sufficient rights to grant the rights conveyed by this License.

6. Notice of License Copyright: You must update the COPYRIGHT NOTICE portion of this License to include the exact text of the COPYRIGHT NOTICE of any Open Game Content You are copying, modifying or distributing, and You must add the title, the copyright date, and the copyright holder's name to the COPYRIGHT NOTICE of any original Open Game Content you Distribute.

7. Use of Product Identity: You agree not to Use any Product Identity, including as an indication as to compatibility, except as expressly licensed in another, independent Agreement with the owner of each element of that Product Identity. You agree not to indicate compatibility or co-adaptability with any Trademark or Registered Trademark in conjunction with a work containing Open Game Content except as expressly licensed in another, independent Agreement with the owner of such Trademark or Registered Trademark. The use of any Product Identity in Open Game Content does not constitute a challenge to the ownership of that Product Identity. The owner of any Product Identity used in Open Game Content shall retain all rights, title and interest in and to that Product Identity.

8. Identification: If you distribute Open Game Content You must clearly indicate which portions of the work that you are distributing are Open Game Content.

9. Updating the License: Wizards or its designated Agents may publish updated versions of this License. You may use any authorized version of this License to copy, modify and distribute any Open Game Content originally distributed under any version of this License.

10. Copy of this License: You MUST include a copy of this License with every copy of the Open Game Content You Distribute.

11. Use of Contributor Credits: You may not market or advertise the Open Game Content using the name of any Contributor unless You have written permission from the Contributor to do so.

12. Inability to Comply: If it is impossible for You to comply with any of the terms of this License with respect to some or all of the Open Game Content due to statute, judicial order, or governmental regulation then You may not Use any Open Game Material so affected.

13. Termination: This License will terminate automatically if You fail to comply with all terms herein and fail to cure such breach within 30 days of becoming aware of the breach. All sublicenses shall survive the termination of this License.

14. Reformation: If any provision of this License is held to be unenforceable, such provision shall be reformed only to the extent necessary to make it enforceable.

15. COPYRIGHT NOTICE
Open Game License v 1.0a Copyright 2000, Wizards of the Coast, Inc., Copyright 2003, Bottled Imp Games.

Afterword: If you liked this book, mail us at: imp@bottledimpgames.com. Tell us what you thought of it. Find the Vampires FAQ at www.bottledimpgames.com.